Protestantism

Protestantism

A concise survey of Protestantism and its influence on American religious and social traditions.

Hugh T. Kerr, Editor
Professor Emeritus
Princeton Theological Seminary

Barron's Educational Series, Inc. / Woodbury, New York

All inquiries should be addressed to:
Barron's Educational Series, Inc.
113 Crossways Park Drive
Woodbury, New York 11797

Library of Congress Catalog Card No. 76-16065

Paper Edition
International Standard Book No. 0-8120-0665-8

Library of Congress Cataloging in Publication Data
Main entry under title:
Protestantism.
 Includes bibliographies.
  1. Protestantism—Addresses, essays, lectures.
I. Kerr, Hugh Thomson, 1909-
BX4815.P74   280'.4   76-16065
ISBN 0-8120-0665-8

Contents

PART III — THE SPECTRUM OF BELIEF

PART IV — CURRENT PROBLEMS AND ISSUES

Preface

The intent of this book is to provide a panoramic view of the religious movement known as Protestantism. In keeping with the many varieties of Protestant life and thought, the book is made up of a collection of essays written by recognized authorities. Of course, not everything of importance could be included, but the range and depth of the articles in this selection assure an accurate and authentic introduction to the subject.

There is a deliberate mix, in the essays that follow, of old and new, difficult and elementary, historical and doctrinal. But each item included contributes to the unity of the whole collection.

Designed as a general introduction, as are the other volumes in the Barron's World Religions Series, this overview of Protestantism can be used as a text for teachers and students. As a text it is adaptable, and the suggestions for further reading in the annotated bibliography indicate additional approaches that may be explored. It is tempting to correct the older masculinist terminology of yesterday, making the language of these readings more "inclusive." But we cannot rewrite the historic, classical texts of the past. We can only reflect that sex-inclusive language, as of now, is expected and will soon be everywhere accepted.

Each selection is introduced with a brief preface by the editor. These prefaces, read in sequence, form a brief survey of the Protestant landscape. The editor has written several books on Protestantism, has taught students for 35 years, and edits a religious quarterly that demands constant intellectual involvement with all kinds of religious movements. The authors of the essays included in this book need make no such immodest claims. They are well known and highly respected; and they write with authority, grace, and conviction.

Acknowledgments

Grateful acknowledgment is made to the following for permission to reprint the articles that appear in this book:

Abingdon Press for the article "American Protestant Theology, 1900-1970" by Deane W. Ferm. From *Religion in Life*, Vol. XLIV, No. 1 (Spring, 1975). Copyright 1975 by Abingdon Press. Also for portions of *The American Churches: An Interpretation* by William Warren Sweet. Copyright 1948 by Stone & Pierce (Abingdon Press). Also for the table "Membership Change 1952-1971" on page 9, reprinted from *Yearbook of American and Canadian Churches 1975* by Constant Jacquet. Copyright 1975 by the National Council of Churches of Christ. Used by permission of Abingdon Press.

American Enterprise Institute for Public Policy Research for Peter Berger's bicentennial address "Religion In A Revolutionary Society." In conjunction with publication of *American's Continuing Revolution: An Act of Conservation.* Copyright 1975 by the American Enterprise Institute for Public Policy Research. Reprinted by permission.

Association Press for excerpts from *Primer for Protestants* by James H. Nichols. Copyright 1947; and *Church Cooperation and Unity in America* by Samuel M. Cavert. Copyright 1970 by Association Press. Reprinted by permission.

Beacon Press for an excerpt from *The Reformation of the 16th Century* by Roland H. Bainton. Copyright 1952 by Beacon Press. Reprinted by permission of Beacon Press.

Christian Century Foundation for excerpts from "Toward a Feminist Theology" by Sheila D. Collins. Copyright 1972 by the Christian Century Foundation. Reprinted by permission from the August 2, 1972 issue of *The Christian Century.*

Church History for excerpts from "The Protestant Quest for a Christian America, 1980-1930" by Robert T. Handy. From *Church History*, Vol. XXII, No. 1 (March, 1952). Reprinted by permission.

Harper & Row, Publishers for an excerpt from *The Sun and the Umbrella: A Parable for Today* by Nels F. S. Ferré. Copyright 1953 by Harper & Row, Publishers, Inc. Reprinted by permission of the publisher. Also for excerpts from *Why Conservative Churches are Growing* by Dean M. Kelley. Copyright 1972 by Dean M. Kelley. Reprinted by permission of the publisher.

Harvard University Press for excerpts from *The New England Mind: The Seventeenth Century* by Perry Miller. Reprinted by permission of the publishers from Perry Miller, *The New England Mind: The Seventeenth Century*, Cambridge, Mass.: Harvard University Press, copyright 1939 by Perry Miller; 1967 by Elizabeth W. Miller.

Holt, Rinehart & Winston for excerpts from *Protestantism* by Martin E. Marty. Copyright 1972 by Martin E. Marty. Reprinted by permission of the publisher.

Oxford University Press for excerpts from *The Spirit of Protestantism* by Robert McAfee Brown. Copyright 1965 by Oxford University Press, Inc. Reprinted by permission.

Paraclete for the article "Our Heritage" by William W. Menzies. From *Paraclete*, Vol. 9, No. 1 (Winter 1975). Reprinted by permission.

Princeton University Press for excerpts from "Protestantism" by John A. Mackay from *The Great Religions of the Modern World* by Edward J. Jurji. Copyright 1946. Reprinted by permission of Princeton University Press.

Charles Scribner's Sons for excerpts from *Religion in America* by Winthrop S. Hudson. Copyright 1965 Charles Scribner's Sons.

The Seabury Press for excerpts from *God of the Oppressed* by James H. Cone. Copyright 1975 by The Seabury Press, Inc. Used by permission of the publisher.

Society for Religion in Higher Education for the article "Religious Symbols and Our Knowledge of God" by Paul Tillich. From *The Christian Scholar*, Vol. 38, No. 3 (September 1955). Reprinted with permission.

Westminster Press for excerpts from *Human Liberation in a Feminist Perspective – A Theology* by Letty M. Russell. Copyright 1974 by Letty M. Russell. Used by permission of The Westminster Press.

World Council of Churches for the article "Conversion — A Personal Revolution" by William F. Graham. From *The Ecumenical Review,* Vol. XIX, No. 3 (July 1967). Reprinted by permission.

Protest As Reform

Hugh T. Kerr

Religions are notoriously difficult to define. With good reason. Digging up historical roots can tell us something, but not everything. Rites and worship forms, creeds and codes of conduct, even language and geography—all can contribute to a definition. Still the essence can elude our grasp. While preachers sermonize and theologians rationalize, mystics and contemplatives, as well as just average worshippers, may very well disdain definitions of any kind.

The outward trappings of religion are easy to catalogue, but the inner spirit defies exact analysis. That is surely why outsiders, trying to look inside at what makes believers tick, often describe what they think they see as peculiar, odd, mysterious, irrational, or even perhaps as just plain crazy. Shouting Methodists of frontier days would find the ceremony and liturgy of Episcopalians stultifying and repressive; Presbyterians, who love to do everything decently and in order, would find freewheeling Baptists unpredictable and volatile; charismatics and Pentecostals, speaking in tongues and physically moved by the Spirit, could not be expected to sit still in a silent Quaker meetinghouse.

Protestantism has contributed its quota of intangibles to the fascinating game of religious definition. But curiously enough, Protestantism has always prided itself on being extremely simple and easy to understand. After all, it insists on only a few elemental tenets: the authority of the Bible, the centrality of Jesus Christ, and the importance of faith for both personal and social life. True enough, but that hardly explains why Protestantism erupted with such explosive force in the sixteenth century, why it attacked the Roman Catholic Church with such vehemence, and why in subsequent centuries it divided and subdivided into more than 200 denominations—each with specific and individual definitions of the essence of the faith. Here is where we must call on history for what it can provide.

When Martin Luther nailed his Ninety-five Theses on the church door in Wittenberg, Germany, in 1517, he "protested" against certain Roman Catholic beliefs and customs—notably the current practice of selling indulgences. Luther was a Catholic monk at the time, and his Theses were suggested as topics for theological debate among his fellow Catholic clergy. A few years later, in 1529, at a local legislature, known as the Diet of Speyer (Spires), a "protestation" was made by some followers of Luther against a political decision that would have established the Catholic Church as the only officially recognized church in the area.

But the terms Protestant and Protestantism did not come into general use until many years later. In Germany, the disciples of Luther were known as Lutherans or Evangelicals; in Switzerland, the followers of John Calvin were called Calvinists or Reformed; in Great Britain, members of the Church of England called themselves Anglicans or Episcopalians, and other non-Catholics were simply lumped together as nonconformists. Slowly Protestantism emerged, especially in America, as an umbrella term to cover all those churches and sects that differed in some way from Roman Catholicism. The difference was partly negative (protest) and partly positive (reformation).

The *negative* side of Protestantism was directed against what were regarded as abuses within Catholicism, such as the reputed immorality and ignorance of the clergy, the worldly wealth and power of the Vatican, and the pyramiding of doctrines and practices not originally associated with early Christianity. So Protestants protested against the authority of the Pope by exalting the Bible; they objected to clerical monasticism by affirming the sanctity of common life; they rejected the Catholic practices of veneration for the Virgin Mary and the saints and magnified the lordship of Christ; they repudiated five of the seven Catholic sacraments and the doctrine of purgatory simply because they were not founded in Scripture; while retaining the sacraments of baptism and eucharist, they denied the Catholic doctrine of the mass and the use of Latin in the liturgy.

Protestants, especially in the formative years of the sixteenth and seventeenth centuries, were protesting against what they took to be bigness, corruption, and monopoly in the ecclesiastical establishment. As minority dissidents against the power structure of the day, they criticized the oppression of the Roman clergy against the common people and the accretion of doctrines and regulations that were, in their view, self-serving and discriminatory. So Luther translated the Bible into German, the common language of the people; Calvin rewrote the civil laws of the city of Geneva; Knox arranged a confrontation with Mary, Queen of Scots.

What the early Protestants seemed most concerned about were the defection, the immorality, and the unspiritual character of the church of their own day; and they vented their most violent language upon all such conditions. "It is a horrible and frightful thing," wrote Luther in a characteristic passage, "that the ruler of Christendom, who boasts himself vicar of Christ and successor of Saint Peter, lives in such worldly splendor that in this regard no king nor emperor can equal or approach him." Calvin spared the church of his day nothing. "If any one," he said, "will closely observe and strictly examine this whole form of ecclesiastical government, which exists at the present day under the Papacy, he will find it a nest of the most lawless and ferocious banditti in the world."

A first glance at the Reformation creeds and confessions of faith seems to confirm this reactionary attitude. In stating their own beliefs, Protestants appear to have been primarily interested in showing what it was that they did not believe. A notable example of this is found in the so-called Second Scots Confession of 1581, rightly dubbed "The Negative Confession." Here is just one of the condemnatory clauses: ". . .We detest and refuse the usurped authoritie of that Romane Antichrist . . . his tyranous lawes . . . his erroneous doctrine . . . his fyve bastard sacraments . . . his blasphemous opinion of transubstantiation . . . his devilish messe . . . his worldlie monarchie and wicked hierarchie . . . his erroneous and bloodie Decreets."

It is perhaps inevitable, in view of this historical background to define Protestantism in negative terms. The *Oxford English Dictionary* (unabridged), for example, defines a Protestant as: "A member or adherent of any of the Christian churches or bodies which repudiated the papal authority, and separated or were severed from the Roman communion in the Reformation of the sixteenth century, and generally of any of the bodies of Christians descended from them; hence in general language applied to any Western Christian or member of a Christian church outside the Roman communion."

There was, on the other hand, a *positive* side to Protestantism. To protest against something usually implies a strong conviction about something else. Protestants, for the most part, were not hooligans or terrorists. They were not engaged in mindless trashing of sacred traditions in order to protest in a violent way against the church establishment of the times.

Catholics have usually seen Protestants as anti-Roman, but Protestants have always insisted that they were pro-Christian and therefore anti-Roman. From the Protestant perspective, it is as nonsensical to define their movement as non-Catholic as it would be to define the American Constitution of 1776 as non-British or to define those who are registered Democrats as non-Republicans.

Protest against something can also be profession for something. What Protestants were for was, in a word, reform. They wanted the church to be re-formed according to the normative authority of the Bible and the precedents of the early Apostolic church. So Protestantism, on the positive side, meant reformation.

The Protestant reformers of the sixteenth century, such as Luther and Calvin, were not of course the first or only protesters of the ecclesiastical status quo. The names of Wycliffe and Hus are known as pre-reformers; but there were others, such as the Carthusian monk, Dionysius, Jacob of Jüterbock, John of Wesel, Thomas Gascoigne, John Trithemius, and Matthew of Cracow. There were great preachers, also, like Savonarola; learned scholars like Erasmus; and concerted efforts like the Conciliar Movement—all of whom pleaded for reform. But major reform did not come from within Romanism until after the Reformation, and the Protestant protest at the time was met with defiance and increased Catholic rigidity.

As a matter of fact, the reformers did not think of themselves as breaking away from the true Catholic faith or as starting new, independent, or schismatic churches. Luther once urged: "I ask that men make no reference to my name and call themselves not Lutherans but Christians." Calvin wrote: "So highly does the Lord esteem the communion of his church, that he considers everyone as a traitor and apostate from religion who perversely withdraws himself from any Christian society which preserves the true ministry of the word and sacraments."

The various Reformation creeds constantly appealed to the

early creeds of the Apostolic church, such as the Nicene Creed of 325 A.D. The Augsburg Confession (1530), the primary creedal authority of the Lutherans, concludes its discussion of doctrine by noting: "This is about the sum of doctrine among us, in which can be seen that there is nothing which is discrepant with the Scriptures or with the church catholic or even with the Roman Church so far as that Church is known from the writings of the Fathers. This being the case, they judge us harshly who insist that we shall be regarded as heretics." The Second Helvetic Confession of 1566, which circulated among Protestant churches in Switzerland, Hungary, Poland, France, Holland, England, and Scotland, reaffirmed the ancient creeds of the early church and concluded: "Since we are all of this faith and religion, we hope to be regarded by all not as heretics but as catholics and Christians."

The Reformation, in intention at least, was not an attempt to create new doctrines or new churches. The reformers sought to recall the church of their times to the original gospel. That is why Protestantism is sometimes known as evangelical Christianity, because it emphasizes the "evangel" (the Greek word translated as "gospel" in English).

Important and necessary as this lesson in perspective may be, it must be said that thus far we are mostly dealing in the area of ancient history. We may have learned how Protestantism came about in the first place, but we haven't much clue as to the motivating forces or the inner dynamics of modern or contemporary Protestantism. Two factors in the original dispute have changed so radically as to alter the whole picture.

In the first place, Roman Catholicism today—and especially since the late Pope John XXIII convened Vatican Council II (1962-1965)—is very definitely not what it was in the sixteenth century. Many of the accusations hurled by the reformers and later Protestants against the church are no longer pertinent.

In the early years of the Reformation, the disputes between

Catholics and Protestants revolved around such issues as papal infallibility, the secondary authority of the Bible, the redemptive role of the Virgin Mary, the use of Latin in the mass, and so forth. In our own day, some distinguished Catholics, notably Hans Küng of the University of Tübingen, are questioning the whole notion of infallibility; Biblical studies have become a major concern of Catholic scholars; almost no mention of the Virgin Mary was made at Vatican Council II; and English has replaced Latin in virtually all Catholic worship services.

Even recent disputes between Catholics and Protestants have lost much of their force. Protestants used to accuse Catholics of being nonecumenical, uninvolved in programs of social justice, and un-American in their reluctance to accept the separation of church and state. None of these makes any sense today. Catholics are intensely involved in ecumenical movements of all kinds; they take active leadership in social and political programs; and—since John F. Kennedy was elected president—the church and state issue has been largely transcended.

The divisive issues of the 1970s have to do with such disputed matters as abortion, clerical celibacy, ordination of women, busing, and tax-support for parochial schools. Those who are for or against these issues are to be found as much among Protestants as among Catholics, and a specifically religious basis for evaluation is certainly not a major consideration.

In the second place, Protestantism today is definitely not what it was at the time of the Reformation. Some might think it has become too doctrinally soft, but others might complain that the Reformation-begun never became the Reformation-completed. But the fact is that, with rare exceptions, Protestantism no longer defines itself as against Catholicism. It could be said, somewhat ruefully, that one reason for the lessening of opposition toward Catholicism is Protestantism's desperate effort just to survive. Or to put it another way, the traditional disputes between Catholics and Protestants fade into insignificance in view of the massive onslaught of contemporary materialism and secularism. Who has time for intramural religious rivalry when so many today have no religious ties at all?

Today the most severe protesters against Catholic authoritarianism are to be found within the Catholic Church itself. Curiously, at the same time, there are many Protestants who would like to adopt the traditional hard line of Catholicism that, presumably, defines doctrine clearly, distinguishes right from wrong without quibbling, and demands rigid stewardship from church members on pain of excommunication. In any case, Catholics and Protestants no longer waste much time fighting each other: the Catholics are busy worrying about their own infrastructure; the Protestants — especially those in the established denominations — are nervous about the growth of all kinds of freewheeling sects which are now on the edges of things but are taking hold.

There is another aspect of the modern religious scene that requires serious attention. It may be a straw in the wind, pointing out the direction for the tomorrow of Protestantism. We refer to the disruptive forces in the 1960s and 1970s when it became increasingly clear that while the old-time established denominations were either standing still or losing ground, a whole cluster of relatively smaller or lesser known churches and groups were growing and expanding.

The table printed here gives some picture of what has been happening on the church scene in America during the period of nineteen years from 1952 to 1971.[1] Note that the figures in the first column are not for total church membership but for the increase, or decrease, in members over the nineteen-year period.

Three reflections can be made on the basis of this statistical report. First, the so-called established denominations were preoccupied during this period, and for at least twenty years previously, in constructing conciliar and ecumenical bodies both nationally and worldwide. This quest for unity, sparked

Membership Change 1952-1971

Denomination	Change in Total Members	% Change 1952-1971
Ch. of God (Cleveland, Tenn.)	164,949	120.9%
Church of Jesus Christ of Latter-day Saints	1,055,787	98.0
Pentecostal Holiness	31,165	75.0
Seventh-day Adventists	186,466	73.8
Ch. of the Nazarene	149,681	60.1
Brethren in Christ	3,360	55.6
Roman Catholic Ch.	15,238,705	51.4
Lutheran Ch. — Mo. Syn.	916,363	49.4
Ch. of God (Anderson)	49,844	47.2
Southern Baptist Conv.	3,693,174	45.5
American Lutheran Ch.	746,395	42.8
Wesleyan Church	23,455	35.9
U.S. Population	*52,514,565*	*34.9*
Christian Reformed	53,958	34.8
Reformed Ch. in Am.	66,919	34.5
Mennonite Church	21,216	31.7
Free Methodist Ch. N.A.	14,488	29.5
Evangelical Covenant Ch. of America	14,720	27.9
Presbyterian Ch., U.S.	190,598	25.6
Unitarian-Universalists	34,829	21.8
Lutheran Ch. in Am.	528,223	21.3
Wisconsin Evangelical Lutheran Syn.	65,278	20.6
Episcopal Church	487,877	19.2
Moravian Church	8,503	17.5
Friends USA	12,014	12.6
Un. Presbyterian Ch., U.S.A.	235,980	8.8
Un. Methodist Ch.	495,621	5.2
Evangelical Congregational Ch. ...	1,206	4.2
Ch. of the Brethren	-8,171	-4.3
Un. Church of Christ	-155,343	-7.7
Cumberland Presbyterian	-7,442	-8.0
Am. Baptist Churches	-140,429	-9.2
Seventh-Day Baptist Gen. Conf.	-1,393	-21.7
Christian Church (Disciples of Christ)	-677,249	-36.9

primarily by Protestants, issued in the World Council of
Churches in 1948, and the ecumenical achievement seemed
to presage a new era of church cooperation everywhere and
at all levels. For some reason, by the 60s and 70s enthusiasm
for the ecumenical movement began to wane. Churches
began to withhold their resources from the expansive social
programs sponsored by the WCC and, once again, the
integrity of individual denominations became more important than ecumenical cooperation. The pluralism of Protestantism no longer seemed such a scandal when everyone was
fighting for mere existence.

The second reflection on the changed religious situation
suggests that the growing and expanding churches and
denominations are very much within the original Protestant
tradition of both protest and reform. Whether proudly
conservative, fiercely independent, or joyously charismatic,
many of these growing churches are repeating what the
reformers in the sixteenth century experienced. They know
what they're against, and they know what they're for. In
either case, the main issue has almost nothing whatever to do
with Roman Catholicism or even with other Protestant denominations.

A third reflection relates to the problem of pluralism. As in
other areas of modern society, we are confronted with a
widespread rejection of big corporate structures and a corresponding acceptance of separate, independent groupings.
Emerging out of the disruption of the late 60s, we see
evidence of this in the youth counterculture, the black power
movement, and the women's liberation movement.

The prospects for the fourth quarter of the twentieth
century must take the problem of pluralism into account. We
will either learn to live with many varieties of social groupings, or we will need to discover some new motivation for
bringing people together in cooperative ways. Religiously,
this means that efforts toward ecumenism will have to live
alongside other religious minorities who reject the big program in favor of doing it their own way. There is little

likelihood that the old-time Protestant denominations will disappear overnight. The so-called Consultation on Church Union (COCU), which includes most of the major churches, may very well achieve a breakthrough and issue in a new form of ecumenical comity. The future of such ecumenical organizations is perhaps an open question. But so too is the future of the growing, burgeoning independent religious bodies whose statistics look so promising. It remains to be seen whether their protest against other churches and traditions will be matched by reform efforts and programs in their own membership.

As the old proverb has it: "Carry from the ashes of the past the fire, not the ashes." Future generations will distinguish better than we can between the fire and the ashes of the current religious situation. Protestantism began as a minority movement and as a power-to-the-people movement. It was opposed to all absolutist claims to truth, including its own. If history teaches anything, there will be a new day for Protestantism when the churches once more know what to protest against and, more importantly, what to stand for. As Peter Marshall, the distinguished chaplain of the United States Senate, once prayed: "O God, help us to stand for something, lest we fall for anything. Amen." That is not the whole story of protest as reform, but it is close to the center.

Notes

1.   Constant H. Jacquet, Jr., ed. *Yearbook of American and Canadian Churches, 1975* (Nashville: Abingdon Press, 1975), pp. 264-5.

Tracing The Family Tree

Robert McAfee Brown

One thing that everyone knows about Protestants is that they come in many varieties. If Martin Luther was the acknowledged progenitor of the whole sprawling Protestant family, subsequent generations of Protestants staked out their own turf and sought to make a name for themselves, regardless of pedigrees and the traditions of their ancestors.

Catholics sometimes assume that this divisive and proliferating trait issued from a hereditary disease within Protestantism. After all, given Luther's doctrine of the "priesthood of all believers," it would be inevitable that some Protestants would interpret this to mean private and independent judgment about anything and everything. But that is only part of the story, and not the most important part at that.

The fact is that the Protestant Reformation in sixteenth century Europe did not spring from a single stem. Protests against medieval uniformity were everywhere in the air. The times were ripe for reform. Luther, in Germany, was doubtless the best known because he was the most vigorous; but he was soon surrounded on all sides, on the Continent and in Great Britain, by protesters.

It should not be surprising that both local and national varieties of the Protestant Reformation took on their own individual characteristics and identifying marks. These were sometimes doctrinal and creedal, sometimes merely geographical and linguistic, but the varieties of original Protestantism in Europe multiplied when these branches were transplanted onto American soil.

The contemporary forms of American Protestantism are simply unintelligible without some awareness of this historical background It is true that transplanted Protestant groups soon acquired an American accent of their own, but we cannot understand the later fruits of Protestantism without unearthing the tangled roots of the Reformation itself.

For assistance, we turn to Robert McAfee Brown, who has been writing for many years about both Protestantism and Catholicism. In his book *The Spirit of Protestantism* (1961), the third chapter is entitled: "The Varieties of Protestantism (a swift catalog of family quarrels, family reunions, and the patience of God)." A digest of that chapter follows. The author was formerly professor of religious studies at Stanford University and the Pacific School of Religion. He was a Protestant observer at Vatican Council II (1962-65) and delivered one of the major addresses at the fifth meeting (in 1975) of the World Council of Churches in Nairobi, Kenya.

As we turn from the sixteenth century and try to describe the present-day Protestant scene . . . , we cannot disguise the fact that there were skeletons as well as treasures in the Protestant closet. The skeleton most difficult to hide is contemporary Protestantism's divided character, and we must have the honesty to start with it.

The first Christians knew nothing of "denominations." They had their various factions, to be sure, as Paul's Corinthian correspondence makes lamentably clear, but for a brief time at least "they were not divided, all one body they." The subsequent history of Christendom, however, has been marked (and marred) by the tendency of Christians to take issue with one another, separate from one another, and form rival Christian communities. There was a considerable amount of this in the early centuries, more than is usually recognized, and a very serious rupture between East and West in A.D. 1054, which is still perpetuated in the division between Eastern Orthodoxy and the rest of Christendom. The Protestant Reformation of the sixteenth century produced another such rupture. . . .

The tragic thing about this is that Christians do not divide for petty reasons. New Christian groups always feel that they are either conserving an ancient truth, or combating a modern error, or doing both. At the time of division they may have been doing God's will. But whether denominational divisions that may have been historically justified in the past can still be justified today is another question entirely—a burning one for the Protestant conscience.

There are difficulties in any attempt to "schematize" the divisions into which modern Protestantism has fallen. Even at the risk of over-simplification, however, the attempt must be made, and the following five main denominational families are suggested.

1. The *Lutherans* are the oldest Protestant group with a self-conscious identity. The Lutheran churches came into being as a result of Luther's reforming activity in the early sixteenth century in Germany, when Luther and his followers put fidelity to the gospel above fidelity to medieval ecclesiasticism. Lutheran churches have always put central emphasis upon Scripture as the source of the gospel, and have understood the gospel particularly in terms of belief in justification by faith alone. This means that Lutheranism gives a high priority to right doctrine; so important is doctrine, indeed, that a number of different Lutheran groups exist, each feeling that the other compromise the truth at some important point. Lutheranism managed to conserve more of the elements of pre-Reformation liturgy than most other conti-

nental Protestant groups, and is thus characterized by a rich liturgical worship. In virtue of its doctrine of the separation of the "two realms" (e.g., the church and the magistrate), Lutheranism has historically inclined to an attitude of political quietism, an attitude now being rethought as a result of the church's necessary resistance to nazism.

2. Churches in the *Reformed* or *Presbyterian* tradition have arisen from the reformation activity in countries other than Germany, notably Switzerland, France, Holland, Hungary, and Scotland. The spiritual father of the Reformed family is John Calvin (1509-64), a French convert who spent most of his Protestant life in Geneva, preaching and teaching, and taking an active part in the political life of the city. Like Lutheranism, the Reformed faith is motivated and informed by central attention to Scripture. Scripture witnesses to Jesus Christ, whose reality is conveyed to believers by Scripture, sermon, and sacrament. One of the greatest contributions of the Reformed family has been its stress on biblical preaching and its concerted emphasis on the sovereign grace of God. Reformed doctrine has also emphasized church order as one of the marks of the church, and the offices of pastor, teacher, elder, and deacon derive from an attempt to conform to New Testament practice. The name "presbyterian" signifies the form of government of many Reformed churches. *Presbuteros* is the Greek word for "elder," and Presbyterian churches are governed by elders, elected to serve in the local churches and in larger representative bodies from local churches, known as presbyteries.

3. A third denominational family includes those within the *Anglican* or *Episcopal* tradition. Many of these describe themselves as Protestants or Evangelicals. The Anglo-Catholic wing, however, disavows the Protestant label, and agrees with Roman Catholicism on almost all points of doctrine save papal infallibility. This diversity of theological belief within Episcopalianism, while the despair of those who try to de-

scribe it simply, is one of the sources of its greatness, for the church has managed to conserve within its diversity many of the best features of historical Catholicism and Protestantism. For this reason many of its communicants feel that it can serve as the "bridge church," or the *via media*, between other groups in Christendom.

As the name Anglican implies, the historical roots of the church are to be found in the English Reformation, where the reforms were less radical than those on the Continent—a fact that makes Anglicans particularly conscious of their continuity with the past. As the name "Episcopal" implies, the church is governed by bishops (*episkopos* is the Greek word for "bishop"), and episcopal ordination is a distinguishing mark of its ministry. Another distinguishing characteristic of the Epsicopal family is *The Book of Common Prayer*, one of the liturgical treasures of Christendom, which is used at all services of worship, and from which other Protestant groups unblushingly borrow liturgical materials.

4. Another Protestant family, more diverse than any of those mentioned so far, can be identified as the family of *free churches*. The free churches were usually formed, as the name would suggest, in the face of oppression by established churches from whose domination the free churchmen wished to be released, so that they could preach and worship as they felt they should. The story of the free churches is a story of faith bought at the price of suffering and persecution. The theological convictions of free churchmen were often nurtured in the Calvinist wing of Christendom known as Puritanism. Originally the Puritans were members of the Church of England who wanted to "purify" worship of Romanizing tendencics, and who put biblical truth above human creeds and traditions. But this Calvinist-Puritan impulse became much broader than the Church of England, and has led in many directions.

Among the many free church groups, the following are particularly worthy of mention:

The *Congregationalists* and *Baptists* share an understanding of the church as a "gathered community," i.e., a voluntary association of believers. The name of each group indicates the emphasis it has particularly stressed. In *Congregationalism,* the government of the churches is vested in the "congregational meeting," where all members may discuss and vote on the policies to be pursued by the individual church. Contemporary Congregationalism has greater doctrinal latitude than was true in the seventeenth century, and creeds are usually considered as testimonies to faith rather than tests of faith. The *Baptists* have practiced "believer's baptism" rather than infant baptism; i.e., baptism administered to those of mature years who have made public profession of faith, in accordance to what is felt to have been the New Testament practice. Baptists have considerable variety on other points of doctrine, and today the different Baptist groups comprise the largest denominational family in the United States. Historically, Baptists have had a special concern for religious liberty and the separation of church and state.

The Society of Friends or *Quakers* are difficult to fit into a Protestant scheme, and are often classified as a "sect group," since they lack such normal characteristics of a church as sacraments, ordained ministers, or creedal affirmations. They stem, however, from left-wing Puritanism, having pushed the Puritan antisacramental emphasis to the extent of denying any sacraments at all. The spiritual father of Quakerism is the Englishman George Fox (1624-90), whose religious doubts and dissatisfactions with established religion were resolved by a series of mystical experiences which led him to rely on the "inner light," or the "seed of God within," rather than on external forms. In line with this emphasis there is no formal order of worship at Quaker meetings. Members of the group sit silently, waiting for the leading of the Spirit before getting up to speak. Quakerism has exercised influence on other Protestant groups all out of proportion to its small numbers, particularly through the expression of an acute social conscience and a consistent pacifist testimony.

The *Methodists* owe their historical identity to the spiritual leadership of John Wesley (1703-91), an Angelican clergyman whose "heart was strangely warmed" upon hearing a reading from Luther's Preface to Paul's Letter to the Romans, and who subsequently engaged in widespread evangelism throughout England. Wesley's converts and followers organized groups of their own within the Church of England. When Methodist activity spread to America and there was need for more ministers, Wesley finally took the bold step of ordaining them himself. From this time on, Methodism was distinct from the Church of England, although Wesley himself never left the church. Methodism stresses the doctrine of sanctification and the experience of salvation. "Christian perfection" is the goal of Methodist living, and Methodism places particular stress on personal religion and social responsibility.

The Christian Churches (Disciples of Christ) were founded in America in the nineteenth century by Thomas Campbell (1763-1854) and his son Alexander Campbell (1788-1886), for which reason its members are sometimes called "Campbellites." The driving force behind the history of the Disciples has been a desire for Christian unity based on the example of the early church, stressing the authority of the Bible, the practice of believer's baptism, and weekly celebration of the Lord's Supper. Doctrinally the church has remained flexible ("no creed but Christ") and its members have been active in the struggle for church unity.

5. Problems of description and classification are difficult enough with the free churches, but they are even more difficult when we turn to a final and heterogeneous family, the *sects*. The sects have been done a particular injustice by Protestant historians, who usually see them as no more than aberrations from the "central stream" of the Reformation.

During the Reformation period many of the sect groups were called "Anabaptists," a term of derision meaning "rebaptizers." The term was not strictly accurate; the Anabaptists did not feel that they were "re-baptizing" at all, for they did not consider that infant baptism had been a true baptism. The sectarians believed that the state was corrupt, and that the church should be separated from the world. For this reason, the name "separatist" was often applied to the sect groups. As a result, the sects often formed small communities, usually striving for economic self-sufficiency in order to be relieved of compromise with the evil world outside. Pacifism was a strong plank in most sectarian platforms. Very often the sect groups believed that the millennium was about to be inaugurated and that they must prepare the evil world for this imminent catastrophe. They tried to pattern their life on that of the primitive church in the New Testament, particularly as found in the book of Acts. But they also felt a strong dependence upon the Holy Spirit, who was believed to give direct guidance to members of the sect groups. Confusion between the voice of the Spirit and the desires of the sectarians was often a source of difficulty. Some of these groups became more solidly organized than others, and many of them, such as the Mennonites and Hutterites, survive to the present day.

But not all of the sect groups of the present day trace their roots back to the Reformation. Many of them are of quite recent origin. An emotional type of religous conversion is usually normative for membership in these groups, and those converted expect the imminent return of Christ in judgment. They make repeated use of a few biblical passages to support their position and believe intensely in the present and direct guidance of the Holy Spirit. As a rule they have little social concern, putting their emphasis on keeping "unspotted from the world." Most of the contemporary sect groups proliferate rapidly, each new faction trying to recapture the "purity" which has been lost by its contaminated forebears. Other sects, however, gain stability, and with the passage of time tend to become virtually indistinguishable from other denominations. . . .

Most Protestants belong to one of the first four denominational families just described, and the differences that separate them from one another are less than the similarities that unite them. It is a hopeful sign that there are often greater affinities between members of different denominations than exist within a given denomination itself. . . .

If there is any sure proof of the patience of God, it is in the fact that he has endured the varieties of Protestantism for four centuries. If there is any sure sign of the humility of God, it is in the fact that he has been willing to make use of the feeble instrument of organized Protestantism. If there is any sure indication of the power of God, it is in the fact that through the Protestant churches Jesus Christ has become a reality in countless lives. If there is any sure pointer to the compassion of God, it is in the fact that he deigns to make use of the humblest offerings of his divided flock.

It is such facts as these that enable Protestants to look ahead in hope, no matter how demonic may seem to be the ways men thwart God's will. For it is by his finger that the demons are cast out.

The Soul And Heart Of Belief

John A. Mackay

The roots of churches and denominations can be traced historically, but religious faith is more than history. It is a mysterious amalgam of beliefs and doctrines that gives substance and conviction to the heart and soul. Protestants are often accused of being so divided among themselves that they cannot be expected to agree on anything. But that is a caricature. For one thing, Protestants and Catholics hold many tenets in common, and among the major Protestant traditions there is a well-defined creedal consensus.

John A. Mackay was born in Scotland, studied in Spain, served as a missionary in Latin America, and in recent years was the distinguished president of Princeton Theological Seminary. He has been connected with almost every significant theological and ecumenical movement throughout the world. The author of ten books, two in Spanish, he has been especially concerned with highlighting and magnifying the central convictions of faith, drawing upon the classic traditions of the past but moving ahead into the issues of today.

"The Soul and Heart of Belief" is taken from a chapter on

"Protestantism" in *The Great Religions of the Modern World*, edited by Edward J. Jurji (1946).

It is an impressive, albeit unhappy, fact that the Christian religion, the most influential and aggressive of the great religions of mankind, has been represented for the past four hundred years by three separate traditions, Eastern Orthodoxy, Roman Catholicism, and Protestantism. These traditions, while they all derive from a comon source and are one in essential Christian loyalties, differ from one another in very important respects.

The Christian tradition which took historical form most recently is known by the general name of Protestantism. In its institutional expression, Protestantism is the youngest of the three Christian traditions. To be more specific, it is that Christian tradition which owes its ecclesiastical form, its confessional position, its spiritual attitude to the attempt made in the sixteenth century to give a more adequate expression to Christianity than that which was current at the time. The historic endeavor to restore the Christian religion to its native, pristine glory, is commonly called the Protestant Reformation. This revolutionary movement in the field of religion became the source of a diversified expression of Christianity. Because of its variegated character, Protestantism as a phenomenon in history is difficult to define. "If we are thinking of a purely historical definition of Protestantism," says Ernst Troeltsch, "we soon recognize that for Protestantism as a whole, it cannot be immediately formulated." From the viewpoint of its inner religious spirit, however, as distinguished from that of its outer diversified expression, Protestantism can be readily defined.

Some important facts should be held in mind as we undertake this study. While Protestantism emerged in history at a given time and under special circumstances, its ideas and spirit were not a creation of the sixteenth century. For these it claims high antiquity. It was the contention of the Protestant

Reformers and continues to be the contention of their succes-
sors, that the religious emphases that began to be made in
that century were not discoveries of new truth, but rather
recoveries of ancient truth. The Reformers did not regard
themselves as discoverers but as restorers. They did not think
of their work as opening up new paths, but as reopening old
paths, great highways of truth, which in the course of
Christian history had been abandoned or grown over. Their
emphasis from the beginning was positive, not negative.

The term "Protestant," it is true, suggests, at first thought, a
negative attitude. It has been interpreted as an attitude of
pure dissent from a positive position. Nothing could be more
untrue, historically and etymologically, to the famous "Protest" which was presented at the Diet of Spires in 1529, and
which gave its name to the new religious movement. The
German princes and the representatives of the fourteen free
cities which had embraced the principles of the religious
reform did not "protest" against ideas; they appeared in the
role of "protestants" because a curb had been placed upon the
free propagation of truths which were decidedly positive in
character. Etymologically, moreover, "protest" means dissent
only in a secondary sense. The essence of the word is to "state
as a witness," to "aver," "to make solemn affirmation." As we
engage, therefore, in the study of what Protestantism is, it is
well that our minds be disabused of the idea that what will
engage our attention is a negative dissent from a positive
position. The genius of Protestant Christianity is affirmation,
not negation. . . .

Amid and beneath all the diverse manifestations of Protestantism in history, we discover certain major emphases which
together constitute the inmost core of Protestant faith and
life.

The supreme authority of the Bible. Protestantism emerged in
history with the affirmation that the Bible, the Scriptures of
the Old and New Testaments, rather than tradition or the
Church, constitutes the supreme authority in all questions
relating to Christian faith and practice. This affirmation was

directed against the authority of the Roman Catholic Church, particularly the papacy, which had vested in itself the authority formerly exercised by the Ecumenical Councils. The Protestant Reformers proclaimed that authoritative knowledge of God and his will is derived from a study of Holy Scripture. The Bible, which in the medieval Church had existed only in a Latin version, was now translated from the original Hebrew and Greek into the several languages of the West. It soon began to be studied not only by churchmen and scholars but also by the common people. The presupposition that underlay the translation of the Scriptures into the vernacular tongues of Europe, and later of the whole world, was and continues to be, that the Holy Spirit, under whose inspiration the writers of the sacred record had done their work, would lead humble souls to a saving knowledge of God. Tradition, which had come to be regarded as coequal in authority with the Bible as a source of our knowledge of God, and the Church, which had become the proximate rule of faith and the supreme interpreter of revelation, were now studied and judged in the light of the Bible.

The restoration of the Bible to the supreme place of religious authority which it had occupied in the early Church has had far-reaching implications for Protestant thought and life. One implication touches the meaning of divine revelation. The classical Christian affirmation is that God has spoken. The eternal silence has been broken. The inscrutable mystery has been unveiled. There is a word from the Lord. Truth exists. This truth is redemptive truth. It has taken the form of great redemptive deeds wrought by God in behalf of man, and of luminous prophetic words which interpreted those deeds and made clear to man the nature and will of God for his salvation. The record of those deeds and words we have in the Bible. The core of the Bible and the clue to its understanding is the gospel. The gospel is the good news of what God has already done for man in Christ, and is ready to do for any person who believes the record concerning Jesus Christ, the Saviour. They only, however, really understand the Bible and attain a knowledge of God and his redemptive will who come to the study of Holy Scripture not because of intellectual curiosity but through a deep concern to discover authoritative answers to the agonizing questions about God, sin and destiny.

Biblical truth is moreover personal truth. Being a book about redemption, the Bible is supremely interested in answering the quest of a person who comes to it with the query, "What must I do to be saved?" This question is answered in the form of an encounter between God and the earnest reader in such wise that the centuries are telescoped, and the redemptive encounter takes place again. Not only so: from the hour of the great encounter onward, it is in and through the Bible that the Christian soul holds communion with God. Through the Bible also, the will of God is revealed to the Christian for his behavior in the concrete process of living. The Bible is, therefore, not only the supreme source of our knowledge of God and the supreme theater where God and man meet; it is also the chief medium of our communion with God and the chief guide in the proper conduct of life.

As regards an understanding of biblical truth, the Bible is to be interpreted in terms of categories which are native to itself. Being a book about redemption, that is to say, about the supernatural disclosure of God to men as a redeeming God, the Bible cannot be understood in terms of any categories and forms of thought which are alien to the basic presupposition that God revealed himself in a redemptive manner in the life of Israel. Basic for a true understanding of the Bible is the recognition, for example, that one of its central categories is that of a "covenant" between God and his people whereby he promises to bless them and they promise to do his will. Moreover, being a book about redemption, the Bible is authoritative only in its own particular sphere. As a document with a history, it is to be studied and investigated with the most rigorous historical and scientific criteria. Under such scrutiny, a flood of light has been thrown upon the origin of the biblical records, as also upon the elements that entered into Israel's religion. The important thing about the Bible is, however, that whereas the human, often all too human, elements are abundantly present, God used lowly and unworthy people and religious elements of a plebeian and even exotic character, to communicate himself and his purpose to men. His self-communication moved progressively from the early origins of Israel's history through the great prophets of Israel and Judah, took personal and absolute form in Jesus Christ, and was perfected in the Apostolic era of the Spirit. Revelation as a whole is bound together by the central reality of the Redeemer, so that there is a sense in which one can call the Bible a book about Jesus Christ. It is in the measure in which he becomes known in his saving power that the Bible becomes truly understood. While it is not true that the Bible is the "religion of Protestants," as has sometimes been said, it is true that the Bible produced the Protestant Reformation and has inspired and determined the Protestant expression of the Christian religion.

The centrality given to the Bible in Protestant faith and experience exerted a profound influence upon those forms of cultural development which are Protestant in their inspiration. Popular interest in the Bible gave a great impulse to public education. Literacy was promoted in order that men might learn to read the Scriptures. Where the Bible has been diffused, the common people have become literate, while culture in every sphere has been transfigured. In many instances the Bible itself was the first book to be translated into the language of a people. In other instances, a particular translation of the Bible gave classical expression to the language in which it appeared. The great figures, episodes, and teachings of the Book have entered as a creative force into the main stream of many a literature. It is a striking and symbolical fact that Rembrandt and Bach, two of the greatest masters in the hsitory of art (one in painting, the other in music), were Protestants, and that their great creations were directly inspired by the text of Holy Scripture. Both men were profound students of the Bible whose inner meaning they succeeded in interpreting in a way that no other artists have ever done.

The unmediated Lordship of Jesus Christ. The centrality of Christ in Christian thought and experience and the unmediated character of relations between him and the soul of men is a basic Protestant emphasis. Jesus Christ does not submit to control or patronage even by the Church, as the Grand Inquisitor in Dostoevski's famous legend thought he should. He maintains himself in sovereign freedom, using the Church as the agent of his will, but bringing it into judgment when it becomes presumptuous and assumes prerogatives which Christ has never relinquished. A fourfold affirmation makes up the Protestant insight into the meaning and significance of Jesus Christ and his relations with men.

1. *Salvation is obtained through faith in Jesus Christ.* The doctrine of justification by faith has been called the formal principle of Protestantism. Its meaning is this: man is saved, not by ethical striving or achievement, but by the joyous acceptance of God's gift of salvation. Good works do not save men; they are the fruits of men who are saved. God offers to man the complete redemption which was wrought out for him in the life, death, and resurrection of Jesus Christ. To the reality of this redemption, man gives his assent, acquiescing in the fact that he owes salvation not to his own goodness, but to the goodness of another. By an act of consent or commitment, he gives himself to that other, the living Christ, with whom he identifies himself in thought and in life. In this view of faith there are, accordingly, two elements: one, the element of assent by which the mind grasps and acquiesces in what God has done for men in Christ; the other, that of consent or commitment, whereby a man identifies himself wholly with Christ in thought and in life. In saving faith, therefore, there is assent to a proposition, and consent to a person.

Believers in Christ, whoever they may be, enter upon a life of unique privilege and responsibility. They are constituted "priests." As such they have full right or access to God through Christ at all times. It is their corresponding responsibility to live lives of utter dedication to God, in the secular as well as in the religious sphere. The doctrine of the "universal priesthood of believers" is a basic Protestant affirmation.

2. *Jesus Christ is the sovereign Lord of the Church and of the world.* While affirming that Jesus Christ founded a Church which is his body, and that outside this Church there is no salvation, Protestantism affirms that Jesus Christ has not abdicated. He continues to direct affairs in the Church and in the world. As the Lord of the Church, he can bring and does bring the Church into judgment. That being so, a Church that bears the Christian name may so far depart from the mind of Christ in faith and practice, as virtually to become apostate and to be, in the words directed by the Lord of the Church to one of the churches in the Apocalypse, "spewed out" of his mouth. It means also that there may be times when an individual Christian may have to appeal to Jesus Christ against the Church. This is the significance of the famous words of Pascal when he said: "If my letters are condemned in Rome, what I condemn in them is condemned in heaven: to Thy tribunal, O Lord Jesus, I appeal." That was the profoundly Protestant affirmation of a great Roman Catholic saint. It was in the spirit of that affirmation that the Protestant Reformers made their appeal to Jesus Christ himself against those who carried on the affairs of the Church in his name.

Jesus Christ should be equally sovereign in the affairs of the state. It is never legitimate for Protestants to make any pact with, or derive special advantages from, a form of government whose principles run counter to the truths of the Christian religion, or which challenges the right of the Church to proclaim God's truth and to live in accordance with his will.

3. A third affirmation is this. *The concrete figure of Jesus*

Christ as he appears in the gospels, is the normative standard for human life. Whenever, as has frequently happened in Roman, Orthodox, and Protestant circles, the way of life and thought which was characteristic of the historical figure of Jesus is not taken seriously, the quality of Christian living immediately declines. The so-called "Back to Jesus" movement, and that of the "Quest of the historical Jesus," which were Protestant in their inspiration, despite all the great limitations attaching to this approach, gave to the Christian Church the concrete living figure of Jesus in a form in which the Church had never possessed him before. That figure, divested of the elements that belonged merely to his own age, sets before each succeeding generation of men a concrete and authoritative standard of human behavior. While it is true that "Lives of Christ" have been rather autobiographies of their authors than biographies of Jesus, they do enshrine the eternal truth that the most important thing that any man can do is to face the man and to order his life in accordance with the life of Christ.

4. The fourth affirmation regarding Jesus Christ is: *the risen Christ is the perennial source of strength for action.* Protestant piety has stressed the reality of communion with the living Christ, not only on the part of great saints but also on the part of simple believers; not only in the sacraments of the Lord's Supper but amid the routine of daily living. "Lo, I am with you always, even unto the end of the world," said Christ. These are the words which David Livingstone called the "words of a gentleman." A sense of comradeship with the living Christ, to whom one can go at all times for forgiveness and cleansing, for sympathy and for strength, has been one of the chief marks and sources of inspiration of Protestant Christian personality. Because of the overwhelming fact of Christ as the ever present and living Lord, Protestant Christians have not been aware of any necessity to have recourse to the Virgin Mother or to the saints as special intercessors. Having the living Lord himself, they have felt the need of no

other. This Christocentric character of religious experience amid the routine of daily living and in all the great crises of life has been a characteristic of Protestant Christianity.

The witnessing responsibility of the Church. The supreme function of the Christian Church is, in the Protestant view, to bear witness to God. The Church exists to witness to the gospel, the good news of human salvation in and through Jesus Christ. Whenever the Church, as the "Body of Christ," thinks and acts as if it were an end in itself, or engages in activities in which the reality of the gospel does not hold a central position, it fails to fulfill its primary function.

Witness must be borne to the gospel by word and by life. The centrality of preaching, of proclaiming the gospel by word, has been one of the chief characteristics of Protestant Christianity. Ideally speaking, the gospel must be proclaimed with passionate conviction: with conviction because it is true, with passion because it is important and because obedience to it is urgent. It must be proclaimed also with unmistakable clarity in the language of every people. Clarity in the proclamation of the gospel involves a thorough knowledge of the Bible, where such knowledge is obtained; personal experience of the power of the gospel; an adequate theological system in which the gospel is central. The form of speech used in proclamation must be such as to convey the significance of the good news in the most compelling form. The heart of man and the culture of the time must be assiduously studied in order that communication may take place in such a way as to be challenging and luminous.

It is for the Church also to bear witness to the gospel by life. No witness will be more effective than that of personal piety, of spiritual inwardness, of victorious living, on the part of those who profess the name of Jesus Christ. But witness must be borne no less by a deep human or social passion. If men are to take seriously the presentation of the good news about God, goodness must validate the presence of truth; good works must prove the reality of faith. However, personal ethical behavior and Christian philanthropy are not enough.

The Christian Church must proclaim God's righteousness for all human relationships, and must throw its weight at all times upon the side of righteousness.

Everything which the Church does in bearing witness to the gospel by word and by life must have as its principal aim that individuals and communities may respond to the call of God. In order to exist truly, the Church, in accordance with the inner meaning of the term exist, must set out, sally forth, along the highways of life, bearing witness before all men, in every circumstance and in every age, to the good news that God has given a definite and final answer to the agonizing problems of man's life.

The Radical Reformation

Roland H. Bainton

It is a conceit of majorities in power everywhere to assume that dissident minorities are of little importance for the future. During the sixteenth and seventeenth centuries in Europe, Lutherans and Calvinists were so busy fighting the Roman Catholics that they had no time to consider the left-wing groups like the Anabaptists. In Great Britain, the Church of England, having established itself, had little time for the group of Quakers or Friends.

History has a way of vindicating the aims and goals of the little people, and while the left-wing reformation groups never achieved much recognition in Europe, they found receptive soil in America.

Since all such groups took their faith seriously, they rejected infant baptism as an empty ceremony (how can children know what is happening?). Dubbed Anabaptists (or "re-baptizers"), they also tended to remain aloof from state and government, and they were usually peace-loving, dedicated Christians—which of course did not prevent them from being persecuted on all sides.

No one knows more about this left-wing or radical reformation than Roland H. Bainton, the Titus Street Professor of Ecclesiastical

History at Yale University. A Quaker by birth and by choice, he has been especially interested in religious liberty, Christian pacifism, and the whole area of Reformation studies on which he has written more than thirty books.

The passage reprinted here is from his popular text, *The Reformation of the Sixteenth Century* (1952).

The word Reformation is usually referred to the Lutheran movement, the word Reformed to the Zwinglian and Calvinist. The word "restored" would be the most appropriate to apply to those who by opponents were called Anabaptists. Their great word was "restitution." Much more drastically than any of their contemporaries they searched the Scriptures in order to recover the pattern of the early church.

What struck them was that the primitive church had been composed only of heartfelt believers and so far from being united with the state was rather persecuted, despised and rejected, a church of martyrs. So always, said the Anabaptists, must the true Church be reviled, rejected, and crushed. To this the Catholics and equally the Lutherans and Zwinglians replied that of course the Church was persecuted in an age when the government was hostile, but after the conversion of the emperor why should hostility continue? The state had become Christian and the Church could affiliate with the state and embrace the community. The Anabaptists retorted that the formal conversion of the emperor did not Christianize the state. The world remains the world, and if Christians are well spoken of, the explanation can only be that they have abandoned their witness. In the words of an Anabaptist hymn writer:

> "Yes," says the world, "there is no need
> That I with Christ should languish.
> He died for me and by his deed
> He saved me from this anguish.
> He paid for me, this faith can see.
> Naught else need be." . . .

O brother mine, it is not so fine.
The devil said this to thee.

The Anabaptist view rested upon pessimism with regard to the world and optimism with regard to the Church. The world—that is, society at large—will always be the partner of the flesh and the devil, but the Church must walk another road and must exemplify within its fellowship the living and the dying of the Lord Jesus. It must be a community of the saints whose members, though not perfect, yet aspire to perfection and strive mightily. The complaint against the Lutherans and the Zwinglians was that they had not produced a sufficient improvement in life. Promptly came the retort that the Anabaptists were reverting to monasticism and seeking again to win heaven by their good deeds, to which the answer was that they were not seeking to fulfill the law in order to be saved but rather to give proof of their faith by exhibiting its fruits. The kernel of Anabaptism was an ethical urge. If the Catholic Church had improved its morals they might not have found it too hard to return to its fold, whereas Luther said that his objection to the Catholic Church centered not on the life but on the teaching.

The Anabaptists called for a strict morality, and there can be no question that they achieved it. The testimony of their opponents is eloquent. Zwingli said of them, "At first contact their conduct appears irreproachable, pious, unassuming, attractive. . . . Even those who are inclined to be critical will say that their lives are excellent." Zwingli's successor, Bullinger, said that they denounced covetousness, pride, profanity, the lewd conversation and immorality of the world, drinking, and gluttony. A Catholic observed in them "no lying, deception, swearing, strife, harsh language, no intemperate eating and drinking, no outward personal display, but rather humility, patience, uprightness, meekness, honesty, temperance, straightforwardness in such measure that one would suppose they had the Holy Spirit of God."

One notes in these testimonies the witness to their sobriety.

The movement for total abstinence from alcoholic beverages stems from these groups. Not even Catholic monasticism had called for total abstinence. Luther most assuredly did not, but neither did Calvin or Knox. The Anabaptists moved in this direction. . . .

The Church, then, according to these so-called Anabaptists, must be a gathered society, to use the terminology later current among the Congregationalists, and cannot coincide with the community unless of course the community be restricted to adult believers, as was sometimes the case in Anabaptist colonies. . . .

The Church is to be kept pure by discipline and the expulsion of those who do not exemplify the pattern of Christ's conduct. The religious ban, however, was to be the only penalty. The arm of the state should never be invoked. Religious liberty was thus a tenet of the Anabaptists, and they were the first church to make it a cardinal point in their creed.

Furthermore church and state should be separate, inasmuch as the state is concerned with everyone in the community, whereas the Church consists only of the saints. The state was ordained because of sin, but the Church was created for the saved. These propositions entailed the dissolution of the whole structure of medieval society. Luther and Zwingli had never gone so far and recoiled the more because the Anabaptists went on to say that the true Christians must not only forswear an allegiance with the state, but must have nothing whatever to do with it, since the world is the world and remains without hope of ever being Christianized. Luther agreed that society cannot be Christianized, but nevertheless believed that Christians must accept the office of magistrate in order to restrain outrageous villainy. The Anabaptists retorted that the state has indeed been ordained by God on account of sin and to restrain sin, but should be left to be administered by sinners.

Such a position of itself entailed a withdrawal from political life and the separation became all the more marked because the ethic of the Sermon on the Mount was taken literally and made incumbent upon all Christians. The Catholics took it literally but conserved it only through a vocational division whereby its rigoristic precepts applied solely to the monks. Luther rejected this division, insisting that Christian morality is demanded of all, but he regarded the Sermon on the Mount rather as a disposition than a code. The Anabaptists agreed with the Catholics in taking the counsels to the letter and with Luther as to the single standard. Hence all Christians became monks. There was this difference, however, that the Anabaptists did not reject marriage. They repudiated war and capital punishment. Under no circumstances would they wield the sword, nor would they go to law. They would take no oath, for Christ said "Swear not at all," and some held all things in common.

Their whole manner of life was summed up by a Swiss chronicler who was himself impressed although not persuaded: "Their walk and manner of life was altogether pious, holy, and irreproachable. They avoided costly clothing, despised costly food and drink, clothed themselves with coarse cloth, covered their heads with broad felt hats; their walk and conduct was altogether humble. . . . They carried no weapon, neither sword nor dagger, nothing more than a pointless bread knife, saying that these were wolf's clothing which should not be found on the sheep. They would never swear an oath, not even upon demand of the government. And if anyone transgressed, he was excluded by them." . . .

Those who thus held themselves as sheep for the slaughter were dreaded and exterminated as if they had been wolves. They challenged the whole way of life of the community. . . . And the Anabaptists did become numerous. They despaired of society at large, but they did not despair of winning converts to their way. Every member of the group was regarded as a missionary. Men and women left their homes to go on evangelistic tours. The established churches, whether Catholic or Protestant, were aghast at these ministers of both sexes insinuating themselves into town and farm. In some of the communities of Switzerland and the Rhine valley the Anabaptists began to outnumber Catholics and Protestants alike. Would not the growth of people with such views be even more of a menace to public security than the demolition of a city wall? In 1529 the imperial meeting at Speyer declared with the concurrence alike of Catholics and Lutherans that the death penalty should be inflicted upon the Anabaptists.

Menno Simons, one of their later leaders, reported the outcome.

> Some they have executed by hanging, some they have tortured with inhuman tyranny, and afterwards choked with cords at the stake. Some they roasted and burned alive. Some they have killed with the sword and given them to the fowls of the air to devour. Some they have cast to the fishes. . . . Others wander about here and there, in want, homelessness, and affliction, in mountains and deserts, in holes and caves of the earth. They must flee with their wives and little children from one country to another, from one city to another. They are hated, abused, slandered, and lied about by all men.

. . . Then the less balanced spirits came to the fore. Those who had lived under the continual shadow of death in caves and desolate places of the earth began like Muentzer to dream dreams of the birds of the heaven coming to devour the carcasses of the oppressors, of the return of the Lord to vindicate the saints, of the New Jersualem from which the 144,000 of the redeemed should go out to slaughter the ungodly. Whether the Lord would accomplish all this by himself, or whether men should assist, was not altogether clear. Dates for the return of Christ were set and places selected as the New Jerusalem. Melchior Hoffman predicted that in the year 1533 he would be imprisoned for six months in Strasbourg and then the Lord would come. Only the first half of the prediction was fulfilled, and Hoffman languished in prison, speedily forgotten even by his own party. But his ideas moved down the Rhine and in 1534 the town of Muenster in Westphalia was selected as the New Jerusalem. Here for the first and only time the Anabaptists succeeded in taking over municipal government, and not without violence. Under all the strains pacifism succumbed. The Anabaptists marched into the market place prepared to be as sheep for the slaughter, but armed with swords just as a reminder of what they might do if they chose. Whereupon a revelation from the Holy Ghost instructed them to choose that which they might. Catholics and Lutherans were expelled; the saints began their reign.

Leadership fell to those who sought to restore not only the New Testament but also the Old. They were like Zwingli in stressing the continuity between the new and the old Israel of God. But then they began to revive the eccentricities of the prophets and the immoralities of the patriarchs. Some Anabaptists in Holland ran around naked in imitation of the prophet Isaiah who walked naked as a sign. Another Anabaptist, also in imitation of Isaiah, went to the fireplace and lifted a hot coal to his lips. Instead of being able to say like the prophet, "Woe is me, I am undone, for I am a man of unclean lips," he was too burned to say anything for a fortnight. At Münster the aberration took the form of a reinstatement of polygamy after the example of Abraham, Isaac, and Jacob. Catholics and Lutherans combined to exterminate the New Jerusalem. The town was taken and all the new Davids and Enochs and Elijahs were put to the rack and the sword.

The whole ugly episode discredited Anabaptism. Despite the fact that for the first ten years under frightful provocation they had been without offense, yet when a handful of fanatics ran amuck the entire party was besmirched with the excesses of the lunatic fringe, and well into the nineteenth century historians of the Reformation did little more than recount the aberrations of the saints rampant.

Despite constant vigilance Anabaptism was not extinguished. Nor did the excesses pervert the character of the movement as a whole. Menno Simons, the founder of the Mennonites, and Jacob Hutter, the founder of the Hutterites, repudiated all of the Muentzer vagaries: polygamy, revolution, and date-setting for the return of the Lord. Anabaptism revived its original principles of a sect separated from the world, committed to following the pattern of the New Testament in simplicity, sobriety, poverty, meekness, and long-suffering. Menno declared that true Christians must "crucify the flesh and its desires and lusts, prune the heart, mouth and the whole body with the knife of the divine word of all unclean thoughts, unbecoming words and actions." There must be no adornment with gold, silver, pearls, silk, velvet, and costly finery. Swords must be beaten into plowshares and love extended even to enemies. Charity must be given to all, and though the faithful be despoiled of their goods they must turn not away.

For the most part in Europe these groups could find no abiding place. In Holland and Switzerland a few survived at the price of a measure of conformity. In Germany they were stamped out. This is one of the greatest tragedies of German history. If only Lutheranism could have been subject to the stimulus of the criticism and competition of the sects, it could never have become so complacent and allied to the established order. The Anglican Church owes an incalculable debt to the Nonconformists. So completely were the Anabaptists exterminated that few Lutherans are aware that the principles of British dissent originated on German soil.

The Anabaptists, however, did survive. They maintained themselves by following the frontier and keeping aloof from bourgeois civilization, industrialism, imperialism, and nationalism. They sought the fringes where social totalitarianism had not yet imposed conformity and the community of saints could live unmolested. Poland and Moravia for a time offered an asylum. Tolerant noblemen were willing to admit tillers of the soil without asking too many questions about their religious convictions. In Moravia religious communist societies with an international complexion were established in small groups of about a hundred. The ideal was not the improvement of the standard of living as in modern communism, but rather to live in accord with Franciscan poverty but on a family basis. The resemblance to monasticism is obvious save for celibacy and later the Shakers were to introduce celibacy in the Protestant community, but the Mennonites and Hutterites have never done so. How close they were, however, to monasticism appears in the case of one group of Anabaptists in Moravia, who in the period of the Counter-Reformation were offered the choice of exile or tolerance of their entire mode of living on the one condition that they accept the mass. The Catholic Church regarded them as a quasi-monastic community.

Those who did not conform, and they were the majority, had to suffer repeated exiles. Some went West, some went East. Pennsylvania received a considerable migration. Other bands traversed northern Germany to Poland, Hungary, and Transylvania, and at length to Russia, until in the late nineteenth century new pressures in the East occasioned fresh movements to the West, to Manitoba, Indiana, Nebraska, and Paraguay. Eternal Abrahams, they have ever loins girt ready to go they know not whither.

On the western frontiers the Anabaptists have preserved their pattern more truly than in the Old World. During the past four centuries they ahve succeeded amazingly in maintaining a community life of their own, cut off from all the corruptions of the world. The buttonless coats, the broad hats, the flowing beards of the Amish set them apart even on their occasional excursions into society. These peculiarities serve like a uniform to distinguish the wearer and guard him against seduction. All the encroachments of the modern society have been stoutly resisted—the railroad, the telephone, the automobile, the movie, the newspaper, especially the comic strips, and even the tractor. Naturally, too, the state school has been regarded as a peril to the community pattern. The old ways have been best preserved where the isolation is greatest and where the opposition is most acute. A segregated community thrives on persecution. It needs something like the ghetto for the preservation of its own morale. Contact with the outside and fraternization insidiously induce conformity. Then the children begin to dress and think like others and to go over to the world. The sect thus becomes the church and the old witness survives only in a warm piety and a nostalgic singing of martyr hymns.

Primacy Of The Bible

Martin E. Marty

It is sometimes suggested that the Protestants of the Reformation exchanged one pope for another. They rejected the authority of the pope in Rome in favor of a paper pope, the Bible. Protestants, of course, have always claimed that the Bible precedes the pope, not only in time but in authority. It is the Bible, therefore, that stands in judgment over all ecclesiastical forms since it has primacy. The Bible, all Protestants would agree, is the supreme court of final appeal.

But Protestant consensus on the Bible's authority does not mean unanimity regarding interpretation. Some Protestants take the creation of the world in six days as literal scientific fact, just as they believe that the whale swallowed Jonah, because that's what the Bible says. Other Protestants insist that the primary message of the Bible has to do with God's redemption of sinful humanity, and that quibbling about dates and historical events only detracts from the main point. Oversimplified, the two views can be described as "literal" and "liberal," with many modifications.

Still, it remains true that for most Protestants, today as for yesterday, the Bible is the sole authority for faith and practice. This basic conviction motivated the reformers to translate the Scriptures into the common languages which people could understand; it inspired a steady succession of biblical commentaries; it prodded pastors to preach expository sermons; it issued in the Protestant passion for education, a learned ministry, and an intelligent and instructed laity. By insisting on the primal authority of the Bible, Protestants also claimed that Christian faith should be literate, rational, and understandable.

But this common conviction did not prevent Protestants from disagreeing among themselves. The reason for this resided in the Bible itself. The interpreter must first decide what text (from many manuscripts) to use and how to evaluate variant readings in the Hebrew and the Greek. The next problem is to be sure of the original writer's intent, not always an easy matter. But beyond these initial steps, the interpreter must relate an ancient message from an alien culture into modern terms for a scientific, technological society.

To unravel some of these issues we need a historian and a theologian. Martin E. Marty is professor of modern church history at the University of Chicago and associate editor of *The Christian Century* magazine. He is a prolific and thoughtful writer and one of the major voices in contemporary American religious thought. The selection which follows is taken from his book, titled simply, *Protestantism* (1972).

The Bible and Protestantism are entwined in a common history after the early sixteenth century. People in revolt against empire and pope, conscious of their new territorialism or nationalism, eager to extricate themselves from Rome but fearing anarchy, needed an authority and found it in the Bible. They needed a sacred symbol and found it in the Book. Most Protestant movements immediately saw the need for the vernacular Scriptures, and reformers had to be linguistic experts, providing a common language for emerging areas or territories.

Printing with movable type in "the age of Gutenberg" was roughly contemporaneous with the early Protestant movement. The evangelical leaders exploited the new invention to propagate their movement by putting out scores of editions of a Book that in a previous age had been denied the laity and many priests for economic reasons if for no other. Dissemination of the Bible, then, was an act of a democratizing spirit and a sign of faith in the ability of people to read and interpret the texts in a faithful and authentic manner. Wycliffe Tyndale, Coverdale, Luther—these and others were busy translators and publishers of the Bible at the dawn of reform.

The German theologian Gerhard Ebeling once suggested that the history of Christianity is simply the history of the interpretation of the Bible. In some respects this seems to be true of Protestantism. The missionary and benevolent movements were born in part of a rereading of the great commission in Matthew's Gospel, the command to teach and baptize all nations. This was an injunction that had been overlooked in much of Protestantism for most of two and a half centuries. The humanitarian endeavors and the formation of societies for propagating the faith and publishing the Bible grew out of men's rereading of that Book and their fusing of a vision of human need and divine command.

Liberal and modernizing theological movements in the age of the Enlightenment or the nineteenth century were reinterpretations of the Bible, often with its supernatural elements removed or minimized. The ecumenical movement in the twentieth century was based in part on a recovery of biblical language, which made interchurch talk comprehensible, and a rereading of the biblical injunctions to give expression to unity, passages which had often been overlooked. . . .

On the matter of regarding and interpreting the Bible itself (as opposed to interpreting various teachings in it), two basically different attitudes have prevailed. One could draw a line through Protestant churches in various countries and find people on both sides of it. The two attitudes toward the Bible are paralleled by differing attitudes toward faith itself. These two deserve examination; it must be remembered that many subtle variations occur within each general school, but two have prevailed.

The first view we shall call liberal, without thereby wanting to connote all the shadings of theological liberalism. By liberal here is meant a generally rather free approach to interpretation, one which, in the words of its advocates, stresses "not the letter but the Spirit."

In the eyes of its enemies, this approach is a modern innovation—though evidences of battles over it are already present within the canon, and early fathers like Irenaeus, Justin Martyr, and Origen could be numbered in its camp. Certainly it has been present from the first generation of Protestantism. Were it not for the confusing associations of the word, it could even be called the traditional view. It retains something of the Catholic sense that the Bible is to be interpreted in the light of the religious and literary traditions, not radically isolated or segregated from its environment and from the rest of learning, literature, and experience. . . .

This school of interpretation considers itself to be particularly Protestant when it stresses the openness of the biblical canon. That is, there has never been complete agreement in the Church about which books belong in the Bible. Certain ones were agreed upon, but there had been protest against others. It was considered theoretically possible at least that other books could be discovered which the Church would regard as belonging in the canon. After all, the canon was itself the product of the Church, and not vice versa. An open canon, it was argued, kept people from idolizing the collection of documents, making a god out of a book, or having an all-purpose code.

At the same time, the liberal always stressed levels of intensity or revelational power within the canon as it came to him. He resists the idea of a doctrine of inspiration which would call him to grant equal hearing to, say, a passage from the book of Esther which had no theological reference and to the Gospel of John. He looks for some divining principle which will throw light on such a varied collection of documents as the Bible is.

The liberal prefers to reproduce the Gospel of John in

calling Jesus and not the Bible itself, "the Word of God," though if proper precautions are first asserted, its spokesmen will refer also to the Bible as the Word of God. They do not want a simple equation between the two, since God's Word in Christ is also something more and somehow other than the book. These Protestants might say, then, that the Bible is not the revelation but is the witness to the revelation, the written testimony to God's Word and his mighty acts. . . .

The literal view has always seen itself to be the higher and more safeguarding version. The Bible does not contain but *is* the Word of God. The Book is not the testimony to a revelation but it is the revelation. The canon is not a partly haphazard collection, but was put together by divine guidance on certain clearly definable lines (e.g., in the New Testament, apostolic authorship). There is a qualitative difference between it and all other literature, and the hermeneutical (interpretive) principles by which one comes to it differ from those which one employs on other great literature. If a book is ascribed to a certain author, he must have written it—even if such an ascription seems to place it outside its own time. If Christ refers to passages from Second Isaiah (Isaiah 40-60) as being "Isaiah," even if they give evidence of having been written 250 years after Isaiah's time, then Isaiah it must be. This is upheld even if it means that a prophet is heard talking in detail in the past tense, and with a different style from what he had earlier used, about events that have not yet occurred. What could it mean for the idea of his divine sonship if Christ called a biblical book by an inaccurate designation, asks the literalist.

The literal approach has always been championed in those circles where Protestant scholasticism, with its sense for logic and sequence and for a substantial (as opposed to existential) view of truth or for a propositional approach to revelation, has been favored. Thus in the seventeenth century period of Protestant dogmatic formulation, when Aristotelian categories that had become familiar in the church through medieval Scholasticism were revived in the service of the church, both Reformed and Lutheran theologians wrote works of dogmatics which located a doctrine of infallible Scriptures as an a priori to other Christian teachings. As this view came to be challenged in the Enlightenment, its adherents became defensive and elaborated it even further. When scientific discoveries seemed to call into question elements of biblical world views, the scientific order had to be challenged. Some literalists did so by compartmentalizing, by living in one mental setting when they encountered science and then moving into an entirely different one when they read the Scripture. Others tried to harmonize the two worlds. When scientific accounts stressed an old world, the literalist took the young-earth pictures of Genesis and suggested that the writers may have meant that the world was created in six aeons, using the terms of six "days" figuratively.

The literal reader accuses the liberal of adapting the Scripture to contemporary opinion, and thus doing it violence. Only hardness of heart and resistance to the Spirit would lead one, he would contend, to place himself and his literary analysis above the Scriptures and Christ. It is clear here again, as so often in Protestantism, that behind the surface issue two approaches of faith are in question. The liberal stresses a kind of subjective-existentialist coming to faith in Christ, after which the scriptural witness is seen to be inspired and revelational. The literal reader stresses the conviction that faith is produced when one comes to have a belief in the trustworthiness of the Bible.

Accusations fly across these party lines. The liberal calls the literal reader obscurantist, fundamentalist, antimodern, and less than trusting in the power of the Spirit. The literal reader sees the liberal as tampering with holy things, making the Bible say what he wants it to. Both try to forget that their approach does not solve everything: for example, Seventh-day Adventists and conservative Baptists share in belief in an inerrant Bible, but differ on almost everything in it, including the days of worship, the question of Old Testament legislation's binding effect, and the millennium. . . .

Concurrent with the rise of modern literary criticism of the text came drastic theological change. . . . A new relativism was afflicting many reflective men, and they became unsure of the salvation account that had been isolated from the contingencies of history in the literalists' view of the biblical narrative.

While all this was occurring, the literal interpreter found all the more reason to resist science and modern philosophy, to feel more beleaguered and defensive as he saw theological faculty after faculty and scholar after scholar go over to the liberal view in even its more extreme forms. The result was a reaction that in America was called fundamentalism, in which the literalistic approach was reinforced and made the touchstone of all theology. The fundamentalist view is well known around the world because of the publicity given evangelists who speak in its name and because it has produced great numbers of "faith missionaries," who operate with a certitude about their truth born of adherence to this vision of the Bible.

There have been reconciling attempts and some common meeting grounds for moderates in both camps in the twentieth century. . . . Still, both camps are wary. The liberal feels that he alone keeps alive the Protestant principle with its resistance to the idolization of the human, the objectification of the spiritual. The literal reader argues strenuously that the alternative is hopelessly subjective and arbitrary; that it offers no defense against modernity's acids and calls into question the reliability of God. If the battle shows no sign of wearing down, let it at least be noted that when Protestants fight, they fight about the Scripture. They remain a people of the Book; both sides read it for reinforcement of their point of view. They want to settle arguments on its basis. In their own peculiar ways, then, they give it honor, as their fathers have done for centuries.

Churches As Social Institutions

H. Richard Niebuhr

Churches and denominations are not only communities of faith and ritual; they exist as social institutions within the current culture. As such, they mirror the historical situation in which they live, and they tend to reflect the values and goals of the secular society that surrounds them.

Using a nineteenth century distinction between church and sect, it can be said that a sect type of religious community arises in protest against an entrenched church type. The church is usually bigger, more nationally distributed, more secure, and so it echoes the life-style of its particular community. The sect breaks away from the church establishment in order to emphasize the radicalness of religious faith and the need for a Christian witness over against the prevailing morality of the culture.

Original Protestantism, and many of its subsequent forms, was a sect. But in time, as so often happens, the protesting group achieved social acceptance, and so the sect became another church.

The relation between churches and culture, how they interact and influence each other, is the special concern of what is known as the sociology of religion. A religious view of churches, for example, would take account of such matters as doctrinal beliefs, ways of worship, and codes of personal conduct. A sociological view of churches would consider what in fact happens in any community where two sets of values may clash and where theological concepts become enmeshed with secular values and the harsh empirical realities of the social caste system.

A pioneering work for American religious thought in this sociological approach was H. Richard Niebuhr's book, *The Social Sources of Denominationalism* (1929; revised ed., 1954). Writing at a time of Protestant disunity and on the eve of the Great Depression, Niebuhr's account of the churches in America is unflattering and pessimistic. Denominational divisiveness, he observed, exerted a negative influence on society, and as sects became churches—and thus more accommodated to the culture—the ethical social witness of religion was mostly ineffectual.

In the later edition of his work, the author revised some of his more gloomy accusations against the churches, because the times had changed. But his initial analysis still makes sense today, and in some ways is even more relevant. H. Richard Niebuhr was the distinguished and widely respected professor of Christian ethics at the Yale Divinity School.

Theological opinions have their roots in the relationship of the religious life to the cultural and political conditions prevailing in any group of Christians. This does not mean that an economic or purely political interpretation of theology is justified, but it does mean that the religious life is so interwoven with social circumstances that the formulation of theology is necessarily conditioned by these. Where theology is regarded only from the ideological point of view, sight is lost of those very conditions which influence the divergence of its forms, and differences are explained on a speciously intellectual basis without taking into account the fundamental reasons for such variations. It is generally conceded that the theology of the first five centuries can be understood only if the psychology of the Greek mind and the social, religious, political, and economic conditions of the Roman empire are apprehended in their relationship to the new faith. One will fail completely to understand Roman Catholicism if one blinds one's eyes to the influence of the Latin spirit and of the institutions of the Caesars upon its conception of Christianity and its formulation of doctrine. The spirit and the doctrines of Lutheranism derive not only from the New Testament but also from Luther's German temperament and from the political conditions of the church in Germany. Calvinism was no less influenced in its temper and theology by national character and by the interests of the economic class to which it especially appealed. Back of the divergences of doctrine one must look for the conditions which make now the one, now the other interpretation appear more reasonable or, at least, more desirable. Regarding theology from this point of view one will discover how the exigencies of church discipline, the demands of the national psychology, the effect of social tradition, the influence of cultural heritage, and the weight of economic interest play their role in the definition of religious truth. The importance of such elements is now generally recognized when the history of nations is under discussion. It is too often disregarded when denominational histories are written or sectarian differences investigated. . . .

One element in the social sources of theological differentiation deserves especial attention. . . . The primary distinction to be made here is that between the church and the sect, of which the former is a natural social group akin to the family or the nation while the latter is a voluntary association. The difference has been well described as lying primarily in the fact that members are born into the church while they must join the sect. Churches are inclusive institutions, frequently are national in scope, and emphasize the universalism of the gospel; while sects are exclusive in character, appeal to the individualistic element in Christianity, and emphasize its ethical demands. Membership in a church is socially obligatory, the necessary consquence of birth into a family or nation, and no special requirements condition its privileges; the sect, on the other hand, is likely to demand some definite type of religious experience as a prerequisite of membership.

These differences in structure have their corollaries in differences in ethics and doctrine. The institutional church naturally attaches a high importance to the means of grace which it administers, to the system of doctrine which it has formulated, and to the official administration of sacraments and teaching by an official clergy; for it is an educational institution which must seek to train its youthful members to conformity in thought and practice and so fit them for the exercise of rights they have inherited. The associational sect, on the other hand, attaches primary importance to the religious experience of its members prior to their fellowship with the group, to the priesthood of all believers, to the sacraments as symbols of fellowship and pledges of allegiance. It frequently rejects an official clergy, preferring to trust for guidance to lay inspiration rather than to theological or liturgical expertness. The church as an inclusive social group is closely allied with national, economic, and cultural interests; by the very nature of its constitution it is committed to the accommodation of its ethics to the ethics of civilization; it must represent the morality of the respectable majority, not of the heroic minority. The sect, however, is always a minority group, whose separatist and semiascetic attitude toward "the world" is reenforced by the loyalty which persecution nurtures. It holds with tenacity to its interpretation of Christian ethics and prefers isolation to compromise. At times it refuses participation in the government, at times rejects war, at times seeks to sever as much as possible the bonds which tie it to the common life of industry and culture. So the sociological structure, while resting in part on a conception of Christianity, reacts upon that conception and reenforces or modifies it. On the other hand the adoption of one or the other type of constitution is itself largely due to the social condition of those who form the sect or compose the church. In Protestant history the sect has ever been the child of an outcast minority, taking its rise in the religious revolts of the poor, of those who were without effective representation in church or state and who formed their conventicles of dissent in the only way open to them, on the democratic, associational pattern. The sociological character of sectarianism, however, is almost always modified in the course of time by the natural processes of birth and death, and on this change in structure changes in doctrine and ethics inevitably follow. By its very nature the sectarian type of organization is valid only for one generation. The children born to the voluntary members of the first generation begin to make the sect a church long before they have arrived at the years of discretion. For with their coming the sect must take on the character of an educational and disciplinary institution, with the purpose of bringing the new generation into conformity with ideals and customs which have become traditional. Rarely does a second generation hold the convictions it has inherited with a fervor equal to that of its fathers, who fashioned these convictions in the heat of conflict and at the risk of martyrdom. As generation succeeds generation, the isolation of the community from the world becomes more difficult. Furthermore, wealth frequently increases when the sect subjects itself to the discipline of asceticism in work and expenditure; with the increase of wealth the possibilities for culture also become more numerous and involvement in the economic life of the nation as a whole can less easily be limited. Compromise begins and the ethics of the sect approach the churchly type of morals. As with the ethics, so with the doctrine, so also with the administration of religion. An official clergy, theologically educated and schooled in the refinements of ritual, takes the place of lay leadership; easily imparted creeds are substituted for the difficult enthusiasms of the pioneers; children are born into the group and infant baptism or dedication becomes once more a means of grace. So the sect becomes a church. . . .

The evils of denominationalism do not lie, however, in this differentiation of churches and sects. On the contrary, the rise of new sects to champion the uncompromising ethics of Jesus and "to preach the gospel to the poor" has again and again been the effective means of recalling Christendom to its mission. This phase of denominational history must be regarded as helpful, despite the break in unity which it brings about. The evil of denominationalism lies in the conditions which make the rise of sects desirable and necessary: in the failure of the churches to transcend the social conditions which fashion them into caste organizations, to sublimate their loyalties to standards and institutions only remotely relevant if not contrary to the Christian ideal, to resist the temptation of making their own self-preservation and extension the primary object of their endeavor.

The domination of class and self-preservative church ethics over the ethics of the gospel must be held responsible for much of the moral ineffectiveness of Christianity in the West. Not only or primarily because denominationalism divides and scatters the energies of Christendom, but more because it signalizes the defeat of the Christian ethics of brotherhood by the ethics of caste it is the source of Christendom's moral weakness. The ethical effectiveness of an individual depends on the integration of his character, on the synthesis of his values and desires into a system dominated by his highest good; the ethical effectiveness of a group is no less dependent on its control by a morale in which all subordinate purposes are organized around a leading ideal. And the churches are ineffective because they lack such a common morale. . . .

The lack of an effective, common, Christian ethics in the churches is illustrated by the manner in which they have divided their loyalties in each national crisis in the history of America and allied themselves with the struggling partisans of parliament and marketplace. During the American Revolution the rector of Trinity Church, New York, wrote to an English confrere, "I have the pleasure to assure you that all the society's missionaries without excepting one, in New Jersey, New York, Connecticut, and, so far as I learn, in the other New England colonies, have proved themselves faithful, loyal subjects in these trying times; and have to the utmost of their power opposed the spirit of disaffection and rebellion which has involved this continent in the greatest calamities. I must add that all the other clergy of our church in the above colonies though not in the society's service, have observed the same line of conduct." On the other hand, he testifies, the Presbyterian ministers, with singular uniformity, are promoting by preaching and every other effort in their power "all the measures of the congress, however extravagant." In any case, and this applies also to Congregationalists, Baptists, Methodists, and the other churches in the revolutionary colonies, one hears no word of a common Christian system of values to which all can express allegiance. Each religious group gives expression to that code which forms the morale of the political or economic class it represents. They function as political and class institutions, not as Christian churches.

The case was not different in the slavery crisis. Methodism had carried an antislavery doctrine in its platform from the very beginning, but even Whitefield urged the desirability of eliminating from the charter of Georgia the prohibition of slavery and when Methodism became the church of the slaveholder as well as of the poor tradesman it soon divided into a Northern and a Southern branch although the gradual emasculation of the antislavery clause in the old program was designed to maintain peace at the expense of principle. So it was also with Baptists and Presbyterians. Again the interests of economic class bent to their will the ethics of the Christian church and it was unable to speak a certain word on the issue of slavery. When the irrepressible conflict came the various denominations, as was to be expected, showed themselves to be the mouthpieces of the economic and sectional groups they represented. . . .

Almost always and everywhere in modern times the churches have represented the ethics of classes and nations rather than a common and Christian morality. Evident as this is in the crises, it is no less true of the times between crises. In the issues of municipal and national elections, on the questions of industrial relationships, of the conservation or abrogation of social customs and institutions—including the prohibition issue—the denominations have been the religious spokesmen of the special nonreligious groups with which they are allied.

For the denominations, churches, sects, are sociological groups whose principle of differentiation is to be sought in their conformity to the order of social classes and castes. It would not be true to affirm that the denominations are not religious groups with religious purposes, but it is true that they represent the accommodation of religion to the caste system. They are emblems, therefore, of the victory of the world over the Church, of the secularization of Christianity, of the Church's sanction of that divisiveness which the Church's gospel condemns.

Denominationalism thus represents the moral failure of Christianity. And unless the ethics of brotherhood can gain the victory over this divisiveness within the body of Christ it is useless to expect it to be victorious in the world. But before the Church can hope to overcome its fatal division it must learn to recognize and to acknowledge the secular character of its denominationalism.

The Colonies In The Divine Destiny

Winthrop S. Hudson

The story of Protestantism in America begins simply enough. The early colonists brought their doctrinal and church traditions with them, and, with very minor exceptions, these were the classic Reformation creeds and forms of worship. There were, of course, differences within colonial Protestantism, and in the new land the newfound freedom from restraints of all kinds prompted the older traditions to strike out in new ways. The basic religious toleration enjoyed by the colonies (and which was the main reason most of them came into existence) was not only a principle of faith but an economic necessity. If a colony were to enrich the homeland, as was expected, then differences of creed or ways of worship must not be allowed to interfere with economic development. But even more important for the development of the new land was the built-in theological conviction that a divine destiny was being fulfilled. Freedom demanded responsibility and hard work; many peoples and traditions opened doors of opportunity; a spirit of expectancy

57

was in the air; the churches lived under a mandate of divine mission. Though creeds and beliefs might differ, all the colonists were united in the sure conviction that God had an unfolding and glorious purpose for the new world.

The excerpt which follows comes from Winthrop S. Hudson's widely used standard history, *Religion in America* (1965). The author is professor of church history at the Rochester Center for Religious Studies. He has served as president of the American Baptist Historical Society and is the author of several works dealing with the American religious scene.

The fact that the American colonies were English colonies meant, first of all, that the colonists in background if not always in active affiliation would be predominantly Protestant. Even the non-English minorities—the Scots, the Scotch-Irish, the Germans, the Dutch, the French, and the Swedes—were almost wholly Protestant in background. Only in Maryland was there a significant number of Roman Catholics and even in Maryland they were a minority. Judaism was limited to a handful of tiny congregations. Thus, to the extent that the mind of colonial America was shaped by a religious faith, it was shaped perforce by Protestantism. . . .

The fact that the American colonies were English colonies also explains in large measure the multiplicity of religious bodies which was so prominent a feature of the English colonial scene in contrast to the religious uniformity which prevailed in the French and Spanish domains, for a deliberate policy of religious toleration was adopted by the English colonial authorities.

At the outset, to be sure, it was assumed that there would be and should be uniformity of religion in the new settlements; but in keeping with the whole system—or lack of system—of English colonial administration, the instructions at this point were not always observed. The Separatists who landed at Plymouth in 1620, for example, had set sail with the permission of the Virginia Company to establish a settlement within its territory, even though a second Virginia charter stated that no one, such as the Separatists, who refused to take the oath of supremacy should be allowed to embark for Virginia. Within a relatively brief time this administrative laxity was transformed into an explicit policy of toleration, and in no colony other than Virginia did the English authorities even attempt to impose a pattern of religious uniformity. When such attempts were made in the colonies, as in Massachusetts Bay, it was by the colonists themselves, and it was in spite of rather than because of English policy.

One important factor determining the tolerant attitude of the English government was the economic advantage to be gained by a policy of toleration. From the point of view of the English government, the colonies were commercial ventures designed to contribute to the wealth and prosperity of the mother country. The great need if they were to be profitable was to attract settlers who would provide the manpower to exploit the untapped resources of field and forest. Jails were emptied to provide colonists, the impoverished were sent out, adventurers were enlisted. But it soon became obvious that those who suffered from disabilities at home because of their religious profession would be prime recruits if they could be induced to leave the homeland by the prospect of greater freedom abroad.

The Dutch had early discovered the economic folly of adopting rigorous measures to suppress religious dissent, and Peter Stuyvesant was rebuked for attempting to institute such a policy in New Amsterdam. The Dutch authorities informed him that his "vigorous proceedings" should be discontinued lest he "check and destroy" the population. The secret of the prosperity of old Amsterdam, he was reminded, was the moderation displayed by the magistrates in dealing with religious minorities, with the result that "people have flocked" from every land "to this asylum." He was informed that a similar policy should be pursued in New Amsterdam. "It is our opinion that some connivance would be useful; that the consciences of men, at least, ought ever to remain free and unshackled."[1]

English policy was of a piece with the Dutch. This is self-evident in the grants that were made to Lord Baltimore and William Penn, but the clearest statement of the motivation which lay behind the policy is to be found in a communication from the Lords of Trade in London to the Council of Virginia: "A free exercise of religion . . . is essential to enriching and improving a trading nation; it should be ever held sacred in His Majesty's colonies. We must, therefore, recommend it to your care that nothing be done which can in the least affect that great point."[2] Non-English settlers were welcomed and some were even recruited with the promise of freedom to establish their own religious institutions. Most of these non-English groups arrived relatively late in the colonial period and they constituted, proportionately, a small segment of the total population, but they did serve to give added variety to the religious spectrum.* . . .

One of the facts of life in the New World was that a new beginning had to be made, and for most of the churches this new beginning had to be made by individual clergymen recruiting their own congregations out of a population that was largely unchurched. The ready-made congregations of early New England and the parishes created by legislative fiat in Virginia were not typical. Elsewhere there were neither closely knit bodies of believers already in existence nor parishes established by law. Nor was there any ecclesiastical body close at hand to supervise and regulate the life of the churches. Furthermore, because of the diversity that prevailed, the clergy often had to compete for the allegiance of the people. Far removed from the status-giving context of an ordered church life and dependent upon what support they could enlist among the laity both for the formation and the

---

*The great influx of the Germans and Scotch-Irish, the major non-English elements in the population, occurred during the last third of the colonial period.

maintenance of the congregations they served, the only real authority the clergy possessed was the authority they could command by their powers of persuasion and the force of their example. Given these circumstances, it is scarcely surprising that the laity soon began to exercise a decisive voice in church affairs, with "everything," as Henry M. Muhlenberg (1711-87) was to explain, dependent "on the vote of the majority."[3]

Even in New England, where churches had been constituted at the outset with ministers as a "speaking aristocracy" and congregations reduced to a "silent democracy," this state of affairs did not long persist. Men who had gained independent status as property holders by clearing their own land with flintlocks close at hand were not the type to be unduly submissive, and their self-assertiveness soon stripped the New England clergy of much of their independence. The same process was at work in Virginia where lay vestries gained effective control by neglecting to present the clergy to the governor for permanent induction into office, thus retaining, as the Archbishop of Canterbury complained, the right to hire and fire them like "domestic servants."[4] . . . .

A full century before disestablishment stripped away the lingering traces of the parish structure in New England, Jonathan Edwards (1703-58) had recognized that its days were numbered and had called upon his fellow Congregationalists to return to their initial emphasis upon the church as a covenanted community of convinced believers. When certain privileges were retained until the first decades of the nineteenth century, the defenders of the attenuated establishment that survived during these final years found it necessary to adopt all the techniques of the "gathered" churches in order to carry on a rear guard defense of its few remaining prerogatives.

The "techniques of the 'gathered' churches" is a key phrase, for it calls attention to the necessity that was laid upon the churches to win support and gain recruits by voluntary means. No longer could they depend upon people being automatically members of the church and subject to its discipline. The churches had to utilize all their powers of persuasion if they were to maintain and perpetuate themselves. The techniques they devised to this end were many and varied: the fostering of revivals, the organization of mission societies, the establishment of Sunday schools, the development of programs of visitation, the publication of tracts, and more recently the utilization of advertisements in periodicals. This vigorous evangelistic and instructional activity, imposed upon the churches by their status as "gathered" groups of convinced believers, was to become one of the most distinctive features of American church life. And in the end, in order to maintain themselves on this basis, some of the churches—most notably the Roman Catholic church—felt compelled to embark on the even more ambitious venture of establishing weekday schools for the complete education of their children. . . .

The prominence of religious radicals and left-wing groups in America has frequently been noted, and it is not surprising that they should have come to the New World in disproportionate numbers. Members of the established churches in Europe could only view the situation in America with some dismay, for the necessity to make a new beginning forced them to improvise and served to shatter many of their previously cherished patterns of ecclesiastical life. In New Amsterdam, for example, Jonas Michaelius (b. 1584) was acutely conscious of the coercions imposed by the conditions of life in a new land, and he felt compelled to explain the irregularities which attended the formation of his church. "One cannot," he wrote to the authorities at home, "observe strictly all the usual formalities in making a beginning under such circumstances."[5] The nonestablished churches of Europe, however, were in a reverse situation. They welcomed the opportunity to make a new beginning free from the restraints to which they were subjected at home. This was the great attraction which enticed the Mennonites and the Moravians to risk the hazards of beginning life anew in the American wilderness. It was this prospect also which exerted so strong an appeal to that hardy band of Pilgrims who settled at Plymouth in 1620 and encouraged the founders of Massachusetts Bay Colony in 1629 to undertake their "great migration."

The necessity to make a new beginning was seen by these minority groups as something more than a mere negative release. It was an opportunity to undertake a positive work of construction. William Penn (1644-1718) could never have launched his "holy experiment" in England where the existing patterns and institutions of a settled community would have dictated compromises from the start. He needed an opportunity to begin anew where there would be "room," as he puts it, for "such an experiment," and it was this opportunity that was given him in America.

The significance of the opportunity to make a new beginning can be seen most clearly through the eyes of those who sailed with the Winthrop fleet to Massachusetts Bay. Michaelius had had to "make do" in New Amsterdam, but the early New Englanders had had to "make do" at home. In England they had been compelled to adjust to the irregularities imposed upon them by the requirements of the established church, and the shift to the New World was viewed by them as a release from this bondage. "It is one thing," explained John Cotton (1564-1652), "for . . . members of the church loyally to submit unto any form of [church] government when it is above their calling to reform it"; it is quite another matter for them to "choose a form of government and governors discrepant from the rule." The Great Migration had been organized with the specific purpose of providing them with this freedom to "choose," and John Winthrop (1588-1649) standing on the deck of the *Arbella* made explicit the duty that was thus laid upon them. It was to "bring into familiar and constant practice" that which they previously had been able to "maintain as truth in profession only." Their purpose was clear. "We go," said Francis Higginson (1536-1630), "to practice the positive part of church reformation."[6]

America was for them, as it was to become for others, a land of opportunity, a land where a wide door of liberty had been set open before them. No longer were they to be compelled to resort to devious expedients, as they had been at home, in order to avoid "corruptions." This necessity had been lifted. But more important was the freedom they possessed to undertake a radical reconstruction of church life to conform to what they regarded as the plain prescriptions of God's "most holy Word." The goal was a full and complete restoration of the primitive church in all its pristine glory. This was their opportunity, and they were determined to take advantage of it. Looking back in 1677 to the early days of settlement, Increase Mather (1639-1723) declared: "There never was a generation that did so perfectly shake off the dust of Babylon . . . as the first generation of Christians that came to this land for the Gospel's sake."[7]

The early New Englanders were seeking freedom for themselves alone, but others found in America an equal freedom to "shake off the dust of Babylon." There was and there continued to be space enough for everyone.[8] It was this sense of being freed from the necessity to give heed to compromising restraints in making a new beginning that was to give a perfectionist cast to much of American religious life and to foster the uninhibited experimentation by smaller fringe groups that was to be the dismay of European churchmen. . . .

A new beginning is always a heady experience that breeds an eager expectancy among those who participate in it. Hopes are kindled and, as imagination takes over, the future becomes pregnant with possibility. This was doubly true of the new beginning that was made in America, for European peoples had always lived with the hope—sometimes faint but never absent—that the Lord's promise in Isaiah and Revelation to "make all things new" would some day be fulfilled. And the very term "New World," which was used to describe the setting in which they were making their new beginning, was calculated to remind them of the Lord's promise.

Since every Englishman had been taught from childhood to view the course of history as predetermined by God's overruling providence, no one could regard the colonizing activity in America as an ordinary venture. As early as 1613, William Strachey was insisting that God had kept America hidden for a purpose and that those who had established the small settlement in Virginia were but pursuing a course of action which God had foreseen and willed and was now carrying to its foreordained completion.[9] This purpose of necessity was related to God's final act of redemption, for this was the end toward which all history was directed.

The specific understanding of the past which illumined God's activity in the present was that which had been made the common possession of all Englishmen by John Foxe's "Book of Martyrs"—a volume that in 1571 had been placed by official decree in every cathedral church for all to read and was later to have a place of honor beside the Bible in every Protestant home.* Through the eyes of Foxe the shifting course of past events was seen to be a movement within a set pattern which God had adopted as a means of instructing mankind in the ways of righteousness. Throughout the centuries there had been alternating periods of impiety and faithfulness, corruption and reform, decline and renewal. After a long period of decline in which darkness had been demonstrated to be the only result of the folly of unrighteousness, Foxe pointed out that by 1300 God had begun to summon his servants to a renewed witness to him and thus to

---

*The first edition of 1554 was a small octavo volume which recounted the martyrdoms of the precursors of the Protestant Reformation, and to these accounts of martyrdoms under Mary Tudor were soon added. By the time it reached its final form in 1583, it was a folio of almost 2,500 pages and its full title had become *Acts and Monuments of Matters Most Special and Memorable, Happening in the Church, with an Universal History of the Same.* See William Haller. "John Foxe and the Puritan Revolution," in *The Seventeenth Century: Studies in the Hsitory of English Thought and Literature from Bacon to Pope,* by Richard F. Jones and others (Palo Alto, Calif., 1951); and also Haller's *The Elect Nation* (N.Y., 1963).

serve as harbingers of the new dispensation which was to be inaugurated with the Protestant Reformation.

When a full century had passed after the posting of the Ninety-five Theses by Martin Luther, it had become clear to scattered groups in England that Foxe had been overoptimistic in his estimate of the immediate outcome of the Reformation. The godly forces in Europe had proved to be unequal to the task to which God had summoned them. Why this should be so, they could only speculate; it was evident that God intended to pursue a new tactic to effect the final thrust into the new age.

The early New Englanders shared this sense of disappointment and as they reflected upon the significance of their venture in the New World they felt certain that it was to implement God's over-all design that they had been sent, as Samuel Danforth (1626-74) put it, on an "errand into the wilderness." When old England "began to decline in religion," declared Edward Johnson (1598-1672), Christ raised "an army out of our English nation, for freeing his people from their long servitude" and created "a new England to muster up the first of his forces in." This new England, he continued, "is the place where the Lord will create a new heaven and a new earth in, new churches and a new commonwealth together."[10]

God had "sifted a whole nation" in order to plant his "choice grain" in the American wilderness, but his purpose was more far-ranging than merely to enable them to escape the inhibitions they had suffered at home. They were not fleeing from persecution; they were executing a flank attack upon the forces of unrighteousness everywhere. Their role, John Winthrop had reminded them, was to be "a city set on a hill" to demonstrate before "the eyes of the world" what the result would be when a whole people was brought into open covenant with God. As part of God's program of instruction, they were to provide the nations with a working model of a godly society and by the contagion of their example were to be God's instruments in effecting the release from bondage of all mankind.[11]

The New Englanders, however, were not alone in the conviction that America had a decisive role to play in God's plan of redemption. William Penn was equally convinced that God intended his "holy experiment" to be "an example . . . to the nations" and a means of forwarding the remodeling of life everywhere. And Samuel Purchas's history of Virginia, written in 1625, begin its account of that colony's varied experiences with Adam and Eve in order to "show how God had so managed the past that English colonization in the present was the fulfillment of his plan."[12] Even Roger Williams (1604?-84), "the New England firebrand" who dissented at several crucial points from his neighbors in the Bay Colony, lived in daily expectation of a new dispensation.

This understanding of the decisive role that America was to have in the divine economy was appropriated and popularized in the eighteenth century by leaders of the Great Awakening. . . .

Jonathan Edwards, reflecting upon the outbreak of the revival, was convinced that "this work of God's Spirit, so extraordinary and wonderful, is the dawning or at least a prelude of that glorious work of God so often foretold in Scripture, which in the progress and issue of it shall renew the world of mankind." He saw the Awakening as the vindication, after so many successive disappointments, of the earlier expectation that the final act of God's work of redemption would begin in America. And if "in any part of America," he continued, "I think if we consider the circumstances of the settlement of New England, it must needs appear the most likely of all American colonies to be the place whence this work shall principally take its rise."[13] Whatever other leaders of the revival may have thought of Edwards's speculation as to the precise point at which the new age would first manifest itself, they shared his belief that God's Spirit was making itself felt in an unusual way and that God had a special destiny in store for America.

This mood of eager expectancy was to continue to be characteristic of American religious life. Having escaped in so many ways the limitations of a bounded existence, men and women were easily persuaded of the reality of unlimited possibilities. The hope of all things being made new, in the course of time, was often subtly secularized and frequently restated in political terms. But the conviction remained that somehow this was God's country with a mission to perform. For the churches this sense of mission was the source of much of their restless energy as they sought to keep abreast of the westward tide of migration and to make sure that the United States would fulfill its calling as a godly nation.

Notes

1. The text of the letter is printed in W.W. Sweet, *Religion in Colonial America* (New York: Scribner's Sons, 1942), pp. 151-2.

2. William S. Perry, ed., *Historical Collections Relating to the American Church* (Hartford, 1871-78), I, 379-81.

3. Henry Melchior Muhlenberg, *The Journals of Henry Melchior Muhlenberg* (Philadelphia: Muhlenberg Press, 1942), I, p. 67. For a perceptive discussion of this point, see Sidney E. Mead, "The Rise of the Evangelical Conception of the Ministry," in *The Ministry in Historical Perspectives*, ed. H. Richard Niebuhr and D.D. Williams (New York: Harper and Row, 1956), pp. 212-8.

4. Elizabeth Davidson, *The Establishment of the English Church in Continental American Colonies* (Durham, N.C.: Duke University Press, 1936), p. 19.

5. His letter is printed in H. Shelton Smith, et al., eds., *American Christianity: An Historical Interpretation with Representative Documents* (New York, 1960-63), I, 56-9.

6. See Perry Miller, *Orthodoxy in Massachusetts* (Cambridge, Mass.: Harvard University Press, 1933), pp. 137, 146. Winthrop's address, "A Model of Christianity," is printed in *The Puritans*, ed.

Perry Miller and T.H. Johnson (New York: Harper and Row, 1963), I, pp. 195-9; and in Smith, Handy, Loetscher, *American Christianity*, I, pp. 97-102.

7.   Quoted by W.W. Sweet, *Religion in Colonial America* (New York: Scribner's Sons, 1950), p. 2.

8.   For a discussion of the significance of geographic space, see S.E. Mead, "The American People: Their Space, Time, and Religion," *Journal of Religion*, XXXIV (1954): 244-55; reprinted in S.E. Mead, *The Lively Experiment* (New York: Harper and Row, 1963).

9.   Perry Miller, *Errand into the Wilderness* (Cambridge, Mass,: Harvard University Press, 1956), pp. 111, 117.

10.   J.F. Jameson, ed. *Johnson's Wonder-working Providence, 1628-1651* (New York: Scribner's Sons, 1910),pp. 23, 25. A portion of Johnson's narrative is in Perry Miller, ed., *The Puritans* (New York: Scribner's Sons, 1938), I, pp. 143-62.

11.   Smith, Handy, and Loetscher, eds., *American Christianity*, I, p. 102; Miller and Johnson, eds., *The Puritans*, I, p. 199. Perry Miller discusses this "errand" in *Errand into the Wilderness*, p. 11 f.

12.   Miller, *Errand into the Wilderness*, p. 115. See also Wright, *Religion and Empire*, pp. 115-33.

13.   *Work of Redemption, The Works of Jonathan Edwards* (Worcester, Mass,: I. Thomas, 1808-09), II, pp. 153, 158.

God's Controversy With
New England

Perry Miller

The Puritan "establishment," if we can call it that, in New England
has always been a source of lively debate. In many ways, the Puritans
in the seventeenth century magnified as virtues what later interpreters often regarded as vices. Weren't they stolid, aloof, unfeeling,
repressed, sour? Though partly true, the popular opinion that the
Puritans were mostly misanthropes and spoilsports has been challenged in more recent research. The late Perry Miller at Harvard,
with some colleagues such as Samuel Eliot Morison and Kenneth
Murdock, initiated a reevaluation of the Puritan way of life, and this
new appreciation is now everywhere acknowledged by historians. It
was just because the Old World offered little evidence of future
possibilities for the Reformation movements of the sixteenth century
that the Puritans took seriously their awful responsibility to fulfill the
divine destiny in New England. Theologically, they thought in terms
of a covenant whereby God's providence in opening up the new land
was to be met by moral earnestness, hard work, and a no-nonsense

style of life. Of course, if the divine side of the bargain was guaranteed, human frailty and sin all too often broke the equitable relation, hence, in the vivid language of a Puritan poet, God had not only a contract with New England but a "controversy."

The essential text on American Puritanism is Perry Miller's *The New England Mind: The Seventeenth Century* (1939). The passage that follows is taken from the final chapter. The absence of footnotes to identify the many quotations is deliberate. As the author notes: "It is a matter of complete indifference or chance that a quotation comes from Cotton instead of Hooker . . . ; all writers were in substantial agreement." Perry Miller, who died in 1963, was Cabot Professor of American Literature at Harvard University. Among his other works are *Jonathan Edwards, Orthodoxy in Massachusetts, The Transcendentalists,* and (with T.H. Johnson) *The Puritans.*

Greek and Roman historians never ceased to marvel that so small a band as charged at Marathon or manned the ships at Salamis overcame the Persian hosts. Being pagans, and knowing nothing of the providence of the true God, they ascribed the victory to fortune, but we, said Increase Mather, who have the Scripture to instruct us, know the real cause of those astounding triumphs: angels fought in the ranks of the Greeks. Just as Homer described a physical presence of the Gods in the battles before Troy, so the pastor of the Second Church in Boston conceived that the Grecians "were secretly and invisibly animated by Angels." By such lights did Puritans read history. The record of humanity was to them a chronicle of God's providence, exactly as occurrences in nature or in the heavens were significations of his governing will. Nothing that men had ever done was without a spiritual import, for the power that created the world continually guided and directed all worldly events; though men acted of their own volition, they always fulfilled his intentions. Even events which at first sight seemed contrary to God's interests proved, upon closer analysis, to have served his ends. The onslaught of the Turks might appear to the casual or atheistical student a victory for the powers of darkness, but to Increase Mather the finger of God was obvious even in their successes. When the Holy Roman Emperor "was minded to destroy his Protestant Subjects, God let loose the great Turk upon the Empire, and so diverted the evil designs against his people, which had been long preparing, and were become ripe for execution." The Puritan scholar studied all history, heathen or Christian, as an exhibition of divine wisdom, and found in the temporal unfolding of the divine plan that the entire past had been but a sort of prologue to the enactment of the New England commonwealths. . . .

We can appreciate the New Englanders' sense of their own role in the cosmos only when we realize that they believed the Reformation to be a cumulative and still expanding force in the seventeenth century, but were also convinced that in Protestant countries of Europe it had not gone more than half way and could proceed no further until it received further guidance. For the moment, the first onslaught having dislodged erroneous doctrines, the Protestant ranks were in confusion and were losing their advantage; they were falling into the anarchy of Anabaptism and Antinomianism or being betrayed by Arminianism into a disguised Popery. In order that the disorganized troops of righteousness might be rallied anew and the lines reformed, there was desperate need of a plan of battle. The doctrinal positions won by Luther and Calvin had to be reinforced by the more concrete program of polity, and New England had been reserved in the divine strategy to furnish Protestantism with a model for the final offensive of the campaign. If the New Englanders' estimate of their own importance seems ludicrous or pathetic to us, we must remember that we no longer read history in the light of piety, and we forget that from their point of view several thousand years of human experience pointed unmistakably to their existence and defined their task. They did not, at least in the first settlements, regard themselves as fleeing from Europe but as participating to the full in the great issue of European life; they did not set out to become provincial communities on the edge of civilization but to execute a flanking maneuver in the all-engrossing struggle of the civilized world. The Lord was granting them the greatest opportunity afforded to any people since the birth of Christ, the chance "to enjoy Churches, and Congregational Assemblies by his Covenant, to worship him in all his holy Ordinances," such a privilege indeed as "for 1260 years, the Christian world knew not the meaning of it . . . but this the Lord vouchsafeth to us this day, above all Nations that have power of the civill sword." We, the people of New England, wrote Peter Bulkeley, "are as a City set upon a hill, in the open view of all the earth, the eyes of the world are upon us, because we professe our selves to be a people in Covenant with God." Our function is to walk so that all the nations will say, "Onely this people is wise, an holy and blessed people"; the Lord has purposely kept us few, weak, and poor, so that we may excel in grace and holiness alone. . . .

But no sooner was the divine order completed, and the ultimate work of reformation performed, than the first signs of faltering appeared among the people. The younger generation, according to Cotton, were coming of age in the 1640s without coming into their fathers' spirit, and young men were manifesting their irreverence by wearing their hats when the Word was read in the congregations; but still worse, the founding saints themselves were proving to be "not so lively in their profession as they were wont to be many yeares agoe." Some who for piety had been "marvellous eminent in our native Country" were discovering, often to their genuine distress, that here they could not pray so fervently or hear the Word with so much profit: "They wonder what is become of their old prayers . . . and of their lively spirits in holy duties." In the 1640s there commenced in the sermons of New England a lament over the waning of primitive zeal and the consequent atrophy of public morals, which swelled to an incessant chant within forty years. By 1680 there seems to have been hardly any other theme for discourse, and the pulpits rang week after week with lengthening jeremiads. We have precious little evidence from which to reconstruct the ordinary daily life of the communities, yet we can in effect trace the chronology of their social and material growth, of their economic evolution, through the expanding array of vices, sins, and naughty practices enumerated by the ministers. From Cotton's mild complaint of disrespectful hats and his deploring the dry springs of fervor, the list of evils accumulated into a staggering index of criminality: worldliness, fornication, uncleanness, drunkenness, hypocrisy, formality, oppressing of debtors by creditors, usury and profiteering, the wearing of wigs and luxurious clothes, Sabbath-breaking and cock-fighting, rudeness and incivility among the young, and a general "degeneracy from the good Manners of the Christian world." Horror was piled upon horror when the people wished, like dogs returning to their vomit, to celebrate Christmas, when fortune-tellers could make a living in New England, and when at last there were rumors of a brothel in Boston. In 1662 Michael Wigglesworth achieved his best verse in a work entitled *God's Controversy with New-England,* representing the monarch of creation wringing his hands in unavailing distress over the languishing state of New England: could these be the men, he marveled; who at his command forsook their ancient seats to follow him into a desert?

> If these be they, how is it that I find
>   In stead of holiness Carnality,
> 'In stead of heavenly frames an Earthly mind,
>   For burning zeal luke-warm Indifferency,
> For flaming love, key-cold Dead-heartedness,
>   For temperance (in meat, and drinke, and cloaths) excess?

In one sense, however, the heavens had no cause to be astonished. They knew, and the Puritan clergy had learned, enough of the influence of material circumstances upon the spirits of men to perceive physical reasons for the retrogression. When there is a storm at sea, said Shepard, every man is ready and will be pulling his rope, "but when a calm, they go to their cabins, and there fall asleep"; in England the storm of conflict had aroused every man of faith to mighty exertions, but in New England, after the first hardships of settlement were over, "We have all our beds and lodgings provided, the Lord hath made them easy to us." At home, when the saints were being deprived of true ordinances, they had longed after them with lively hearts, but now that "the Lord hath freed us from the pain and anguish of our consciences," they were taking sermons and lectures for granted. It had become especially appropriate, John Cotton asserted in his last years, to preach in Boston upon Ecclesiastes and to drive home its refrain of the vanity of earth, because men "that have left all to enjoy the Gospel, now (as if they had forgotten the end for which they came hither) are ready to leave the Gospel for outward things." . . .

The best of saints, as God learned from bitter experience in Palestine, cannot be trusted too long with material favors; they let themselves become ensnared and wax wanton and secure. In individuals such declensions can be forgiven in the name of Christ, but when a whole people abuse their blessings, they must be punished, and a nation can be dealt with only here and now. A people in agreement with the Lord have "bound themselves to yield obedience to all his commands," and consequently "when . . . they depart from his obedience . . . they therein depart from their Allegiance." We cannot assume that God's children are at fault because they meet with afflictions in their particular concerns, "for the design of these is very often for their trial," but "when God brings sore and wasting Calamities of Sickness, Famine, and War, on a professing people . . . God is not angry without a cause." Personal dispensations are on a level of grace, where justice is replaced by mercy, but for an entire community within a covenant, the law of justice is still in effect. A good covenanted society prospers in this world, a bad one gets what it deserves. . . .

New England ministers denounced the sins of the land and expanded the list of its crimes until the bystander, judging by the light of reason, might well have supposed the limit to be exceeded. The clergy were less ready to draw such an inference; they would prophesy that the time was at hand when the Lord would bring his controversy with New England to a crisis, and constantly warned their congregations that this or that moment was the last opportunity to save themselves by repentance and reformation, but they could not announce flatly that the time had passed and that all hope should be abandoned. If they were ever publicly to make this admission, they would be surrendering their reason for being; having commenced on the assumption that they were leading a covenanted people, and that a covenanted community could win God's favor by its moral efforts, the churches could not, during the seventeenth century, confess that there was no longer any reason why this particular community should strive to be holier than others. The great end toward which the theory aspired, the moral which the leaders worked to instill into the minds of the people, citizens or inhabitants, was the principle of communal responsibility. When a commonwealth breaks covenant with God, Thomas Shepard declared, it casts him off, and a people taken together as a commonwealth are able so to cast him off, though the grace imparted to individuals is irresistible. A fellowship can forsake the covenant of its own volition, and does so whenever it fails to keep touch "with God, in sincere, exact, and holy obedience, answerable to the means and mercy he bestows upon us, and the care and kindness of the Lord towards us." Well into the eighteenth century the notion was still being dinned into the ears of legislators, as when Grindal Rawson in 1709 explained to the General Court that while the privileges of a people in compact with God are great, "so also are their Duties and Obligations," that where others might just as well sin to their hearts' content because they would gain little in the way of public good by their virtues,

A Covenant People are not left at their Liberty, whether they will Love, Fear, Serve and Obey the Voice of God in his Commands, or not. They are under the highest, and most awful Obligations imaginable to the whole of Covenant duty; not only from Gods express Command and Precept, who is their King, Lord, and Lawgiver; but also, by virtue of their own Professed Subjection unto God . . . They are therefore most Solemnly cautioned to take heed to themselves, and beware, lest they should forget and forsake the Lord, his Worship, Fear and Service; because by this means they would assuredly forfeit all those desirable blessings, which a course of Obedience would crown them with, and pull down upon themselves the just rebukes, and terrible revenges of Heaven.

The people of New England could thus survey the past in the light of their tribal covenant, see the course of history coming to a predestined climax in themselves, and yet argue that they were not necessarily fated to follow the pattern into an equally inevitable decline. They could assert that the first generation had done all the good that was ever to be done, and yet reasonably expect the children to walk faithfully in the righteous steps of the fathers. A society, considered apart from its component individuals, was lifted by its covenant out of the flux of nature, set above the laws of physics, an exception to the cycles of history. Others acquired wealth where it was to be found and depended on circumstance; New England was assured in advance that the land and sea would offer them possibilities for exploitation, "let all the whole course of second causes bode never so ill," God's word had been passed, "and he will never recede from it." Others might grow rich, and thereby become depraved; New Englanders were awarded riches for their holiness, and were under no necessity of being corrupted. They were swinging free in time and space, masters of their own destiny, their fate in their own hands to make or mar at will. In a universe created by absolute power, ruled by unlimited prerogative, funded upon a perfect and immutable pattern of ideas, in which grace alone could extricate men from the web of necessity—grace which was dispensed regardless of merit—in such a universe an entire people could still be informed that they had taken upon themselves an agreement with the Lord and that their physical and material career depended from day to day upon their moral conduct. Success and morality here were linked together as nowhere else in the world by a specific promise of the same God who elsewhere regulated success or failure without the slightest regard to civic virtue.

Religion Goes West

William Warren Sweet

Even if some in Massachusetts were self-deceived about it, New England was not the whole of the New World. It has perhaps always been an Eastern conceit that everything beyond the Atlantic seaboard must be largely derivative, including religious ideas, churches, and the life of the spirit. But as soon as some hardy souls pushed beyond the Allegheny Mountains, another world in the West appeared. And, curiously, while whole populations streamed across the plains, the major religious traditions back East were reulctant to go West. The Puritans, the Congregationalists, the Unitarians, the Presbyterians, the Quakers, and the Episcopalians mostly "stayed at home," for various reasons. It was left to the Baptists and the Methodists to move with the western tide of migration and, at the same time, to imprint their trademarks upon the new frontier. Both Baptists and Methodists were unencumbered with the baggage of ecclesiastical bureaucracy or theological requirements. They were free and easy compared to their more entrenched competitors back East, and they were thus more adaptable to the wild and woolly

West. Stressing individual faith, repentance and conversion, personal piety rather than creedal assent, a plain but holy life style, the Baptist preachers and Methodist circuit riders made converts wherever there were people; and they built churches all across the land.

The story of religion's role in the winning of the West has only emerged slowly within the past thirty years or so. Credit for the telling must go, in large part, to William Warren Sweet who almost singlehandedly carved out a niche for research in American church history. Teaching at the University of Chicago and at Southern Methodist University, Sweet is recognized as the dean of church historians. He has amassed an impressive series of documentary chronicles, much of it relating to religion on the frontier. In a small, popular book, growing out of some lectures given in England, Dr. Sweet summed up his basic findings regarding religion on the frontier. The following passage comes from that book, *The American Churches: An Interpretation* (1947).

───────────────

For the first two generations following independence the most outstanding fact in the history of the United States was the westward movement of population; the building of new communities; the forming of new territories; the admission of new states into the Union. From 1791 to 1821 eleven new states were added to the original thirteen—and the most important work performed by the American churches during this formative period was that of following this restless and moving population with the refining and uplifting influences of religion. The first danger which always accompanies any great migration of people, as Horace Bushnell so well pointed out more than a hundred years ago, is that of reverting to barbarism. Cut off from the restraints and refining influences of the old home and of the old home communities, with their churches and schools and family relationships, and living under rude and uncouth conditions, many a frontier family lost track of the Sabbath and gave up all attempts at refinement and decency in living. Many frontier communities became notorious for lawlessness, rowdyism, gambling, swearing, drinking, and fighting. Travelers in the trans-Allegheny west in the early part of the last century were often "terrified at the drunkenness, the vice, the gambling, the brutal fights, the gouging, the needless duels they beheld on every hand."[1] Their social gatherings, such as logrollings, house-raisings, and even weddings and funerals often degenerated into drunken orgies, where

> There was lots of swearing,
> Of boasting and daring,
> Of fighting and tearing.

For at least fifty years following independence a vast struggle was going on from the Alleghenies to the Mississippi River between civilization and Christian morality on the one hand and barbarism on the other, and upon the outcome of that struggle hung the fate of the new nation.

Let us glance for a moment at the religious forces which were available to meet this crisis.

At the head of the list were the Congregationalists, the largest and most influential religious body at the end of the colonial period. Established by law in Massachusetts, Connecticut, and New Hampshire, Congregationalism possessed about 700 congregations and had a native and American-trained ministry. Next in point of size were the Presbyterians with some 600 congregations, and they too possessed a well-educated ministry, mostly American-trained. Ranking third in point of size were the Baptists, ministering primarily to humble and unchurched people, but growing rapidly as a result of that fact and their development of a devoted farmer-preacher type of ministry. Fourth on the list were the Episcopalians, though at the moment under a cloud of suspicion due to the unpopularity which the struggle for independence had brought upon them. There were also some 295 Quaker meetings; 250 Dutch and German Reformed congregations; some 200 Lutheran congregaions; perhaps some fifty or sixty congregations of German sectaries; a bare fifty Roman Catholic; and thirty-seven Methodist circuits, then nominally still a part of the Anglican communion. Such were the forces of organized religion in the new nation upon which the responsibility was largely placed of saving America for Christian civilization.

It was the way in which the task of following the population westward was faced by these several religious bodies that was to determine which of the churches were to become large and which were to remain small; which were to be sectional and which were to be national. It was perhaps unfortunate that the two most privileged religious bodies of the colonial period, the Congregationalists and the Episcopalians, failed to take advantage of the opportunities and responsibilities that the great westward movement presented. Neither of them at the beginning took a national view of their task. Both also were handicapped by an unfortunate superiority complex, which came naturally from the fact that both had been state churches and possessed privileges and social status which in the long run was to prove a handicap rather than an advantage to their growth and influence. Their appeal was, to a large degree, limited to the more prosperous groups, and they became, in a sense, apostles only to the genteel.

Others of the colonial religious bodies faced other handicaps. The Dutch, the German Reformed, and the Lutherans, together with the German sectaries, were still foreign-language bodies, and thus their activity and their appeal was limited to a particular class of people. As a consequence, they did not possess a national view of their task as they were destined to continue to minister only to small sections of the population—to people of their own language and cultural background. The Presbyterians were also handicapped in somewhat the same way. Their ministers on frontier preaching tours sought out communities where people of Scotch or Scotch-Irish background were to be found, and were not greatly concerned with communities in which there were no people of their own kind. To a large degree also the Congregational home missionaries were inclined to seek out

communities of New England settlers, and made little effort
to reach a cross section of frontier society. The Quakers, after
their adoption of the birthright membership in 1734, soon
lost their burning missionary zeal and settled down to become
a smug, self-satisfied, and economically prosperous social
group.

Thus it was that the great task of following the population west, by a sort of process of elimination, came to be
more and more the responsibility of the churches of the
poor—principally the Baptists and Methodists, and to a
limited degree the Presbyterians. These three American
churches made the greatest moral and religious impact upon
the first two generations of the American frontier. Each had
its own method of performing its frontier task. The Baptist
farmer-preacher came along with the people pushing westward. He was sent by no church organization, and though
with little or no formal education he preached the gospel, as
he understood it, to his neighbors and what he lacked in
education he partly made up in earnestness and devotion.
The Presbyterian minister in the early West was at least half a
schoolteacher. He was generally a man of education, the
popular sentiment of the community where he resided compelled him to open a school. The Baptist preacher must make
his own living and thus he divided his energies between his
farm and his church, his plow and his pulpit; the Presbyterian
schoolteacher-preacher divided his time between his school-
teaching and his preaching; the Methodist circuit rider, on
the other hand, gave all his time to his religious activities. On
great circuits, sometimes as large as three or four hundred
miles around, he preached at least once every day in the
week, with the possible exception of Monday, and during the
course of a single year traveled many thousands of miles. So
closely did the Methodist system enable the circuit preacher
to follow the moving population that not infrequently a
circuit rider would call at a settler's cabin before the mud in
the stick chimney was dry or the weight poles were on the
roof. Methodism was so organized as to be able to follow step

by step this moving population, and to carry the gospel even to the most distant cabin. It alone could be present whenever a grave was opened or an infant was found in its cradle.

The relative effectiveness of these most important religious bodies may be visualized by some statistics. In the census of 1820 there were some 21,000 Methodists in Kentucky; over 20,000 Baptists; the Presbyterians had 3,700 members; while all other bodies numbered not more than 500; and this proportion pretty generally prevailed throughout the trans-Allegheny region. By 1850 the Methodists had become the largest Protestant body in America, with a membership of 1,324,000; the Baptists numbered 815,000; the Presbyterians came third with 487,000; the Congregationalists fourth with 197,000; the Lutherans had 163,000; the Disciples 118,000; and the Episcopalians 90,000. . . .

The Methodists of those days were possessed of a burning zeal for the advancement of the Kingdom of God. As was said of the early Quakers, so it could be said of them—the gospel was as a hammer and an anvil in them. It drove them forth into every nook and corner of the needy land, and they considered the vast continent as their parish. Although the smallest and most humble of American religious bodies at the opening of the national period, the Methodists were the first to achieve a national organization suited to an indefinite geographic expansion.

Another reason which helps explain Methodism's success was its catholicity. It built no ecclesiastical or theological fences to keep men out.

There is no such thing as a distinctive Methodist theology. Those churches which possess the historical confessions have been contemptuous of Methodism in the past, and many of them still are, because of this fact. This does not mean, however, that Methodists have not been interested in theology or considered it of slight importance. Methodists have in fact produced some very respectable theologians on both sides of the Atlantic. There was no other religious body in seventeenth-century England that gave more attention to the discussion to theology than did Wesley's conferences. But he was always careful to preface these discussions with the statement: "You must not expect me to come to your opinion, nor will I expect you to come to mine. We can no more think alike than we can see or hear alike." There was but one condition of membership to Methodist societies—the desire to flee from the wrath to come. Wesley took pride in the fact that no doctrinal tests were ever laid down. On many occasions he stated:

> Methodists do not impose, in order to their admission, any opinions whatever. Let them hold particular or general redemption, absolute or conditional decrees; let them be churchmen, or dissenters, Presbyterians or Independents, it is no obstacle. Let them choose one mode of baptism or another, it is no bar to their admission. The Presbyterian may be a Presbyterian still; the Independent and Anabaptist use his own worship still. So may the Quaker; and none will contend with him about it. They think and let think. One condition, and only one is required—a real desire to save the soul. Where this is, it is enough; they desire no more; they lay stress upon nothing else; they only ask, "Is thy heart herein as my heart? If it be, give me thy hand."

None of the divisions that have occurred in American Methodism have been due to differences in theology; and one of the principal reasons why the Methodists alone of the three great churches which divided over the slavery issue have been able to heal that greatest of all schisms in American Protestantism, is largely due to that fact. There were no basic theological differences among the three Methodist bodies which came together in 1939 to form the present Methodist Church. . . .

Pretty generally, the great evangelical churches in America have gone forward on the assumption that man and God must work together to build a decent world; that no situation could be so bad but that man with God's help could do something about it. In the face of frontier hardships and dangers, surrounded by crude and raw conditions of life, which of necessity must always accompany pioneering, the western pioneers, like the New England Puritans, succeeded in maintaining a cosmic optimism even in the midst of anguish. They were too busy waging war against sin, too intoxicated with the exultation of the never-ending conflict, to find occasional reverses, however costly, a cause for deep and permanent discouragement.

One of the principal charcteristics of America from the beginning, and particularly during the period of the settlement of the trans-Allegheny regions and the great prairie plains beyond, has been an immense optimism. Opportunity has been a charmed world throughout our history. It is not incorrect to say that the greatest accomplishment of the American people has been the conquest of the continent. Not only has the mere filling in of vast unoccupied areas with a teeming population been a notable achievement, but far more notable has been the establishment throughout the nation of American democratic, political, and social institutions; and if the story of American industrial achievements is a fascinating romance it is not more so than is that of the story of the founding and development of American educational and cultural institutions. Naturally, out of such a background have come optimistic and positive attitudes toward life; the attitude that no obstacle is too great to be overcome in any realm.

Here certainly is one of the roots of the American emphasis upon social Christianity; the influences which have come directly out of frontier experiences. It is significant that those churches that have been the strongest supporters and promoters of the social gospel are those which came to power and influence as a consequence of their successful coping with the frontier—the Baptists, the Methodists, the Presbyterians, the Disciples, and the Congregtionalists. It was in the pioneering period that they learned the necessity of making application of Christian principles to society. Frontier Baptist, Methodist, and Presbyterian churches disciplined members not only for personal lapses, such as drunkenness and immorality, but also brought them to book for fraudulent business dealings, such as selling unsound horses, removing boundary stones, or cutting down corner trees. Frontier preachers took part in politics, as a matter of course, and it was perfectly normal and natural that the first governor of Ohio—Edward Tiffin—should have been a Methodist local preacher, and that one of the early governors of Kentucky was a Baptist farmer-preacher. Peter Cartwright was a member of the Illinois legislature for two terms, and while there introduced the first measure for the establishment of a state college. He was in active politics for many years; he was high in the councils of the Jacksonian party and in 1846 was their candidate for Congress, running against Abraham Lincoln. Thus religion tended to permeate all frontier society, and when new frontiers arose, created by the new industrial developments and the rise of the great cities, the movement to bring religion to bear upon the new social problems thus created was not something new, but was simply the revival of a frontier emphasis applied to a much more complicated and difficult social situation.

Notes

1. For information on the moral disintegration found on the early frontier, see W.W. Sweet, "The Churches as Moral Courts of the Frontier," *Church History*, March 1933, pp. 3-21.

Church And Culture — Give And Take

Robert T. Handy

Cutting a wide swath through another section of American history, roughly the century from 1830 to 1930, we soon discover that church and culture were in constant competition. The homogenous character of early New England and the rough and ready individualism of the Western frontier gave way little by little to sectionalism and secularism. The Civil War was the ultimate and tragic disruption of the country into two warring sections. As the States squared off in the death struggle, so also did the churches (mainly the Presbyterians, the Methodists, and the Baptists). Ignited by slavery, the war only served to victimize even further those who were eventually "emancipated." White church leaders, preachers, and theologians argued—from the Bible—on both sides. Black churches struggled to maintain some semblance of identity. The big denominations grew even bigger as they tried to meet the increasing pluralism with more efficient organization. But the relation between church and culture was becoming more and more ambiguous. In trying to Christianize the culture, the churches often found themselves being acculturated and, unconsciously, adopting the value system of the secularized society. For the Protestant churches, as for the nation as a whole, it was a confusing century, punctuated at one end by a divisive bloodbath and, at the other, by a paralyzing depression.

For an overview of this give and take between church and culture, we can turn to Robert T. Handy's *The Protestant Quest for a Christian America, 1830-1930*. The author is professor of church history at Union Theological Seminary, New York. He has served as president of the American Society of Church History and is the author of numerous works on American religious life. With H. Shelton Smith and Lefferts A. Loetscher, Dr. Handy has edited a substantial and widely used work: *American Christianity: An Historical Interpretation with Representative Documents* (1960, 1963).

The Protestantism that faced post-Civil War America was far from being a static entity continually being challenged by external forces. Rather it was an aggressive, dynamic form of Christianity that set out confidently to contront American life at every level, to permeate, evangelize, and Christianize it. The results of this Protestant thrust were ambivilant: on the one hand there were some notable achievements, but on the other there was an entanglement and partial envelopment by an incrasingly pluralistic and secularized culture.

The middle third of the nineteenth century, roughly the years 1830-1860, was a period in which conservative, sectarian, evangelical Protestantism was a dominant force on the American scene. The French observer de Tocqueville remarked that "in the United States the sovereign authority is religious and consequently hypocrisy must be common; but there is no country in the world where the Christian religion retains a greater influence over the souls of men than in America. . . ."[1] A domestic observer, Robert Baird, gave evidence repeatedly in his massive study of the vast hold of the evangelical churches on American life.[2] Recent study has underlined how important the traditional faith and morality of Protestantism was as a force in pre-Civil War America. The attempt to understand the cataclysm of the Civil War itself leads directly to a consideration of the antislavery movement which grew out of and was stamped with the pattern of pietistic Protestantism. Analyses of the national faith in democracy point to the decisive sway of Christian ideas; Professor Ralph H. Gabriel notes that "the foundation of this democratic faith was a frank supernaturalism derived from Christianity. The twentieth-century student is often astonished at the extent to which supernaturalism permeated American thought of the nineteenth century."[3] The cultural dominance of Protestantism was illustrated in the transition to a public tax-supported school system. This transition was palatable to Protestants because the schools were rather clearly Protestant in orientation, though "nonsectarian." Protestant cultural leadership was reflected in the realm of higher education also—as a report in 1857 stated it, "We might go through the whole list of American colleges, and show that, with here and there an exception, they were founded by religious men, and mainly with an eye to the interests of the Church."[4] Historians whose major interests are not religious sometimes react with some surprise when they are forced to recognize how widespread Protestant influence was in the first part of the nineteenth century. Professor Whitney R. Cross, for example, in his recent and useful work, *The Burned-over District,* records how widespread the circulation of religious journals was in the first part of the nineteenth century and how avidly they were read. He comments, "Now that theology is a very nearly dead subject, one finds it extremely difficult to realize how such journals could have an extensive appeal. But appeal they did, in demonstrable fashion. . . ."[5]

The great revivals of 1857-59 provide further evidence of the power and prestige of evangelical Protestantism; a recent student of the revivals has noted that "there was remarkable unanimity of approval among religious and secular observers alike, with scarcely a critical voice heard anywhere."[6] There were, of course, Protestant groups whose interpretation of Christianity was not that of the conservative evangelicals, but they were small in comparison. The latter dominated the religious press, which had grown more than had the secular press in the twenty years before 1865, both in number of periodicals and in circulation.[7] Protestantism was fully committed to and profited from the principle of religious liberty and the voluntary method in religion, anticipating continued progress on this basis. Finally, orthodox Protestantism had grown up with the individualism that characterized nineteenth-century America, had contributed to its rise, and found it thoroughly congenial. In the words of Henry May, "Organized Protestantism supported the dominant economic beliefs and institutions even more unanimously than it accepted the existing form of government."[8] In many ways, the middle third of the nineteenth century was more of a "Protestant age" than was the colonial period with its established churches.

At the close of the Civil War there were approximately 5 million Protestant church members out of an estimated population of some 32 million. Protestantism's influence, of course, extended far beyond its actual membership; the vast majority of Americans were encompassed in popular if not in ecclesiastical Protestantism.[9] The Protestants were an aggressive, self-confident, and surprisingly homogeneous group. To be sure, they were divided into denominations among which considerable tension could arise, yet there was a fundamental similarity. De Tocqueville stated that "they all differ in respect to the worship which is due to the Creator; but they all agree in respect to the duties which are due from man to man. Each sect adores the Deity in its own peculiar manner, but all sects preach the same moral law in the name of God."[10] As the denominations faced their country they saw no reason why their influence should not continue to grow and their numbers increase, and they set out to evangelize and Christianize every aspect of American life. Their tremendous drive scattered churches across the West; church extension and church building were major focal points of Protestant concern throughout the nineteenth century. The restless energy of expanding Protestantism made possible the steady growth of the denominations and the erection of elaborate denominational structures. The inner dynamic of Protestantism led to the extension of existing cooperative agencies and societies as well as the development of many new ones devoted to the promotion of revivals, the advancement of good causes, the furtherance of education, and the expansion of missions, home and foreign. The desire to permeate the life of America with the leaven of Christianity led to the adoption and imaginative use of such new instruments as the YMCA.[11] This religious drive to Christianize the nation was a phase of the energy that characterized American life in general at that time, but the evangelical fervor of the Protestant denominations intensified it.

As Protestantism set about the task of permeating and Christianizing American life, the very seriousness of the effort magnified the tendency of churches to absorb the characteristics of those whom they served. The culture they were trying to Christianize grew steadily less homogeneous after the Civil War. The horrors of reconstruction widened the chasm between South and North; the great denominations of those sections, striving to reach every level of their respective sections, identified themselves warmly with their people and the broken spiritual ties were not healed. In the North and East particularly, the impact of evolutionary and historical thinking began to upset many, especially those of the educated classes. Their churches came to feel the obligation to understand the new conditions and mediate the gospel to such folk. Henry Ward Beecher, whose genius apparently lay largely in his ability to express to perfection what his huge congregations were thinking, declared: "The providence of God is rallying forward a spirit of investigation that Christian ministers must meet and join. There is no class of people upon earth who can less afford to let the development of truth run ahead of them than they."[12] Ministers who moved in the circles where such currents were flowing tried to stand between the new modes of thought and the old theology; it was from among the ardent evangelicals that the liberal pioneers came. The full secularity to which the new ways of thinking could run was not then clear, and the older theology was often expressed in intransigent and stylized forms that repelled Christians sensitive to the needs of their day. Hence liberalism arose not so much from outside as from within, as prominent evangelicals seeking to live out their faith moved among people troubled by new intellectual trends.[13] In the major denominations of the North particularly, the liberal trend was evident in the late nineteenth century, at times painfully evident.

A great deal of Protestant America, of course, lived in rural and small town areas where the new winds blew faintly, and where the cyclones of the cultural centers had warned the faithful to erect storm signals. Hence the same post-Civil War years that are marked by the leftward trend are also characterized by the rightward movement of a counter-reformation which was rooted in the conservative, evangelical, revivalistic Protestantism of the earlier nineteenth century, but showing a hardening and a narrowing of that tradition. Again, we see Protestant zeal at work. We see the Protestant churches identifying themselves with the concerns of the people, matching themselves to their level. The conservative reaction was of course by no means limited to the small town and rural areas; it swept into the great urban centers where city conditions were severing people from their cultural roots and where many of the city masses had a longing for the religious securities of their rural youth. An early dramatic expression of the conservative reaction was a hugely attended Prophetic Conference in New York in 1877, followed by one eight years later in Chicago. At these conferences the liberal drifts and compromises made with the world were deplored; the prophetic and premillennial doctrines were vigorously proclaimed. The rightward trend was strengthened by the appeal to the authority of the infallible Bible. This stream of conservative thought was especially evident in the great Bible conferences: Niagara, Winona, Rocky Mountain. The conservative trend was supported and carried both to the greatest cities and the tiniest hamlets of America by the host of revivalists of the late nineteenth and early twentieth centuries. One student of revivalism, writing twenty-five years ago, noted that "if collected in one volume with only a paragraph apiece, the revivalists of the last fifty years would form a book that would dwarf an unabridged dictionary. . . ."[14]

The Christian social movements which arose in the years after the Civil War shared in the Protestant quest for a Christian America; their attention was focused on the economic, social, and political aspects of the nation's life, where revolutionary transformations were going on. . . .

There were crucial differences in theology and social philosophy between social gospel and conservative Protestants, but both groups strove to make America Christian. The Christian social movement was not only a response to external pressure; it was also a redirection, varied and often slow and cautious, of the inner vitality of Protestantism. Hence even at the point of its greatest validity, the challenge-response view must be used with care.

Despite its zeal and energy, Protestantism's dominance in culture and education, so evident at the mid-nineteenth century mark, had ebbed by the 1920s. Many who had come from Protestant backgrounds had become estranged from the church or grown indifferent to it; secularization was clearly on the increase. Protestant thought, especially in certain liberal circles, was showing the effect of culture, more than the reverse.[15] The racial, sectional, and class lines that were still drawn within Protestantism suggest rather disturbingly that the Protestant effort to permeate and Christianize society had not had too profound an effect even on its own social fabric. The tide, flowing strongly in Protestanta favor in mid-nineteenth century, had clearly turned by the third decade of the twentieth century. At least part of the complex reasons for this can be seen in the operation of sociological forces which changed the structure of both Protestantism and the society in which it moved, and which diluted and dulled the Protestant thrust. . . .

In effect, the church was in part remolded on the associative principle in the face of a segmented, pluralistic, associative culture. By this culture the Protestant thrust was diluted, blunted, absorbed. Though the churches, with their charactristic strengths and weaknesses and their varying definitions of themselves, strove zealously to penetrate and permeate American life, their impact was in some measure fragmented and disrupted by the nature of the society in which they worked. All this helps us to understand why Protestantism lost ground, why cults and sects have mushroomed since the Civil War, why denominations have often limited their ministrations to a given racial or nationality group, why local churches have often served a particular community interest. The associative nature of society in combination with the tendency of churches to identify themselves with the interests of the folk they serve contributed to the peculiar situation of American Protestantism, whereby the churches became entangled in cultural, racial, and class barriers instead of transcending them. Protestantism hoped to permeate and Christianize a society, but was instead partly enveloped by it.

Notes

1. Alexis de Tocqueville, *Democracy in America* (New York: Alfred A. Knopf, 1945), I, p. 303.

2. Robert Baird, *Religion in America* (New York: Harper & Brothers, 1856), esp. pp. 536 ff., 586 f., 658 ff.

3. Ralph H. Gabriel, *The Course of American Democratic Thought: An Intellectual History Since 1815* (New York: The Ronald Press Co., 1940), p. 14.

4.   Quoted by Donald G. Tewksbury in *The Founding of American Colleges and Universities Before the Civil War* (New York: Teachers' College, 1932), p. 56.

5.   Whitney R. Cross, *The Burned-over District: The Social and Intellectual History of Enthusiastic Religion in Western New York, 1800-1850* (Ithaca, New York: Cornell University Press, 1950), p. 108.

6.   J. Edwin Orr, *The Second Evangelical Awakening in Britain* (London: Marshall, Morgan & Scott, Ltd., 1949), p. 21.

7.   Winfred Ernest Garrison, *The March of Faith: The Story of Religion in America Since 1865* (New York: Harper & Brothers, 1933), p. 10.

8.   Henry F. May, *Protestant Churches and Industrial America* (New York: Harper & Brothers, 1949), p. 6.

9.   H. Paul Douglass, "Religion—The Protestant Faith," in Harold E. Sterns, ed., *America Now: An Inquiry into Civilization in the United States* (New York: Charles Scribner's Sons, 1938), pp. 505-27.

10.   De Tocqueville, *Democracy in America,* I, p. 303.

11.   See C. Howard Hopkins, *History of the Y.M.C.A. in North America* (New York: Association Press, 1951).

12.   Ernest Trice Thompson, *Changing Emphases in American Preaching* (Philadelphia: Westminister Press, 1943), p. 86.

13.   See Daniel Day Williams, *The Andover Liberals: A Study in American Theology* (New York: King's Crown Press, 1941); see also George Hammar, *Christian Realism in Contemporary American Theology* (Uppsala: A.B. Lundequistska Bokhandeln, 1940), especially the note on page 153, where the author stresses the evangelical center of Rauschenbusch's liberal theology.

14.   Grover C. Loud, *Evangelized America* (New York: Dial Press, 1928), p. 257.

15.   See Arnold Nash, ed., *Protestant Thought in the Twentieth Century* (New York: Macmillan Co., 1951).

Emerging Black Consciousness

W.E.B. Du Bois

Until recently, when historians tried to relate the story of the Negro churches in America, they almost always used categories derived from white church traditions. Black slaves were expected to adapt to white ways—including religion; and that meant some variety of Protestantism. After the Civil War, presumably, the development of the various Negro denominations simply imitated the larger, white traditions already well established. But we have learned more recently that the narrative is not so simple as that. Black historians have insisted that the deeper dimensions of religious life have been largely obscured by the white disposition to regard the black experience as derivative and secondhand. The shift in language from "Negro" to "black" symbolizes something more than a verbal nicety of distinction. It indicates that blacks are no longer willing to be identified by a white-bestowed epithet. And many of the roots of this new emerging black consciousness lie deep in the soil of the black religious experience.

At the turn of the twentieth century, a prophetic black voice could be heard foretelling the future of the old-time Negro churches. But not many heard or listened. Today, the prophet's words are like a newsreel of what has been happening. William Edward Burghardt Du Bois (1868-1963) wrote *The Souls of Black Folk* in 1903. Among other things, he was able to see deeply into the inner soul of religious experience and how this was expressed for black folk through the "preacher," the "music," and the "frenzy"—all three of which were essential ingredients of Negro church life. Du Bois was also aware that black religious experience, no matter how Baptist or Methodist, had intimate associations with African animism, nature worship, and tribal community life. As early as 1903, Du Bois anticipated a division in the black community where some blacks would opt for protest and even anarchy, while others would be content to make it as much as possible in the white world, even if this meant hypocrisy.

W.E.B. Du Bois was certainly one of the most literate and articulate blacks of his time. Editor, teacher, author, he was one of the founders of the NAACP and received the International Peace Prize in 1952. A Phi Beta Kappa graduate from Fisk and Harvard Universities, he taught Latin and Greek at Wilberforce University before moving on to the University of Pennsylvania and Atlanta University.

This excerpt from *The Souls of Black Folk* is reprinted from *The Black Church in America,* edited by Hart M. Nelsen, Raytha L. Yokley, and Anne K. Nelsen (1971).

It was out in the country, far from home, far from my foster home, on a dark Sunday night. The road wandered from our rambling log house up the stony bed of a creek, past wheat and corn, until we could hear dimly across the fields a rhythmic cadence of song—soft, thrilling, powerful, that swelled and died sorrowfully in our ears. I was a country schoolteacher then, fresh from the East, and had never seen a Southern Negro revival. To be sure, we in Berkshire were not perhaps as stiff and formal as they in Suffolk of olden time; yet we were very quiet and subdued, and I know not what would have happened those clear Sabbath mornings had some one punctuated the sermon with a wild scream, or interrupted the long prayer with a loud amen! And so most striking to me, as I approached the village and the little plain church perched aloft, was the air of intense excitement that possessed that mass of black folk. A sort of suppressed terror hung in the air and seemed to seize us—a pythian madness, a demonaic possession, that lent terrible reality to song and word. The black and massive form of the preacher swayed and quivered as the words crowded to his lips and flew at us in singular eloquence. The people moaned and fluttered, and then the gaunt-cheeked brown woman beside me suddenly leaped straight into the air and shrieked like a lost soul, while round about came wail and groan and outcry, and a sense of human passion such as I had never conceived before.

Those who have not thus witnessed the frenzy of a Negro revival in the untouched backwoods of the South can but dimly realize the religious feeling of the slave; as described, such scenes appear grotesque and funny, but as seen they are awful. Three things charcterized this religion of the slave—the preacher, the music, and the frenzy. The preacher is the most unique personality developed by the Negro on American soil. A leader, a politician, an orator, a "boss," an intriguer, an idealist—all these he is, and ever, too, the center of a group of men, now 20, now 1,000 in number. The combination of a certain adroitness with deep-seated earnestness, of tact with consummate ability, gave him his preeminence, and helps him maintain it. The type, of course, varies according to time and place, from the West Indies in the sixteenth century to New England in the nineteenth, and from the Mississippi bottoms to cities like New Orleans or New York.

The music of Negro religion is that plaintive rhythmic melody, with its touching minor cadences, which, despite caricature and defilement, still remains the most original and beautiful expression of human life and longing yet born on American soil. Sprung from the African forests, where its counterpart can still be heard, it was adapted, changed, and intensified by the tragic soul-life of the slave, until, under the stress of law and whip, it became the one true expression of a people's sorrow, despair, and hope.

Finally the frenzy, or "shouting," when the spirit of the Lord passed by, and, seizing the devotee, made him mad with supernatural joy, was the last essential of Negro religion and the one more devoutly believed in than all the rest. It varied in expression from the silent rapt countenance or the low murmur and moan to the mad abandon of physical fervor—the stamping, shrieking, and shouting, the rushing to and fro and wild waving of arms, the weeping and laughing, the vision and the trance. All this is nothing new in the world, but old as religion, as Delphi and Endor. And so firm a hold did it have on the Negro, that many generations firmly believed that without this visible manifestation of the God there could be no true communion with the Invisible.

These were the characteristics of Negro religious life as developed up to the time of emancipation. Since under the peculiar circumstances of the black man's environment they were the one expression of his higher life, they are of deep interest to the student of his development, both socially and psychologically. . . .

In the South, at least, practically every American Negro is a church member. Some, to be sure, are not regularly enrolled, and a few do not habitually attend services; but, practically, a proscribed people must have a social center, and that center for this people is the Negro church. The census of 1890 showed nearly 24,000 Negro churches in the country, with a total enrolled membership of over 2.5 million, or ten actual church members to every twenty-eight persons, and in some Southern states one in every two persons. Besides these there is the large number who, though not enrolled as members, attend and take part in many of the activities of the church. There is an organized Negro church for every sixty black families in the nation, and in some states for every forty families, owning, on an average, $1,000 worth of property each, or nearly $26 million in all.

Such, then, is the large development of the Negro church since emancipation. The question now is: What have been the successive steps of this social history and what are the present tendencies. First, we must realize that no such institution as the Negro church could rear itself without definite historical foundations. These foundations we can find if we remember that the social history of the Negro did not start in America. He was brought from a definite social environment—the polygamous clan life under the headship of the chief and the potent influence of the priest. His religion was nature worship, with profound belief in invisible surrounding influences, good and bad, and his worship was through incantation and sacrifice. The first rude change in this life was the slave ship and the West Indian sugar fields. The plantation organization replaced the clan and tribe, and the white master replaced the chief with far greater and more despotic powers. Forced and long-continued toil became the rule of life, the old ties of blood relationship and kinship disappeared, and instead of the family appeared a new polygamy and polyandry, which, in some cases, almost reached promiscuity. It was a terrific social revolution, and yet some traces were retained of the former group life, and the chief remaining institution was the priest or medicineman. He early appeared on the plantation and found his function as the healer of the sick, the interpreter of the unknown, the comforter of the sorrowing, the supernatural avenger of wrong, and the one who rudely but picturesquely expressed the longing, disappointment, and resentment of a stolen and oppressed people. Thus, as bard, physician, judge, and priest, within the narrow limits allowed by the slave system, rose the Negro preacher, and under him the first Afro-American institution, the Negro church. This church was not at first by any means Christian nor definitely organized; rather it was an adaptation and mingling of heathen rites among the members of each plantation, and roughly designated as Voodooism. Association with the masters, missionary effort, and motives of expediency gave these rites an early veneer of Christianity, and after the lapse of many generations the Negro church became Christian.

Two characteristic things must be noticed in regard to this

church. First, it became almost entirely Baptist and Methodist in faith; second, as a social institution it antedated by many decades the monogamic Negro home. From the very circumstances of its beginning, the church was confined to the plantation, and consisted primarily of a series of disconnected units; though, later on, some freedom of movement was allowed, still this geographical limitation was always important and was one cause of the spread of the decentralized and democratic Baptist faith among the slaves. At the same time, the visible rite of baptism appealed strongly to their mystic temperament. Today the Baptist Church is still largest in membership among Negroes, and has a million and a half communicants. Next in popularity came the churches organized in connection with the white neighboring churches, chiefly Baptist and Methodist, with a few Episcopalian and others. The Methodists still form the second greatest denomination, with nearly 1 million members. The faith of these two leading denominations was more suited to the slave church from the prominence they gave to religious feeling and fervor. The Negro membership in other denominations has always been small and relatively unimportant, although the Episcopalians and Presbyterians are gaining among the more intelligent classes today, and the Catholic Church is making headway in certain sections. After emancipation, and still earlier in the North, the Negro churches largely severed such affiliations as they had had with the white churches, either by choice or by compulsion. The Baptist churches became independent, but the Methodists were compelled early to unite for purposes of episcopal government. This gave rise to the great African Methodist Church, the greatest Negro organization in the world, to the Zion Church and the Colored Methodist, and to the black conferences and churches in this and other denominations.

The second fact noted, namely, that the Negro church antedates the Negro home, leads to an explanation of much that is paradoxical in this communistic institution and the morals of its members. But especially it leads us to regard this institution as peculiarly the expression of the inner ethical life of a people in a sense seldom true elsewhere. Let us turn, then, from the outer physical development of the church to the more important inner ethical life of the people who compose it. The Negro has already been pointed out many times as a religious animal—a being of that deep emotional nature which turns instinctively toward the supernatural. Endowed with a rich tropical imagination and a keen, delicate appreciation of nature, the transplanted African lived in a world animate with gods and devils, elves and witches; full of strange influences—of good to be implored, of evil to be propitiated. Slavery, then, was to him the dark triumph of evil over him. All the hateful powers of the underworld were striving against him, and a spirit of revolt and revenge filled his heart. He called up all the resources of heathenism to aid—exorcism and witchcraft, the mysterious Obi worship with its barbarious rites, spells, and blood sacrifice even, now and then, of human victims. Weird midnight orgies and mystic conjurations were invoked, the witch-woman and the voodoo priest became the center of Negro group life, and that vein of vague superstition which characterizes the unlettered Negro even today was deepened and strengthened.

In spite, however, of such success as that of the fierce Maroons, the Danish blacks, and others, the spirit of revolt gradually died away under the untiring energy and superior strength of the slave masters. By the middle of the eighteenth century the black slave had sunk, with hushed murmurs, to his place at the bottom of a new economic system, and was unconsciously ripe for a new philosophy of life. Nothing suited his condition then better than the doctrines of passive submission embodied in the newly learned Christianity. Slave masters early realized this, and cheerfully aided religious propaganda within certain bounds. The long system of re-pression and degradation of the Negro tended to emphasize the elements in his character which made him a valuable chattel: courtesy became humility, moral strength degenerated into submission, and the exquisite native appreciation of the beautiful became an infinite capacity for dumb suffering. The Negro, losing the joy of this world, eagerly seized upon the offered conceptions of the next; the avenging spirit of the Lord enjoining patience in this world, under sorrow and tribulation until the great day when He should lead His dark children home—this became his comforting dream. His preacher repeated the prophecy, and his bards sang—

> *Children, we all shall be free*
> *When the Lord shall appear!*

This deep religious fatalism, painted so beautifully in "Uncle Tom," came soon to breed, as all fatalistic faiths will, the sensualist side by side with the martyr. Under the lax moral life of the plantation, where marriage was a farce, laziness a virtue, and property a theft, a religion of resignation and submission degenerated easily, in less strenuous minds, into a philosophy of indulgence and crime. Many of the worst characteristics of the Negro masses of today had their seed in this period of the slave's ethical growth. Here it was that the home was ruined under the very shadow of the church, white and black; here habits of shiftlessness took root, and sullen hopelessness replaced hopeful strife. . . .

It is difficult to explain clearly the present critical stage of Negro religion. First, we must remember that living as the blacks do in close contact with a great modern nation, and sharing, although imperfectly, the soul-life of that nation, they must necessarily be affected more or less directly by all the religious and ethical forces that are today moving the United States. These questions and movements are, however, overshadowed and dwarfed by the (to them) all-important question of their civil, political, and economic status. They must perpetually discuss the "Negro problem"—must live, move, and have their being in it, and interpret all else in its light or darkness. With this come, too, peculiar problems of their inner life—of the status of women, the maintenance of home, the training of children, the accumulation of wealth, and the prevention of crime. All this must mean a time of intense ethical ferment, of religious heart searching and intellectual unrest. From the double life every American Negro must live, as a Negro and as an American, as swept on by the current of the nineteenth while yet struggling in the eddies of the fifteenth century — from this must arise a painful self-consciousness, an almost morbid sense of personality and a moral hesitancy which is fatal to self-confidence. The worlds within and without the veil of color are changing, and changing rapidly, but not at the same rate, not in the same way; and this must produce a peculiar wrenching of the soul, a peculiar sense of doubt and bewilderment. Such a double life, with double thoughts, double duties, and double social classes, must give rise to double words and double ideals, and tempt the mind to pretence or revolt, to hypocrisy or radicalism.

In some such doubtful words and phrases can one perhaps most clearly picture the peculiar ethical paradox that faces the Negro of today and is tingeing and changing his religious life. Feeling that his rights and his dearest ideals are being trampled upon, that the public conscience is ever more deaf to his righteous appeal, and that all the reactionary forces of prejudice, greed, and revenge are daily gaining new strength and fresh allies, the Negro faces no enviable dilemma. Conscious of his impotence, and pessimistic, he often becomes bitter and vindictive; and his religion, instead of a worship, is a complaint and a curse, a wail rather than a hope, a sneer rather than a faith. On the other hand, another type of mind, shrewder and keener and more tortuous too, sees in the very strength of the anti-Negro movement its patent weaknesses, and with Jesuitic casuistry is deterred by no ethical considerations in the endeavor to turn this weakness to the black man's strength. Thus we have two great and hardly reconcilable streams of thought and ethical strivings; the danger of the one lies in anarchy, that of the other in hypocrisy. The one type of Negro stands almost ready to curse God and die, and the other is too often found a traitor to right and a coward before force; the one is wedded to ideals remote, whimsical, perhaps impossible of realization; the other forgets that life is more than meat and the body more than raiment. But, after all, is not this simply the writhing of the age translated into black — the triumph of the lie which today, with its false culture, faces the hideousness of the anarchist assassin?

Today the two groups of Negroes, the one in the North, the other in the South, represent these divergent ethical tendencies, the first tending toward radicalism, the other toward hypocritical compromise. It is no idle regret with which the white South mourns the loss of the old-time Negro—the frank, honest, simple old servant who stood for the earlier religious age of submission and humility. With all his laziness and lack of many elements of true manhood, he was at least open-hearted, faithful, and sincere. Today he is gone, but who is to blame for his going? Is it not those very persons who mourn for him? Is it not the tendency, born of reconstruction and reaction, to found a society on lawlessness and deception, to tamper with the moral fiber of a naturally honest and straightforward people until the whites threaten to become ungovernable tyrants and the blacks criminals and hypocrites? Deception is the natural defense of the weak against the strong, and the South used it for many years against its conquerors; today it must be prepared to see its black proletariat turn that same two-edged weapon against itself. And how natural this is! The death of Denmark Vesey and Nat Turner proved long since to the Negro the present hopelessness of physical defense. Political defense is becoming less and less available, and economic defense is still only partially effective. But there is a patent defense at hand—the defense of deception and flattery, of cajoling and lying. It is the same defense which peasants of the Middle Ages used and which left its stamp on their character for centuries. Today the young Negro of the South who would succeed cannot be frank and outspoken, honest and self-assertive, but rather he is daily tempted to be silent and wary, politic and sly; he must flatter and be pleasant, endure petty insults with a smile, shut his eyes to wrong; in too many cases he sees positive personal advantage in deception and lying. His real thoughts, his real aspirations, must be guarded in whispers; he must not criticize, he must not complain. Patience, humility, and adroitness must, in these growing black youth, replace impulse, manliness, and courage. With this sacrifice there is an economic opening, and perhaps peace and some prosperity. Without this there is riot, migration, or crime. Nor is this situation peculiar to the southern United States, is it not rather the only method by which undeveloped races have gained the right to share modern culture? The price of culture is a lie.

On the other hand, in the North the tendency is to emphasize the radicalism of the Negro. Driven from his birthright in the South by a situation at which every fiber of his more outspoken and assertive nature revolts, he finds himself in a land where he can scarcely earn a decent living amid the harsh competition and the color discrimination. At the same time, through schools and periodicals, discussions and lectures, he is intellectually quickened and awakened. The soul, long pent up and dwarfed, suddenly expands in newfound freedom. What wonder that every tendency is to excess—radical complaint, radical remedies, bitter denunciation or angry silence. Some sink, some rise. The criminal and the sensualist leave the church for the gambling hell and the brothel, and fill the slums of Chicago and Baltimore; the better classes segregate themselves from the group life of both white and black and form an aristocracy, cultured but pessimistic, whose bitter criticism stings while it points out no way of escape. They despise the submission and subserviency of the southern Negroes, but offer no other means by which a poor and oppressed minority can exist side by side with its masters. Feeling deeply and keenly the tendencies and opportunities of the age in which they live, their souls are bitter at the fate which drops the veil between; and the very fact that this bitterness is natural and justifiable only serves to intensify it and make it more maddening.

Between the two extreme types of ethical attitude which I

have thus sought to make clear wavers the mass of the millions of Negroes, North and South; and their religious life and activity partake of this social conflict within their ranks. Their churches are differentiating—now into groups of cold, fashionable devotees, in no way distinguishable from similar white groups save in color of skin; now into large social and business institutions catering to the desire for information and amusement of their members, warily avoiding unpleasant questions both within and without the black world, and preaching in effect if not in word: *Dum vivimus, vivamus.*

But back of this still broods silently the deep religious feeling of the real Negro heart, the stirring, unguided might of powerful human souls who have lost the guiding star of the past and seek in the great night a new religious ideal. Some day the awakening will come, when the pent-up vigor of 10 million souls shall sweep irresistibly toward the goal, out of the Valley of the Shadow of Death, where all that makes life worth living—liberty, justice, and right—is marked "For White People Only."

What Would Jesus Do?

James H. Smylie

At the turn of the twentieth century, many middle-American church people were worried about relating personal faith to the everyday problems of life. With increasing industrialization and commercial competition, the middle class grew more affluent but many also became more anxious. The satisfactions of personal piety can hardly be enjoyed in the midst of glaring poverty, injustice, and human degradation.

In the churches of the middle class, the accent fell on experiential religion and the warm feeling of assurance and salvation. The figure of Jesus as savior-redeemer was central; and the popular hymns of the time expressed the intimate bond between believer and Lord— "Jesus, Savior, pilot me," "Jesus, the very thought of Thee," "I need Thee every hour," "What a friend we have in Jesus," "More love to Thee, O Christ," "Abide with me," and so forth. For many, this experience of inner comfort was enough; but for others the figure of Jesus not only promised peace and joy but challenged complacency and called for self-sacrifice.

A dramatic illustration of this dilemma between personal piety and moral conscience was provided in a modest religious novel entitled *In His Steps.* The chapters grew out of a series of Sunday evening sermons preached by the Reverend Charles M. Sheldon of the Central Congregational Church, Topeka, Kansas. The book was first published in 1897. It was an immediate and unexpected success. It has gone through dozens of editions, is still in print today, and is one of the phenomenal best-sellers of all time.

The point of the story revolved around a small group of committed church people who agreed to govern their lives and confront all their daily decisions by asking themselves the simple question: "What would Jesus do?" The results for those who took the "pledge" were usually agonizing and upsetting, but spiritually (if not materially) rewarding.

A digest of the novel, with some interpretive commentary, is given in the selection that follows. It comes from an article, "Sheldon's *In His Steps:* Conscience and Discipleship," published in *Theology Today* (April, 1975). The author of this article, James H. Smylie, is professor of American church history at Union Theological Seminary, Richmond, Va., and editor of the *Journal of Presbyterian History.*

Charles M. Sheldon's religious novel, *In His Steps,* grew out of a series of Sunday evening sermons preached in the minister's Central Congregational Church, Topeka, Kansas. One of the all-time best-sellers, *In His Steps* was originally addressed to the young people of Sheldon's congregation, to the members of the Christian Endeavor Society, and to students from Washburn College. The biblical text for the sermon series was 1 Peter 2:21—"For even hereunto were ye called: because Christ also suffered for us, leaving us an example, that ye should follow in his steps." The homilies, in story form, were printed serially, beginning 5 November 1896, in *The Advance*, a Congregational weekly. The novel has long been considered one of the great American tracts because of its widespread distribution. . . .

It did for the "Social Gospel" movement what T.S. Arthur's *Ten Nights in a Bar Room* and Harriet Beecher Stowe's *Uncle Tom's Cabin* did for the temperance and antislavery movements. The basic story: The Reverend Henry Maxwell, pastor of the First Church in Raymond, is preparing, on Saturday, his Sunday sermon on the text of 1 Peter 2:21 in which he is discussing the atonement as personal sacrifice. He intends to emphasize the doctrine "from the side of example," giving illustrations from the life and teachings of Jesus and showing how "faith in the Christ helped to save men because of the patterns or character he displayed for their imitation."

The minister is interrupted by a vagrant, who has lost his wife, lost his job, and is separated from his daughter. On Sunday, this same man hears Maxwell preach his sermon as he worships with the congregation. He interrupts the worship to comment on the sermon and to ask what the pastor and congregation mean when they sing "Jesus, I my cross have taken, all to leave and follow thee." Later he dies in Maxwell's home. He makes such an impression on the pastor that on the next Sunday, Maxwell invites members of his church to volunteer to take a pledge for a year. They are to ask themselves in every situation of life, "What would Jesus do?" and to carry through on their conclusions regardless of the cost to themselves.

A number of persons meet after church in a type of church-within-the-church, to speak about their commitment. These include, among others, Virginia Page, a wealthy heiress; Edward Norman, a newspaper editor; Alexander Powers, a businessman; and Donald Marsh, a college president. The novel focuses on families in First Church and on the Rectangle in Raymond, a vacant lot in the middle of the city's saloon and slum district, and the scene of a revival. Then it shifts to Chicago's mansions and tenements as the influence of the pledge spreads. There is romance in the book for the young people. Converted girl, Miss Winslow, who sings at the First Church and at the revival meeting, finally accepts boy, Virginia Page's brother, who is finally converted and takes the pledge along with Rachel. The novel has to do with the way in which these people attempt to follow after Jesus as the pattern for their lives and the texts of the Bible which suggest this as a model for Christian ethics. . . .

Sheldon wrote in the period of the success hero, symbolized

by Andrew Carnegie, a poor immigrant who made good and who was celebrating his rise to prominence in the "Gospel of Wealth." Carnegie enunciated as the divine laws of his success, individualism, competition and the accumulation of wealth, and the trusteeship of riches. Horatio Alger, an older contemporary of Sheldon, fictionalized this rise from tenement slum to millionaire's mansion with luck and pluck in his novels about "Ragged Dick" and "Tattered Tom." William T. Stead published *If Christ Came to Chicago* in 1894 and spotlighted the "Chicagoan Trinity," George M. Pullman, Marshall Field, Philip Armour, the "great gods" of the "Mecca of Mammon." When Sheldon's young people, affluent themselves and surrounded by these stories of success, met with him on Sunday evening, he presented to them another hero, one who called them to service and sacrifice of a different kind. . . .

In his attempt to motivate and give direction, Sheldon casts his morality play in a familiar mold. He deals with a number of cases of conscience. The term, "case of conscience," is an old one used in Protestant casuistry to deal with problems in economics, politics, and social relations. . . . Each case involves a personal response, but touches corporate life and highlights some of the challenges which Christians had to face in a rapidly changing society. Each case involves a person who pays the cost of discipleship, and in doing so, shows how his or her life impinges upon the larger community, often separating them from family and friends.

Case of Conscience I. Virginia Page is a wealthy heiress, a woman of the leisure class, who lives in a mansion in Raymond with her grandmother. Her problem is the stewardship of her inheritance, or trusteeship as Andrew Carnegie put it in his article on wealth in 1889. This was a nagging problem for Virginia after she took the pledge, asking herself "What would Jesus do?" with her money. She is drawn more and more to the Rectangle and takes up playing the organ for the revival meeting there and to accompany Rachel Winslow.

During the course of one of the revivals a fallen girl by the name of Loreen comes under conviction for sin and is converted. Virginia knows that this girl cannot go back into the slums in which she was involved in her trade, and a plan for the use of her wealth begins to take place. Virginia takes Loreen home. She comes up against the resistance of her grandmother, who had already shown hostility toward the conception of Jesus as a sacrifice. Sheldon, using Matthew 10:35 ("For I am come to set a man at variance against his father, and the daughter against her mother, and the daughter-in-law against her mother-in-law"), shows how attempts to follow after Jesus, often separate members of the same household. Virginia's grandmother protests bringing "scum" into the home, insists that her grandchild send Loreen to an "asylum for helpless women" for the sake of the Page reputation. Virginia protests that society is not her god. She keeps Loreen, and tells her grandmother that if she does not like it she may leave. Grandmother packs up for parts South.

The most sensational scene in the whole novel takes place when Virginia takes Loreen back to the Rectangle for a meeting. An angry crowd threatens them. Loreen pushes Virginia out of the path of a flying bottle, but is killed by the object herself — she dies a vicarious sacrifice. Sheldon blames the drunken crowd. But he also blames "Christian America" for permitting the conditions in which Loreen could be exploited and murdered.

Virginia decides to use the bulk of her wealth, in cooperation with her brother, who has also been converted, to transform the Rectangle. She studies the methods of Christian work in city slums and decides to build wholesome lodging-houses, refuges for poor women and shop girls. To her friend Rachel Winslow she proposes a Musical Institute. With this use of her wealth, including her own personal involvement in the enterprise, she hopes to make "reparation" for Loreen.

Case of Conscience II. Virginia also uses part of her fortune to undergird Edward Norman's experiment in responsible journalism. Norman is a newspaper editor who is moved by Maxwell's suggestion and takes the pledge. He asks himself what Jesus would do in running a modern newspaper — in a day of popular penny-papers, yellow journalism thriving on sensationalism, and the Sunday special. Sheldon introduces the chapter in which he described Norman, struggling with this question, with the text of 1 John 2:6 ("He that saith he abideth in him ought himself also so to walk, even as he walked"). The author admonishes that those who say they abide in Christ ought to walk as he walked. He decides that Jesus would strive to print only such news and only those advertisements which were fit to print, and do so on every day except Sunday.

In attempting to deal with his Christian responsibilities, Norman decides that he will not run stories which pander to the masses, such as the account of a very brutal prizefight. He decides not to carry liquor and tobacco advertisements, since by doing so he would contribute to the continuation of habits and forces in the community he felt were detrimental to it. He also decides to do away with a very profitable Sunday edition and to print the special Sunday features on Saturday.

Norman determines that probably Jesus would work out a method of profit-sharing with editors, reporters, pressmen, and all who contribute anything to the life of the paper. When he advises his subordinates about his decisions, he is considered insane, an idiot, a fool, bent on bankrupting the whole business with such an absurd moral standard. Although Norman feels the financial loss almost immediately, he nevertheless persists in his experiment in responsible editing. Moreover, as Virginia Page helps him, he determines to support through his editorials the causes of two other men who have taken the pledge and who have determined to follow Jesus in the reforming of the society.

Case of Conscience III. Alexander Powers, a member of Maxwell's congregation, is part of middle management. He runs a railroad shop and supervises the work of about three hundred men. He also must decide what it means to walk as Jesus walked in his work, to take up his cross daily (Mark 10:21). He and his wife and daughter are security oriented, and have learned to enjoy luxury and a good place in Raymond society. At first he decides that he needs to improve the working conditions of his men. He takes a first step by providing a clean place for them to eat their lunches and to hear, for edification, talks on subjects which may help their lives.

By accident, Powers comes across conclusive evidence that his company is engaged in a systematic violation of the newly passed interstate commerce laws of the United States and of state laws passed to prevent railroad trusts. What would Jesus do in this situation? After all, everybody was doing it, in all probability, and what could one man do in the railroad business which made it almost impossible to live by the Christian standard. Everybody would misunderstand him. He would be dragged into court as a witness, he would lose his position, and he and his family would be put in disgrace in society. Powers concludes that he cannot withhold the information. He resigns his job and turns over the documents to the proper authorities. Sheldon acknowledges in a note at this point that a railroad man told him that he could only admire the shrewdness with which the companies violated the law.

Powers is not supported in this decision by his wife and daughter, who refuse to be seen in public. He is in addition to this hurt, misunderstood, misrepresented, and he returns to his old job of telegraph operator at a much lower wage. Powers discovers that a man's "foes are they of his own household," and Jesus is the great divider of life. Powers is supported by the newspaper which praises the sacrifice of one individual who wishes to see equal justice under law — the enforcement of the law against great corporations as well as the weakest of individuals. Powers see the irony of his situation. He knows that it pays a railroad to have in its employment men who are temperate and honest. When it comes to a situation in which one of those temperate and honest employees discovers that the management is engaged in un-Christian, lawless acts, it does not pay. Then Christian temperance and honesty may become a cross for those who blow the whistle on the culprits.

Case of Conscience IV. Donald Marsh also takes the pledge. He is the president of Lincoln College and a longtime professor of ethics and philosophy. His problem of conscience is municipal reform, and his special text seems to be "If any man serve me, let him follow me" (John 12:26). He has to admit that despite his professional concern for ethics, he is a complete stranger to politics. He seems to consider politics, even when he expresses an interest in it, not a high calling from God but a cross he must bear, thus indicating the manner in which the office of civil magistrate had been degraded as a vocation. His experience on the Mount of Transfiguration becomes a way station to a Calvary in city affairs.

He knows that the city is in the hands of corrupt, unprincipled men, controlled in large part by the whiskey men, who have turned city government into a "horrible whirlpool of deceit, bribery, political trickery and saloonism." He decides that the city needs "clean, honest, capable, businesslike city administration," and that he must run for office. Along with other professional people, he has been a political coward, avoiding the "sacred duties of citizenship, either ignorantly or selfishly." He now realizes he must suffer in the fight for clean city life. He agrees with the Italian leader, Mazzini, that he must appeal to his fellow citizens to come and suffer with him in the struggle. In his attempt to organize righteousness against "rum and corruption," he learns from the entrenched politicians by packing a nominating meeting. They were "in the habit of carrying on the affairs of the city as if they owned them and everyone else was simply a tool or a cipher."

Marsh wins in the primary but loses at the polls. Sheldon blames Christians who fail to vote for the narrow margin of the defeat and the continuation of bad government in

Raymond. While the blow to Marsh is a deep one, he continues the administration of the college and his teaching with new attitudes to public affairs. He instructs his students that those who have education have special civic responsibilities, especially for the "weak and the ignorant."

Case of Conscience V. The last case of conscience involves two clergymen in Chicago, where the scene shifts in the last of the novel, Dr. Calvin Bruce (what could be more Presbyterian!) and a "Bishop," who could be either an Episcopalian or a Methodist. These two fall under Maxwell's influence. They take the pledge and ask themselves at the height of their very successful lives: "What would Jesus do?" They have position and prestige. The "Bishop" has considerable possessions. They decide that neither one of them has really paid anything in discipleship and that they have lived apart from the troubles of the city and those who are poor, degraded, and abandoned in this life. They confess that they are haunted by the text of 1 Peter 2:21. The "Bishop" expresses sentiments for them both when he admits that if he had lived in the time of Luther he might have sought God's favor through self-inflicted torture. Here is a touch of masochism, the desire to suffer for suffering's sake. But in the present case the desire is channelled by the two clergymen in their commitment to city mission enterprise.

They reflect on the strange situation in which they find themselves among the Christians whom they have been serving. If they — a "Doctor of Divinity and a Bishop" — would resign charges and go to Bombay, Hong Kong, and Africa to save souls, they would be hailed as heroes of the faith. As they lose themselves in darkest Chicago, for Jesus's sake, they are considered queer. They decide that they cannot be Christians by proxy, and they move to a settlement house in the worst part of Chicago. Here they work with alcoholics, attempting to convert them by identifying with them and assuring them of God's love and their love. Here they attempt to rehabilitate these persons and to provide for those who live in the area a substitute for the saloon, a place where they can meet, talk, and deal with their problems. Here they sponsor teaching and learning, as in the case of one young settlement worker who instructs immigrant women on how to deal with adulterated food. "Martyrdom," the Bishop muses in one place about his case of conscience, "is a lost art with us. Our Christianity loves its ease and comfort too well to take up anything so rough and heavy as a cross. And yet what does Jesus mean? What is it to walk in his steps?"

Sheldon writes about several other cases of conscience in his novel. These indicate the wide range of his interest, and the way in which he was attempting to carry the responsibility of Christian education within his congregation. It is very easy, of course, to make a case against Sheldon for what seems to be a preoccupation with the liquor question and Sabbatarianism. It may be convenient to do this and overlook the fact that he was trying to give some direction in dealing with many of the major issues confronting people in his middle-class congregation and which were on the hearts of many Americans. . . .

Although it is very important to assess these various cases of conscience, we must keep in mind what seems to be Sheldon's primary purpose. He wanted to motivate his hearers and his readers and to give them an option for a life style not very popular in the Gilded Age. Milton Wright, businessman who takes the pledge and runs his retail store as Jesus would run it, put his case of conscience in this way. Would he do business as usual on the basis of the regular code: "Will it pay?" Or could he do business in a different way, to make a living for himself and others, with another question: "What would Jesus do? . . ."

Sheldon's *In His Steps* is still read by people who are looking for a model for ethical decision making. It would be difficult for us to determine who is touched by this novel and how people are touched by it. While Christian ethicists debate weighty matters of right and justice, simple people who have never opened a book in Christian ethics look for a way to move from some faith commitment to action. Some of us cannot always communicate with middle-class America, much less give them moral motivation and moral guidance. Moreover, it occurs to me that those people who are still within the revivalist tradition of Billy Graham or in the charismatic tradition, long for ethical guidance which their leaders do not always give them. Therefore, Sheldon still enjoys a popularity today, for good or ill. His book may perpetuate questionable ideas about following after Jesus as a pattern and an imitation life-style. It may also give a wrong impression about the context in which Christians have to make ethical decisions. Contemporary readers probably do not know about Sheldon's sympathies with Christian socialism or the "social creed" of the Federal Council of Churches. And readers are faced with the problem of correlating Christian faith into life in a society which is vastly different than the one for which Sheldon wrote. But people who read Sheldon may be yearning for some word about Christian behavior, may want to face up to their responsibilities, and may be willing to pay the cost of discipleship.

Mission And Unity —
The Ecumenical Era

Samuel McCrae Cavert

What is known as "the ecumenical movement," the quest for cooperation and unity, was initiated by the Protestant churches. For the first 50 years of the twentieth century, Protestantism in America and throughout the world devoted much of its denominational energies and resources to various experiments in ecumenicity.

It was not until about 1940 that any Eastern Orthodox Church became officially associated with this movement, and it was not until Vatican Council II (1962-65), called by the late Pope John XXIII, that Roman Catholics began to discuss ecumenicity.

There are obvious reasons why Protestantism should have been so caught up in the movement, chief of which were the enervating divisions of denominations, churches, and sects. The statistics of this "scandal of Protestantism" have been documented since 1916 in annual volumes of the *Yearbook of American Churches*.

About 1900, the tide seemed to turn, and some of the broken denominational fragments were put back together again. From the

Federal Council of Churches (1908) to COCU (Consultation on Church Union, 1962), an immense and promising ecumenical activity marked all the major Protestant churches throughout the world.

Part of the ecumenical story relates to various missionary societies and their efforts to coordinate Protestant evangelistic programs. By 1948, the missionary movement and the quest for church unity merged in the newly formed World Council of Churches (WCC).

In the excerpt printed here, the tangled skein of the ecumenical chronicle is skillfully unraveled by an expert in the field. Samuel McCrae Cavert said of his long association with the ecumenical movement: "Among those who had firsthand contacts . . . I am almost the only survivor." He was an official delegate to all the ecumenical church gatherings. The excerpt is taken from his summary statement of the movement, *Church Cooperation and Unity in America: A Historical Review, 1900-1970* (1970).

In America, the churches' support for ecumenicity slackened considerably during the 1960s. This was due partly to declining church membership and financial resources, and partly to resistance to the kinds of social and political positions taken, for example, by the WCC. But the ecumenical movement is still very much alive, in America mostly at the grass-roots level, but elsewhere there is great need for organizational cooperation.

In 1975, the fifth assembly of the WCC was held in Nairobi, Kenya. The location itself indicates the growing importance of the Third World and the redirection of basic problems for all the churches. If churches in the West remain static, or even lose ground, it should be noted that the fastest Christian growth rates in the world are in Africa.

The twentieth century has witnessed a far greater change in the relation of the American churches to one another than is generally realized. By 1900 the Christian community had become fragmented into a bewildering array of self-sufficient and rival denominations. Two generations later this pattern of separation had been succeeded by one of mutual support, extensive cooperation in common tasks, joint administration of certain projects, and lively concern for a fuller form of unity still to be achieved.

The denominational system, as it took shape in America, was not without important values. It made room for a rich diversity both of historic traditions and of ethnic characteristics. It fostered a spirit of freedom and creativity which encouraged each group to develop its own distinctive insights. It was effective in planting churches and schools across a vast unoccupied continent.

But the intense individualism of the system tempted each denominational group to think more of its own advancement than of responsibility for the community as a whole. This resulted in over-churching in many areas and under-churching in others. Worse than the wasteful inefficiency was the divisive influence on the life of the community. Instead of being a force for reconciliation the churches often added one more element of disunity. Most serious of all was an unconscious distortion of the Christian faith and life that arose from emphasis on minor points of denominational difference instead of concentration on the central meaning of the Gospel.

During the nineteenth century the shortcomings of an anarchic denominationalism were overcome in considerable measure by undenominational organizations through which members of the divided churches worked together in various common enterprises. Those who felt a special concern for circulating the Scriptures formed the American Bible Society. Those who were zealous for the religious education of children created the American Sunday School Union and the International Sunday School Association. Those who were impelled to help youth founded the Young Men's Christian Association and the Young Women's Christian Association. Those who were interested in social reform established associations like the American Anti-Slavery Society and the American Peace Society.

In these and other similar movements Christians as individuals joined hands in the nineteenth century by ignoring the denominations and initiating nonecclesiastical societies. The objective, in each case, was not to bring the churches closer together — which seemed out of the question — but to accomplish specific tasks which did not lend themselves to a denominational approach. The types of work thus inaugurated by nondenominational action were often adopted, at a later stage, by denominational agencies, thus causing much organizational confusion. . . .

From the standpoint of overcoming denominational separation the first decade of the twentieth century was a uniquely creative period. Within these few years three different types of unitive concern blossomed into three different movements, each rooted in ecclesiastical soil.

The first movement was one of cooperation among denominational boards and agencies in the interest of more efficient functioning in their own specific fields of operation. It was pragmatic in outlook, focusing on immediate practical objectives and deliberately bypassing theological issues as too divisive. Of this type the Foreign Missions Conference of North America was the earliest example. Beginning in 1893 as a simple annual consultation, it achieved permanent organizational form in 1907 by appointment of a continuous Committee of Reference and Counsel.

The second type of unitive thrust concentrated on the very issues that the first ignored. It was committed to a patient exploration of the doctrinal and ecclesiastical differences which had been responsible for the denominational system and were blocking the way to a united church. The Faith and Order movement, originating in the Episcopal Church in 1910, was the organized expression of this approach to the problems of disunity.

The third type of unitive advance, occupying middle ground between the other two, was federative. It was like the first in putting the main emphasis upon working together in common tasks but it was like the second in being concerned with the relation of the churches to one another as churches. Stressing a spiritual oneness deeper than the denominational divisions, it sought increasing fellowship in Christian life and work, without commitment as to the ultimate forms in which that fellowship would be embodied. The Federal Council of the Churches of Christ in America, created in 1908, represented this form of approach to unity. . . .

The Council won most of its support from forward-looking elements in its diverse constituency. The more conservative elements tended to be indifferent or critical. In some of the denominational assemblies and conventions the question of continuing membership in the Council was a debatable issue. Occasionally one of the small denominations that had not yet developed much sense of social responsibility withdrew, but in general the membership remained remarkably stable. When in 1950 the Federal Council finished its course by uniting with the other interdenominational agencies to establish the National Council of Churches, all of the major denominations that had constituted the original membership in 1908 were still identified with it. . . .

Between the movement for church federation and the movement for organic union represented by Faith and Order a measure of tension prevailed for several years. Some of the sponsors of Faith and Order were fearful that interdenominational cooperation might come to be accepted as a sufficient substitute for union. Many of the supporters of the Federal Council felt that organic union was a utopian dream. A common view among those who were sensitive to the shortcomings of the denominational system was that the two new movements were complementary.

The World Conference on Faith and Order, which finally met in Lausanne in 1927, marked the beginning of a systematic effort in the churches to understand one another at the level of their deepest doctrinal and ecclesiastical differences. It could agree on no solutions of the problems to which it addressed itself but it initiated a continuous process of study and dialogue which has gone on ever since. It was thus a starting point on a new road. The successive world conferences on Faith and Order — held in Edinburgh in 1937, in Lund in 1952, and in Montreal in 1963 —together with the North American Conference in Oberlin in 1957, have created an atmosphere favorable to union and also supplied resources for those engaged in concrete projects of union among certain churches. . . .

The decades of the twenties and thirties were a prolonged testing time for the whole movement for cooperation and unity. The fundamentalist-modernist confrontation produced new divisions. In the Presbyterian Church in the U.S.A., for example, two splinter denominations, the Orthodox Presbyterian Church and the Bible Presbyterian Church, arose. In the Baptist circle the General Association of Regular Baptists and the Conservative Baptist Convention of America were organized as breakaways from the Northern Baptist Convention.

The disruptive effect of doctrinal controversy was felt more within denominations than between them, but the interdenominational agencies could not escape unscathed. Fundamentalists demanded that their particular form of orthodoxy be accepted as a condition of cooperation. Modernists were uninterested in cooperating with those whom they regarded as obscurantist and unprogressive. Between the extremes the central body of Protestants was striving to hold together in the face of the general tension. The Federal Council suffered some setbacks, including the temporary withdrawal of the southern Presbyterians in 1931.

More serious was the rise of two new interdenominational organizations representing groups that criticized the Federal Council for its "liberal" orientation. The less significant of the two was the small American Council of Christian Churches, which was formed in 1941. Aggressive in its denunciation of alleged "apostasy" and "communism" in the mainline churches, it won the support of only the most intransigent fundamentalists, but its militant methods attracted considerable public attention.

The other organization was the National Association of Evangelicals, established in 1942 as a center of cooperative activity among Protestants who felt the need for an explicit commitment to doctrinal orthodoxy. Its membership was made up partly of national denominations, especially of the Pentecostal and Holiness type, and partly of local churches and associations that were not satisfied with current ecumenical trends. Numerically its constituency was not impressive but it clearly revealed that there was a substantial body of Protestants who did not regard the Federal Council as adequately representing them.

Unaligned with any interdenominational structure were certain conservative denominations with large memberships, especially the Southern Baptist Convention and the Missouri Synod Lutherans, which pursued a "go it alone" policy. On the theological left there were smaller bodies that were also outside of the cooperative structures, especially the American Unitarian Association and the Universalist Church of America.

In the midst of this confusing situation the Federal Council experienced inner strain not only from the general theological tension but even more from its activity in fields of social concern. On the one hand, its first defined objective was to "express the fellowship and catholic unity of the Christian church," and in pursuit of this it could well be argued that controversial issues should be avoided. On the other hand, another constitutional objective was to secure "a larger combined influence for the churches of Christ in all matters affecting the moral and social condition of the people, so as to promote the application of the law of Christ in every relation of human life." Efforts to carry out this second objective in industrial, economic, racial, and international affairs were bound to raise highly debatable questions.

The practice of not avoiding controversial issues had been continuous since the first days of the Council. At its inaugural meeting when there was still a strong popular prejudice against the labor movement, the Council had committed itself to the right of workers to organize for the improvement of their condition. As early as 1913 it had opposed legislation discriminating against Orientals on the Pacific Coast. In 1923, when the steel industry still insisted that the twelve-hour day was technically necessary, the Council was characterizing it as "morally indefensible."

In the later twenties and thirties, some of the greatest stress within the Council was not in relation to the industrial and international world but in realms closer to the traditional concern of the churches. A temporary strain was precipitated by an inquiry in 1925 into the way in which the legal prohibition of the liquor traffic was working. A research study concluded that the evils which had led to the adoption of the eighteenth amendment were still far from solution. This so disturbed some of the leaders in denominations that had crusaded for prohibition that sharp argument arose over allowing the research department to publish findings until they had been endorsed by the Council as a whole. A study that evoked even more criticism was made in 1931 by a committee on marriage and the home when it addressed itself to the subject of "Moral Aspects of Birth Control." The committee concluded that a "careful and restrained use of contraceptives by married people is valid and moral." A stormy debate ensued over both the report and the "representative" character of the Council. The view which eventually prevailed was that the Council would serve the churches best by defining "representative" in terms not of a cautious consensus but of the best guidance that their delegated representatives could offer. . . .

During the thirties and forties there were also evidences of a growing trend toward union between denominations not separated by serious doctrinal differences. Three Lutheran bodies combined to form the American Lutheran Church (1930). The Congregational Churches and the Christian Churches (General Convention) joined forces (1931). The Reformed Church in the U.S. and the Evangelical Synod of North America united as the Evangelical and Reformed Church (1934). The Methodist Church (1939) was created by the reunion of three branches that had broken apart in the first half of the nineteenth century. The United Brethren in Christ and the Evangelical Church came together as the Evangelical United Brethren Church (1946). . . .

As the century neared midpoint, the most hopeful approach to greater unity in the immediate future was clearly seen to be along the road of cooperation rather than union.

But the movement of cooperation was handicapped by its segmented character. In addition to the Federal Council of Churches there were almost a dozen agencies responsible for cooperation in particular fields, such as the Home Missions Council, the Foreign Missions Conference, the International Council of Religious Education, and the United Council of Church Women. Each had its roots either in the churches as corporate bodies, as in the case of the Federal Council, or in denominational boards and societies, as in the case of the other organizations. Each was rendering a needed service in its own special area but none represented the total program of cooperative activity. None made visible the life and mission of the American Christian community as a whole.

Why, it began to be asked, should not all these serviceable instruments be united in an inclusive interdenominational body? Would not this both provide a more convincing manifestation of essential oneness and also contribute to better planning and more efficient operation? . . .

The National Council of Churches accordingly came into being at the end of 1950, after approval by twelve interdenominational agencies and ratification of its constitution by twenty-nine denominations. It began its official life on January 1, 1951.*

All of the denominations which had been members of the Federal Council transferred their allegiance to the new body. In addition, three Lutheran bodies — United Lutheran, Augustana Lutheran, and Danish Evangelical Lutheran — became members. This resulted in a pronounced increment

---

*The twelve agencies were the Federal Council of the Churches of Christ in America, the International Council of Religious Education, the Home Missions Council of North America, the Foreign Missions Conference of North America, the Missionary Education Movement of the United States and Canada, the National Protestant Council on Higher Education, the United Stewardship Council, the United Council of Church Women, Church World Service, the Interseminary Movement, the Protestant Film Commission, and the Protestant Radio Commission.

of Lutheran participation in the conciliar movement, both nationally and locally.†

In the realm of structure, the significance of the National Council lay in the creation of a stronger instrument for cooperative planning and action. There was, however, a spiritual significance underlying the practicalities of the development. It revealed a willingness in the merging agencies to surrender separate organizational interests for the sake of a more adequate manifestation of the wholeness of the church. . . .

The number of denominations related to the National Council had a healthy growth. Ten new bodies joined it between 1951 and 1968. Seven of these came from non-Protestant traditions, such as Eastern Orthodox, Old Catholic, and Armenian. The total membership of the Council reached 42 million, approximately that of the Roman Catholic Church in the U.S.

In spite of its widening constituency, the National Council represents by no means all of American Protestantism. There are large sectors which still pursue separatist paths. Conspicuous in this group are one of the two largest denominations, the Southern Baptist Convention, and two large Lutheran Churches, the Missouri Synod and the American. The bodies that remain aloof tend to be of the most conservative outlook, although there are also nonmembers at the opposite end of the theological spectrum, like the Unitarian Universalist Association and the Church of Christ, Scientist. . . .

Probably most people think of the National Council as constantly involved in public affairs. This is, indeed, an important aspect of its life. Increasingly the churches are convinced that they cannot fulfill their mission in the world

---

†For a complete list of the denominations which became charter members of the National Council see Samuel McCrae Cavert, *The American Churches in the Ecumenical Movement: 1900-1968,* pp. 209-210. They had a combined membership of thirty-three million in 143,000 congregations.

without wrestling with such critical issues as justice between the races, world peace in an era of atomic power, and poverty in the midst of affluence. In these and other complex problems the National Council is a center through which the churches are working together, and, naturally enough, it is these activities which attract most attention. Unless, however, they are seen in the perspective of the total functioning of the Council, a distorted image results.

Most of the Council's program has to do with little publicized operations of the churches in their day-by-day ministries in evangelism, education, pastoral work, missions, and social service. Through conferences, consultations, seminars, and workshops it makes available to all the best thinking and experience of each. It publishes materials of which all denominations are in equal need. It carries on studies and research in areas of common concern, a noteworthy illustration of which was the pooling of specialized scholarship that produced the Revised Standard Version of the Bible. It supervises projects that require unified direction, such as overseas relief. It promotes pioneering in new fields, such as experiments in courses about religion in public schools. It is an instrument for maintaining continuous contacts in behalf of Protestant and Orthodox Churches with Roman Catholic and Jewish bodies. It is a channel through which the many denominations, as a group, keep in active touch with secular organizations — cultural, professional, civic — concerned with human welfare. It is, when occasion arises, a spokesman for the churches in relation to government, as in the legal defense of released time for the religious education of children. . . .

In addition to the established cooperative processes among the churches of the National council and their developing rapprochement with the Catholic Church, the sixties witnessed an ambitious effort for complete union on the part of nine major denominations. On the initiative of the United Presbyterian Church in the U.S.A. in 1961, a Consultation on Church Union got under way looking toward a united church that would be "truly catholic, truly reformed and truly evangelical."* The Consultation has held an annual study session of the delegated members for the unhurried exploration of problems and possibilities. In 1966 "Principles of Church Union" were formulated. In 1969 "Guidelines" were issued which point the way to continuity with historic tradition, while strongly emphasizing openness to new problems presented by the world of today. A complete draft of a plan of union was submitted in 1970.

The movement of the American churches toward greater unity started, early in the twentieth century, within Protestantism. After a generation it expanded to include the Eastern Orthodox. In a less organized but vital way it now embraces the Roman Catholic Church also. There are, of course, still churches that are little affected by the movement. Within churches committed to it there is still much uncritical acceptance of preecumenical habits and outmoded patterns. But, after making all the necessary qualifications, a discriminating appraisal must conclude that the denominations are today thinking and acting less as separate and independent groups, more as integral parts of one Christian community.

---

*The participating bodies are the United Presbyterian in the U.S.A., the Episcopal, the United Methodist, the United Church of Christ, the African Methodist Episcopal, the African Methodist Episcopal Zion, the Christian Methodist, and the Presbyterian in the U.S. The Evangelical United Brethren were members until 1968, when they merged with the Methodists, thus reducing the number of denominations in the Consultation from ten to nine.

PART III — THE SPECTRUM OF BELIEF

The Doctrinal Issues:
1900-1970

Deane William Ferm

Protestantism has always been plagued by the variety of its forms. Sometimes — as in the high church Episcopal or Anglican tradition, or within the national Lutheran churches of Germany and the Scandinavian countries — it is difficult to tell what is Catholic and what is Protestant. Other forms of Protestantism, such as the Quakers and the Salvation Army, seem unique, unrelated to anything else. The same is true of doctrinal traditions, creeds, and belief systems. They range from the noncreedal churches, such as Baptists and Methodists, to those families of churches still defining orthodoxy (right opinion) in terms of authoritative "confessions of faith," such as Presbyterians and Lutherans.

In the twentieth century, many of the earlier historic forms of Protestantism changed or were altered by circumstances. But the variety of beliefs continued, and sometimes the panorama of Protestantism presented a picture of doctrinal confusion and internal competition. Some would say that such a description exaggerates the plight of Protestantism. After all, variety can be — in religion as in other things — a sure sign of vitality.

For an overview of the theological landscape during the first three-quarters of our century, Deane Ferm's article provides helpful clues and pointers. Certain doctrinal issues, the Bible and the interpretation of Jesus, for example, have usually dominated the debate among Protestants.

Chaplain and professor of religion at Mount Holyoke College in Massachusetts, Deane William Ferm is a graduate of the College of Wooster and of the Yale Divinity School. He has studied in Sweden, where he became interested in the relation of the churches and modern attitudes toward sexual morality, and as a result wrote a book, *Responsible Sexuality Now* (1971). This article, under the title "American Protestant Theology, 1900-1970," appeared in *Religion in Life* (Spring 1975), pp. 59-72.

Protestantism in the twentieth century has faced major up-heavals in the intellectual, economic, and social spheres as momentous as those of the early sixteenth century. In both periods Christianity could not afford to remain indifferent to these dramatic changes if it were to continue as a vital force in the life of mankind. In order to understand why recent Protestant theology is in some respects so unlike its earlier forms we must be cognizant of the shape of modern thought. We shall concentrate our discussion on the *major* trends on the American scene. . . .

Liberalism

A major Protestant response to the scientific revolution was one of accommodation. Liberalism is that Protestant school of thought which believed that a reinterpretation of the Christian message in accordance with the modern scientific world view was necessary. Liberalism firmly believed that it was faithful to its Christian heritage and indeed enhancing the role of Christ by making his teachings significant to modern man. The basic features of religious liberalism can be summarized in four convictions.

1. *The Scientific Spirit.* Liberalism accepted the methods of inquiry which had proved so successful for human progress. Religious faith must make sense to the mind and personal life of man. Faith in God and Christ could not be separated into a special category of revelation that was not susceptible to the usual tests of inductive inquiry and personal verification. Liberalism affirmed that questions which affected man's destiny needed to have modern answers and that the method that had succeeded in the sciences could work as well in the area of religion.

The scientific method when applied to the study of the Bible meant using the same tests of truth and verification as would be necessary for any other book. Biblical criticism was not new to the twentieth century, especially "lower criticism," which is a study of the texts of the writings to reconstruct as accurately as possible the form and content of the original autographs. This had been done, albeit in a minor way, even before the Reformation. The new feature which gained prominence in the twentieth century was "higher criticism," which asked the deeper questions about the character and purpose of these writings. Queries were raised about the authorship of the books of the Bible, the authenticity of these documents, the theological bias of the writers, and the meaning of the various passages. This kind of persistent inquiry called into question a whole host of assumptions about the Bible that had heretofore been accepted uncritically. Higher criticism thus questioned the authenticity of biblical writings and by implication the role of biblical auhority.

2. *The Authority and Universality of Religious Experience.* For religious liberalism, the primary authority for faith was not the Bible but human experience which

included the total spectrum of man's involvement in and response to the world. It encompassed both the personal and social dimensions. Liberalism also insisted on the importance of reason in understanding experience. Reason was the tool that articulated and organized knowledge in a coherent and comprehensive way. The Bible attained its authority not from special divine sanction, but because it was a record of man's witness to the living God and Christ. The Bible was a human document which contained many different ideas, practices, and customs of men who claimed to know God. This knowledge was potentially available to all men. Christ was the supreme revelation of God, the liberals claimed, because man could best find God through him, not because the Bible said he was. To assert that religious experience was universal was not to claim that all religions were equal, but to affirm that every man ultimately had to determine his own faith according to what he himself had discovered rather than what others, including the church and Bible, had testified as authoritative.

3. *The Importance of Continuity.* For religious liberals the gulf between God and man, revelation and reason, the Bible and other books was no longer acceptable because this dualism often served to protect and defend dogma from the usual tests of rational inquiry and personal confirmation. Liberalism insisted that truth was one. The problem of God was also by analogy the problem of man. Truth could not be compartmentalized. The ways man learned about himself were also the ways he learned about God.

Religious liberalism's advocacy of continuity can be noted in its attitude toward the doctrine of evolution. When Charles Darwin published his *Origin of Species* in 1859 and *The Descent of Man* in 1871, the response from orthodox Christians was quick and denunciatory. What Darwin had suggested, among other things, was that man had evolved from the lower animals through a process of natural selection and the survival of the fittest. Although this teaching was not new, Darwin was able to amass a great amount of evidence in its favor. His claim was a threat to orthodox Christianity because evolution seemed to deny the unique status of man as a special creature of God. For religious liberalism, however, Darwin's teaching served to underscore the continuity of man with God's creation and in no way detracted from God's role as creator. *That* God created the world and everything therein was more important than *how* he created it.

4. *Confidence in Man.* Religious liberalism placed great confidence in man and his potential to overcome his inadequacies and the shortcomings of the social order. He could learn in part about God as he could learn about himself. He could know the truth to a degree. He could change the world for the better. Man was not infallible nor without sin; he would always be limited in his knowledge and would often use his information for selfish purposes. But man did not solve his problems by simply confessing his ignorance or by making a fetish out of his selfishness. Rather, he acknowledged his finitude honestly and humbly and then proceeded with the task of inquiry and social reform. Liberalism stressed man's potential for good rather than his tendency toward evil. It understood the essence of Christianity to be the love of God and man.

The possibility that lay within all men to imitate this divine love was evident in liberalism's emphasis on the social gospel. Liberalism claimed that the source of much of man's difficulties lay in an imperfect social and physical environment. If this environment could be improved, the lot of man would improve, and the social order would then move closer to reflecting God's will. Man as a child of God had the power to eliminate many of the injustices and inequalities which existed in society. The strength of the social gospel movement in the early part of the century was a tribute to the confidence that liberalism had in man himself.

Conservatism

A second major Protestant school of thought made an opposite response to the new thinking. It proclaimed a set of propositions about the gospel of Jesus Christ which in both form and content remained one and the same despite the changing attitudes and world views of mankind. This trend included many shades of interpretation, but for the sake of contrast we shall call it conservatism. Many interpreters have labeled this point of view fundamentalism, but this latter term has been caricatured so badly by liberals as to make it virtually worthless. The term fundamentalism should be reserved for those believers who insisted on a literal interpretation of the words of the Bible. The leading conservative theologians were not literalists. Conservatism can be identified as that movement in Protestantism which upheld the inspired content of the entire Bible. Although conservatism had, like liberalism, always beeen present in the history of Protestantism, it emerged as a self-conscious movement in the decade after 1910.

Reformation Protestantism had insisted that the Bible was the prime authority for Christian belief and practice, but just what this implied had never been precisely defined. For example, Luther had made distinctions among parts of the Bible in terms of their relative value without in any way denying the primary authority of Scripture. Conservatism was reluctant to make such distinctions, preferring to state that God was the author of the entire Bible. Whereas Luther stressed the spirit of the words of the Bible — the Bible is the "cradle of Christ" — as his basis for biblical authority, conservatism put more emphasis on the doctrinal content of biblical authority. Conservatism recognized that twentieth-century man did not have access to the original manuscripts as they were written down by the authors. Errors of translation had crept into the biblical text. But this criticism should not detract from the divine authorship and the objectivity of revelation. There was no place for higher criticism which might call into question some of the basic divinely revealed propositions. To criticize Scripture in such a fashion was to apply human standards to divine authorship, said the conservatives.

What were some of these propositions which conservatives thought essential to the biblical proclamation and which the liberals had relegated to secondary importance? The major doctrines of early Protestantism — the sovereignty of God, the uniqueness of Jesus Christ, the priesthood of all believers — were reaffirmed by the conservatives. But they also insisted on retaining certain propositions about Christ himself, testifying to the indispensable claims of the virgin birth and the deity of Christ. Liberalism, although focusing on Christ, made his teachings central and considered him to be different only in degree from other prophets and men. To the conservatives this denied the uniqueness of the Christian faith. God was in Christ in a way in which he had never been revealed in any other man. Jesus was "very God of very God," the second person of the Trinity. This was the whole point of the incarnation; i.e., God in the flesh. There was a hiatus between man and Christ. For the conservatives the proposition of the deity of Christ was indispensable.

One way of assuring this uniqueness was to assert the virgin birth of Christ as recorded in the Gospels of Matthew and Luke. Christ was born of the Virgin Mary with the Holy Spirit as his father, and to deny this historical fact was to deny the authority of the Bible. The liberals had minimized the importance of the virgin birth; Schleiermacher said that it was superfluous. But for the conservatives this doctrine was crucial, for it preserved the gulf betwen God and man. To deny the virgin birth, i.e., to make Christ corrupt, would be as unthinkable as it would be to accept the doctrine of evolution and thereby reject the sharp difference between man and the rest of God's creation.

The conservatives were equally concerned to affirm the bodily resurrection of Jesus Christ. The implication of liberalism was to deny the importance of the resurrection by shifting the emphasis to the teaching of Jesus. The world view encouraged by modern thinking, the liberals argued, cast doubt on the credibility of bodily resurrection. The conservatives held that according to the biblical witnesses the resurrection was a physical manifestation of the continued presence of Christ on this earth after his crucifixion and descent into hell. Jesus actually appeared to his disciples and to others and was recognized by them. This is historical fact, if we accept the credibility of the biblical testimony.

Another biblical proposition to be endorsed was the substitutionary atonement of Jesus for the sins of the world, the belief that Christ died for the sins of mankind. He substituted his life for the human race and made it possible through his sacrifice on the cross for man to receive forgiveness and to become at one with God, which was man's original status before his fall in the Garden of Eden. Christ was not only a moral example for man to imitate; he was God himself making the supreme sacrifice in order that mankind might be redeemed. Most conservatives also believed in a second coming of Jesus Christ in bodily form to judge man. Christ who had died and was raised from the dead would come again, as the Bible prophesied. . . .

Neo-Orthodoxy

The chief Protestant theology from the late 1930s to the late 1950s has been labeled in various ways: neo-Protestantism, the New Reformation, dialectical theology. The most common designation has been neo-orthodoxy. Its chief concern has been the deliberate attempt to return to the teachings of the early reformers, particularly Luther and Calvin. The theologians representing this position were convinced that liberal Protestantism had perverted its heritage and changed the Christian faith into a religion different from that which was intended by the early reformers. Theirs was a protest against liberalism, but not an affirmation of conservatism, although they held to some beliefs to which conservatism also subscribed. Further, this new movement was essentially a European phenomenon; virtually all of its original leaders were German, Swiss, or English. Its influence on American theology was felt mainly in the theological seminaries and among the intelligentsia but less in the local congregations. It did not gain dominance in the United States until the effects of the depression of the early 1930s began to take their toll on the spirit of man and the social order in which he lived. . . .

1. *The Authority and Unity of the Bible.* In the Bible was to be found a drama of salvation in which God appeared not only as the stage manager of the drama, but also as the chief actor. The Bible was the story of human redemption in which God sought to bring man into a right relationship with him. Biblical history was "his story;" i.e., God's. This bestowal of a supernatural authority on the Bible was the starting point in comprehending the Christian faith. This unique biblical authority was an act of God in his making himself known to man. The Bible was not the attempt on the part of man to know God.

Barth and his followers were not narrow conservatives in their interpretation of the Bible. They did not consider many parts of the Bible to be scientifically accurate or even historically true and believed that the Bible was written by men and not dictated by God. They accepted the results of recent higher criticism, for example, that Moses was not the author of the first five books of the Bible; there were two stories of creation; the Gospel of Mark was written before the other three Gospels; and the apostle Paul probably wrote only a few of the letters attributed to him in the New Testament. Nevertheless, these thinkers declared that there was a supernatural unifying character to the Bible which gave it special status. God "authored" the Bible even though we cannot say precisely how this was done. . . .

2. *The Uniqueness of the Christian Revelation.* If the Bible was authoritative and if the climax to the unified biblical drama occurred in the historical event of Jesus the Christ, then the Christian revelation was unique. This was an act of God, not of man. There never had been a divine revelation to compare with it, and there never would be another like it. The work of salvation had been accomplished. The role of the Protestant Christian was to accept gratefully what God had done and to witness to that revelatory event.

One could admit that other religions had deep insights and significant moral truths, but these other religions did not have the divine Christ-event. Therefore, none of them could be considered sufficient in the way that Christianity was true and complete. Along with this emphasis on the uniqueness of the Christian revelation came a corresponding deemphasis on general revelation, the belief that God had made a significant revelation of himself in other traditions and cultures. The Christ-event had to be the starting point, and to begin anywhere else was simply false. . . .

3. *The Deity of Christ.* The Protestant World Council of Churches originally had as its statement of belief to which member denominations subscribed the confession that they accepted "Jesus Christ as God and Savior." This creed was later expanded to state: "The World Council of Churches is a fellowship of churches which confess the Lord Jesus Christ as God and Savior according to the Scriptures and therefore seek to fulfil together their common calling to the glory of the one God, Father, Son, and Holy Spirit." This affirmation neatly tied together the first three doctrines. If the Bible was our special authority and if the biblical drama reached its climax in God's becoming flesh, i.e., the incarnation of Jesus Christ, then the Christ was in fact "very God of very God," as the ancient creed proclaimed. He was not just a good man or great prophet or special messenger. He was *the event* of

history. The Christian faith proclaimed that God himself died on the cross for the sins of man. . . .

4. *The Sinfulness of Man.* Neo-orthodoxy stressed the sinfulness of man. These theologians argued in this fashion: man's destiny was to live in a right relationship with God and with his fellow men. But man fell far short of his goal. He considered himself as creator rather than accepted his place as creature. Thus, man was a sinner in that he refused to recognize his subordinate role. He was no longer the person that God intended him to be. He had become a prisoner unto himself and his use of reason only served to sink him deeper into the abyss of self-centeredness. There was nothing that man himself could do about his sinful condition. Only God could right this terrible wrong, and God had, in fact, done this through Jesus Christ. God offered man a second chance to be what God wanted him to be. Man's only hope for salvation lay in acknowledging by a sheer act of faith that he was a sinful creature, standing in the need of God's mercy. If he did so, he was "justified by faith," and given a new life in Jesus Christ.

The neo-orthodox emphasis on the sinfulness of man found its most eloquent American interpreter in Reinhold Niebuhr. Niebuhr's most astute contributions were directed to "the nature and destiny of man," the title of his most famous book. He continuously attacked the complacent conscience of modern man that failed to take account of the demonic tendencies of human nature. The sin of pride had so perverted man that it pervaded all his interpersonal relationships. Man's ethical choices had an absolute imperative — the love of God — but his decisions themselves were relative to the human situation and thereby subject to distortion and corruption. Man as a Christian had to act in society even though he knew that his every action would be tainted by sin. Niebuhr often used paradox — "sin is inevitable but not necessary" — to clarify man's ambiguous role. . . .

The 1960s

By the early 1960s neo-orthodoxy had greatly diminished in importance, and although the causes for this collapse are many, perhaps the major reason was its support of a dualistic supernatural theology — a chasm between God and man, faith and reason. It was this "leap of faith" which could not be maintained in the modern scientific world. It assumed the existence of a supernatural order which forever remained beyond the reach of man's reason. It affirmed that a revelation claim must be accepted as "special" and beyond the pale of rational and empirical analysis. Such an assumption no longer made sense in a postsupernatural age. It served to shield the faith from too many soul-searching questions for which this world needed answers. How can the Bible still be our prime authority when there is such wide disagreement as to what constitutes that authority? Can we continue to assert dogmatically the uniqueness and superiority of the Christian revelation in this time of interreligious cooperation? Does not faith divorced from reason lead to superstition? If man stressed too much the transcendence of God, could this not become just a way of justifying a particular revelation claim? These and similar questions had to be answered fairly and squarely, and this was something that neo-orthodoxy had failed to do.

Two religious thinkers were particularly prominent during this period of transition. One of them was Paul Tillich (1886-1965). For Tillich, modern man had to live in creative tension between faith and doubt, theology and philosophy, revelation and reason, the sacred and the secular, the church and the world. Tillich sought to make contact with the unbeliever, to show how the Christian gospel spoke to his condition. He conceived of God as the "being beyond being" who could not be defined or categorized, and the Christian proclamation as the manifestation of the New Being, to which Jesus as the Christ bore witness. Faith was man's "courage to be," to affirm being and meaning despite the threat of nonbeing and insignificance.

Tillich insisted on judging all human assumptions as limited and subject to sin, for only God was beyond corruption. He called this judgment the "Protestant principle." In essence this principle was another way of expressing the conviction of the early reformers of the sovereignty of God. Only God was supreme; all other institutions, dogmas, and individuals were subject to him and him alone. It was this same principle which led Reinhold Niebuhr to point out the relativity of all ethical decisions. . . .

Tillich used the language of both theologian and philosopher to develop his ideas about the nature of God, man, and the world. His unusual breadth of knowledge and his willingness to be receptive to insights from the social and natural sciences made him a respected figure in all segments of the intellectual community. Only the dogmatists of whatever stripe — including some of his own interpreters — failed to appreciate his contributions.

Another theologian whose writings influenced the Protestant theological development of the 1960s was Dietrich Bonhoeffer (1906-1945), a brilliant German theologian who was executed by the Nazis shortly before he would have been freed from prison by the American army. His religious views were never completed in any systematic form, but he wrote sufficiently to stimulate a new cadre of religious thinkers. His ideas were often cryptically presented, as in the following sentences from his *Letters and Papers from Prison:*

> We are proceeding towards a time of no religion at all; men as they are now simply cannot be religious any more.

> If religion is no more than the garment of Christianity . . . then what is religionless Christianity?

> To be a Christian does not mean to be religious in a particular way . . . but to be a man.

> God is teaching us that we must live as men who can get along very well without him.

Bonhoeffer's writings have been widely quoted in recent years to support almost every conceivable theological position. Briefly, he taught that God was calling Christian man to a way of living which would not be dependent on the religious and theological trappings of the past. He reaffirmed Luther's assertion that man is justified not through "religious good works of theology," but through complete trust in God and faithful involvement in the life of the world. Many theologians were more impressed with Bonhoeffer's "man cannot be religious any more" and "we must learn to live without God" than with his unyielding commitment to the God who transcends all human forms and institutions.

The New Secularism

The new secularism succeeded neo-orthodoxy as the leading Protestant theology. Secularism was the conviction that the only real world for man was that of the temporal and transient, a world which could be known through the methods of the natural sciences. Anything beyond this world was either illusory or unknowable; therefore the role of theology had to be limited strictly to the concerns of the secular order. Although this theology exhibited the usual variety apparent in all ideologies, two convictions stood out.

First, the new secularists attacked the doctrine of God and anything which suggested a dimension beyond the human. They were convinced that acceptance of the assumptions of the postsupernatural world meant that God was dead. Their claim was not that God could no longer be experienced but that God was not around to be experienced.

There are some important differences to be noted between the old liberalism and the new secularism. The former accepted the basic affirmations of the Christian gospel and tried to make these teachings palatable to twentieth-century man. The latter no longer could accept these Christian truths, for such ideas seemed alien to contemporary man. The earlier theology never questioned the existence of God, but only whether his presence could be better interpreted to the secular world. This later school was a movement within the church itself which denied God's existence. Radical doubt had now become internalized within the church. Whereas the earlier movement clung to the belief that man was ultimately dependent on God as creator, this new school contended that man himself must take full responsibility and have dominion over creation.

Along with the announcement of the death of God went a curious and uncritical affirmation of the importance of the man Jesus. Jesus as "the man for others" was held up as the best model for humanity. He was the one to whom the Christian turned as the ideal of the good life. Jesus served his neighbor and loved the world, and so should man. In this way the "death of God" theologians dubbed themselves "Christian atheists," rejecting God and accepting Jesus. Their opponents exclaimed that this was like saying, "There is no God, and Jesus is his prophet."

Second, this denial of God was combined with a positive affirmation of man and the secular. Man's first concern was the world in which he lived and died. In this temporal realm man had to find and affirm his faith and hopes. He had to become worldly by involving himself fully in this earthly existence and not fall back on some transcendent power to whom he could turn for help. The "death of God" theologians argued that the scientific and historical categories of reality were the only useful ones. All phases of man's thinking and experience had to be secularized including his religious and theological views. Yet this also meant confidence in solving the problems of the world if man followed Jesus. This faith was "the secular meaning of the gospel." . . .

By the end of the 1960s the "death of God" theology had virtually vanished, its fleeting popularity due in large part to exaggerations of the public press. . . . The weakness of a "death of God" theology had become apparent, for it amounted to an almost complete capitulation to narrow and arbitrary concerns of the modern world. It tended to accept uncritically the notion that secularization was a good thing, a weakness not unlike the liberalism of an earlier period which sought above all an accommodation with the modern scientific world view. . . .

Although it may be hard to conceive of the reality of God in our day, it is even more difficult to comprehend a world without God. This temporal realm must be affirmed, but have we become prisoners to secularism? What is so final about the here and now? Is there a deeper order of reality of which man is a part and which can be experienced by man? And why this rather uncritical emphasis on Jesus as the pattern for living? Do we really know the historical Jesus, and even if we do, why not someone else? If we still insist on keeping Jesus as our model, doesn't that design include faith in God? What happens to prayer and worship which were such vital dimensions to Jesus' religion? Do they become but games that people play or should we not accept them as legitimate aspects of the Jesus model? When we seek to be "relevant," we must ask: relevant to what, to whom, and for what purpose?

The Liberal Challenge

Harry Emerson Fosdick

By far the most disruptive dispute in modern Protestantism was the liberal-fundamentalist controversy in the 1920s and 30s. Scarcely any denomination was spared the acrimony and name-calling, though the Presbyterians and the Baptists more than others were often in the front of the battle, fighting among themselves and with each other. It was not a new doctrinal issue, and, in some ways, it is still with us today. Some interpret the controversy in strictly historical and perhaps geographical terms (the rural South versus the effete North), but the matters of belief at issue were always central and elemental.

The liberals wanted to proclaim the Christian faith in modern terms that would do justice to biblical truth and the historic tradition of the Reformation in the sixteenth century. This meant, among other things, accepting the scientific account of creation, interpreting the Bible according to the best critical methods of literary scholarship, and applying the Christian gospel to all the areas of life — social, economic, and political. So liberals were often called modernists, though by the other side they were dubbed "heretics."

The fundamentalists were deathly afraid that all such accommodations would imperil the faith itself. If science is permitted to supplant the Bible, and if questions in the name of relevancy are to be raised about long-established doctrines, how can we be sure that anything important will be left? If the Scriptures are not the Word of God, "from cover to cover," then what is? Tolerance and ecumenicity are fine, but not at the expense of the gospel.

By the middle of the twentieth century, the groundrules for the debate had shifted somewhat. Liberals experienced traumatic disillusionment as a result of World War II. Instead of rejoicing in the onward and upward climb of modern progress, everything seemed to fall apart.

Fundamentalists now had to fight against a new form of Reformation doctrine, neo-orthodoxy, personified in Karl Barth, who made the Bible even more normative than the old-time literalists. About this time, Reinhold Niebuhr demonstrated how labels can be libels — both sides saw a point the other missed, and each retained a crucial clue to authentic faith.

A dramatic moment in this narrative was the accusation against a young New York preacher that he was subverting the faith. Harry Emerson Fosdick answered back from his pulpit in the First Presbyterian Church of New York. An ardent advocate of liberal ideas, Fosdick was forced out of his Presbyterian church only to reassert himself as the national preacher of the newly established Riverside Church. For more than thirty years, his voice and his influence were virtually uncontested. His published sermons and his books, such as *The Modern Use of the Bible* (1924) and *On Being A Real Person* (1943), spread his fame throughout the land, as did his twenty-year ministry by radio through "National Vespers."

The excerpt printed here is from Fosdick's challenging sermon, "Shall the Fundamentalists Win?" (First Presbyterian Church, New York, May 21, 1922). It was this sermon that precipitated the whole ugly confrontation.

This morning we are to think of the Fundamentialist controversy which threatens to divide the American churches, as though already they were not sufficiently split and riven. A scene, suggestive for our thought, is depicted in the fifth chapter of the Book of the Acts, where the Jewish leaders hail before them Peter and other of the apostles because they have been preaching Jesus as the Messiah. Moreover, the Jewish leaders propose to slay them, when in opposition Gamaliel speaks: "Refrain from these men, and let them alone: for if this counsel or this work be of men, it will be overthrown: but if it is of God ye will not be able to overthrow them; lest haply ye be found even to be fighting against God."

One could easily let his imagination play over this scene and could wonder how history would have come out if Gamaliel's wise tolerance could have controlled the situation. For though the Jewish leaders seemed superficially to concur in Gamaliel's judgment, they nevertheless kept up their bitter antagonism and shut the Christians from the Synagogue. We know now that they were mistaken. Christianity, starting within Judaism, was not an innovation to be dreaded; it was the finest flowering out that Judaism ever had. When the Master looked back across his racial heritage and said, "I came not to destroy, but to fulfill," he perfectly described the situation. The Christian ideas of God, the Christian principles of life, the Christian hopes for the future, were all rooted in the Old Testament and grew up out of it, and the Master himself, who called the Jewish temple his Father's house, rejoiced in the glorious heritage of his people's prophets. Only, he did believe in a living God. He did not think that God was dead, having finished his words and works with Malachi. He had not simply a historic, but a contemporary God, speaking now, working now, leading his people now from partial into fuller truth. Jesus believed in the progressiveness of revelation and these Jewish leaders did not understand that. Was this new Gospel a real development which they might welcome or was it an enemy to be cast out? And they called it an enemy and excluded it. One does wonder what might have happened had Gamaliel's wise tolerance been in control.

We, however, face today a situation too similar and too urgent and too much in need of Gamaliel's attitude to spend any time making guesses at suppositious history. Already all of us must have heard about the people who call themselves the fundamentalists. Their apparent intention is to drive out of the evangelical churches men and women of liberal opinions. I speak of them the more freely because there are no two denominations more affected by them than the Baptist and the Presbyterian.

We should not identify the fundamentalists with the conservatives. All fundamentalists are conservatives, but not all conservatives are fundamentalists. The best conservatives can often give lessons to the liberals in true liberality of spirit, but the fundamentalist program is essentially illiberal and intolerant. The fundamentalists see, and they see truly, that in this last generation there have been strange new movements in Christian thought. A great mass of new knowledge has come into man's possession: new knowledge about the physical universe, its origin, its forces, it laws; new knowledge about human history and in particular about the ways in which the ancient peoples used to think in matters of religion and the methods by which they phrased and explained their spiritual experiences; and new knowledge, also, about other religions and the strangely similar ways in which men's faiths and religious practices have developed everywhere.

Now, there are multitudes of reverent Christians who have been unable to keep this new knowledge in one compartment of their minds and the Christian faith in another. They have been sure that all truth comes from the one God and is his revelation. Not, therefore, from irreverence or caprice or destructive zeal, but for the sake of intellectual and spiritual integrity, that they might really love the Lord their God not only with all their heart and soul and strength, but with all their mind, they have been trying to see this new knowledge in terms of the Christian faith and to see the Christian faith in terms of this new knowledge. Doubtless they have made many mistakes. Doubtless there have been among them reckless radicals gifted with intellectual ingenuity but lacking spiritual depth. Yet the enterprise itself seems to them indispensable to the Christian church. The new knowledge and the old faith cannot be left antagonistic or even disparate, as though a man on Saturday could use one set of regulative ideas for his life and on Sunday could change gear to another altogether. We must be able to think our modern life clear through in Christian terms and to do that we also must be able to think our Christian life clear through in modern terms.

There is nothing new about the situation. It has happened again and again in history, as, for example, when the stationary earth suddenly began to move and the universe that had been centered in this planet was centered in the sun around which the planets whirled. Whenever such a situation has arisen, there has been only one way out: the new knowledge and the old faith had to be blended in a new combination. Now, the people in this generation who are trying to do this are the liberals, and the fundamentalists are out on a campaign to shut against them the doors of the Christian fellowship. Shall they be allowed to succeed?

It is interesting to note where the fundamentalists are driving in their stakes to mark out the deadline of doctrine around the church, across which no one is to pass except on terms of agreement. They insist that we must all believe in the historicity of certain special miracles, preeminently the virgin birth of our Lord; that we must believe in a special theory of inspiration — that the original documents of the Scripture, which of course we no longer possess, were inerrantly dictated to men a good deal as a man might dictate to a stenographer; that we must believe in a special theory of the atonement — that the blood of our Lord, shed in a substitutionary death, placates an alienated Deity and makes possible welcome for the returning sinner; and that we must believe in the second coming of our Lord upon the clouds of heaven to set up a millennium here, as the only way in which God can bring history to a worthy dénouement. Such are some of the stakes which are being driven, to mark a deadline of doctrine around the church.

If a man is a genuine liberal, his primary protest is not against holding these opinions, although he may well protest against their being considered the fundamentals of Christianity. This is a free country and anybody has a right to hold these opinions or any others, if he is sincerely convinced of them. The question is: has anybody a right to deny the Christian name to those who differ with him on such points and to shut against them the doors of the Christian fellowship? The fundamentalists say that this must be done. In this country and on the foreign field they are trying to do it. They have actually endeavored to put on the statute books of a whole state binding laws against teaching modern biology. If they had their way, within the church, they would set up in Protestantism a doctrinal tribunal more rigid than the pope's. In such an hour, delicate and dangerous, when feelings are bound to run high, I plead this morning the cause of magnanimity and liberality and tolerance of spirit. I would, if I could reach their ears, say to the fundamentalists about the liberals what Gamaliel said to the Jews, "Refrain from these men, and let them alone: for if this counsel or this work be of men, it will be overthrown: but if it is of God ye will not be able to overthrow them; lest haply ye be found even to be fighting against God.

That we may be entirely candid and concrete and may not lose ourselves in any fog of generalities, let us this morning take two or three of these fundamentalist items and see with reference to them what the situation is in the Christian churches. Too often we preachers have failed to talk frankly enough about the differences of opinion which exist among evangelical Christians, although everybody knows that they are there. Let us face this morning some of the differences of opinion with which somehow we must deal.

We may well begin with the vexed and mooted question of the virgin birth of our Lord. I know people in the Christian churches, ministers, missionaries, laymen, devoted lovers of the Lord and servants of the Gospel, who, alike as they are in their personal devotion to the Master, hold quite different points of view about a matter like the virgin birth. Here, for example, is one point of view: that the virgin birth is to be accepted as historical fact; it actually happened; there was no other way for a personality like the Master to come into this world except by a special biological miracle. That is one point of view, and many are the gracious and beautiful souls who hold it. But, side by side with them in the evangelical churches is a group of equally loyal and reverent people who would say that the virgin birth is not to be accepted as an historic fact.

To believe in virgin birth as an explanation of great personality is one of the familiar ways in which the ancient world was accustomed to account for unusual superiority. Many people suppose that only once in history do we run across a record of supernatural birth. Upon the contrary, stories of miraculous generation are among the commonest traditions of antiquity. Especially is this true about the founders of great religions. According to the records of their faiths, Buddha and Zoroaster and Lao-Tsze and Mahavira were all supernaturally born. Moses, Confucius and Mohammed are the only great founders of religions in history to whom miraculous birth is not attributed. That is to say, when a personality arose so high that men adored him, the ancient world attributed his superiority to some special divine influence in his generation, and they commonly phrased their faith in terms of miraculous birth. So Pythagoras was called virgin born, and Plato, and Augustus Caesar, and many more.

Knowing this, there are within the evangelical churches large groups of people whose opinion about our Lord's coming would run as follows: those first disciples adored Jesus — as we do; when they thought about his coming they were sure that he came specially from God — as we are; this adoration and conviction they associated with God's special influence and intention in his birth — as we do; but they phrased it in terms of a biological miracle that our modern minds cannot use. So far from thinking that they have given up anything vital in the New Testament's attitude toward Jesus, these Christians remember that the two men who contributed most to the church's thought of the divine meaning of the Christ were Paul and John, who never even distantly allude to the virgin birth. . . .

Consider another matter on which there is a sincere difference of opinion between evangelical Christians: the inspiration of the Bible. One point of view is that the original documents of the Scripture were inerrantly dictated by God to men. Whether we deal with the story of creation or the list of the dukes of Edom or the narratives of Solomon's reign or the Sermon on the Mount or the thirteenth chapter of First Corinthians, they all came in the same way and they all came as no other book ever came. They were inerrantly dictated; everything there — scientific opinions, medical theories, historical judgments, as well as spiritual insight — is infallible. That is one idea of the Bible's inspiration. But side by side with those who hold it, lovers of the Book as much as they, are multitudes of people who never think about the Bible so. Indeed, that static and mechanical theory of inspiration seems to them a positive peril to the spiritual life.

The Koran similarly has been regarded by Mohammedans as having been infallibly written in heaven before it came to earth. But the Koran enshrined the theological and ethical ideas of Arabia at the time when it was written. God an Oriental monarch, fatalistic submission to his will as man's chief duty, the use of force on unbelievers, polygamy, slavery — they are all in the Koran. The Koran was ahead of the day when it was written, but, petrified by an artificial idea of inspiration, it has become a millstone about the neck of Mohammedanism.

When one turns from the Koran to the Bible, he finds this interesting situation. All of these ideas, which we dislike in the Koran, are somewhere in the Bible. Conceptions from which we now send missionaries to convert Mohammedans are to be found in the Book. There one can find God thought of as an Oriental monarch; there, too, are patriarchal polygamy, and slave systems, and the use of force on unbelievers. Only in the Bible these elements are not final; they are always being superseded; revelation is progressive. The thought of God moves out from Oriental kingship to compassionate fatherhood; treatment of unbelievers moves out from the use of force to the appeals of love; polygamy gives way to monogamy; slavery, never explicitly condemned before the New Testament closes, is nevertheless being undermined by ideas that in the end, like dynamite, will blast its foundations to pieces.

Repeatedly one runs on verses like this: "It was said to them of old time . . . but I say unto you;" "God, having of old time spoken unto the fathers in the prophets by divers portions and in divers manners, hath at the end of these days spoken unto us in his Son;" "The times of ignorance therefore God overlooked; but now he commandeth men that they should all everywhere repent;" and over the doorway of the New Testament into the Christian world stand the words of Jesus: "When he, the Spirit of truth is come, he shall guide you into all the truth." That is to say, finality in the Koran is behind; finality in the Bible is ahead. We have not reached it. We cannot yet compass all of it. God is leading us out toward it.

There are multitudes of Christians, then, who think, and rejoice as they think, of the Bible as the record of the progressive unfolding of the character of God to his people from early primitive days until the great unveiling in Christ; to them the Book is more inspired and more inspiring than ever it was before; and to go back to a mechanical and static theory of inspiration would mean to them the loss of some of the most vital elements in their spiritual experience and in their appreciation of the Book. . . .

I do not believe for one moment that the fundamentalists are going to succeed. Nobody's intolerance can contribute anything to the solution of the situation which we have described. If, then, the fundamentalists have no solution of the problem, where may we expect to find it? In two concluding comments let us consider our reply to that inquiry.

The first element that is necessary is a spirit of tolerance and Christian liberty. When will the world learn that intolerance solves no problems? This is not a lesson which the fundamentalists alone need to learn; the liberals also need to learn it. Speaking, as I do, from the viewpoint of liberal opinions, let me say that if some young, fresh mind here this morning is holding new ideas, has fought his way through, it may be by intellectual and spiritual struggle, to novel positions, and is tempted to be intolerant about old opinions, offensively to condescend to those who hold them and to be harsh in judgment on them, he may well remember that people who held those old opinions have given the world some of the noblest character and the most rememberable service that it ever has been blessed with, and that we of the younger generation will prove our case best, not by controversial intolerance, but by producing, with our new opinions, something of the depth and strength, nobility and beauty of character that in other times were associated with other thoughts. It was a wise liberal, the most adventurous man of his day — Paul the Apostle — who said, "Knowledge puffeth up, but love buildeth up." . . .

As I plead thus for an intellectually hospitable, tolerant, liberty-loving church, I am of course thinking primarily about this new generation. We have boys and girls growing up in our homes and schools, and because we love them we may well wonder about the church which will be waiting to receive them. Now, the worst kind of church that can possibly be offered to the allegiance of the new generation is an intolerant church. Ministers often bewail the fact that young people turn from religion to science for the regulative ideas of their lives. But this is easily explicable. Science treats a young man's mind as though it were really important. A scientist says to a young man: "Here is the universe challenging our investigation. Here are the truths which we have seen, so far. Come, study with us! See what we already have seen and then look further to see more, for science is an intellectual adventure for the truth." Can you imagine any man who is worthwhile turning from that call to the church, if the church seems to him to say, "Come, and we will feed you opinions from a spoon. No thinking is allowed here except such as brings you to certain specified, predetermined conclusions. These prescribed opinions we will give you in advance of your thinking; now think, but only so as to reach these results." My friends, nothing in all the world is so much worth thinking of as God,

Christ, the Bible, sin and salvation, the divine purposes for humankind, life everlasting. But you cannot challenge the dedicated thinking of this generation to these sublime themes upon any such terms as are laid down by an intolerant church.

The second element which is needed if we are to reach a happy solution of this problem is a clear insight into the main issues of modern Christianity and a sense of penitent shame that the Christian church should be quarreling over little matters when the world is dying of great needs. If, during the war, when the nations were wrestling upon the very brink of hell and at times all seemed lost, you chanced to hear two men in an altercation about some minor matter of sectarian denominationalism, could you restrain your indignation? You said, "What can you do with folks like this who, in the face of colossal issues, play with the tiddledywinks and peccadillos of religion?" So, now, when from the terrific questions of this generation one is called away by the noise of this fundamentalist controversy, he thinks it almost unforgivable that men should tithe mint and anise and cummin, and quarrel over them, when the world is perishing for the lack of the weightier matters of the law, justice, and mercy, and faith.

These last weeks, in the minister's confessional, I have heard stories from the depths of human lives where men and women were wrestling with the elemental problems of misery and sin — stories that put upon a man's heart a burden of vicarious sorrow, even though he does but listen to them. Here was real human need crying out after the living God revealed in Christ. Consider all the multitudes of men who so need God, and then think of Christian churches making of themselves a cockpit of controversy when there is not a single thing at stake in the controversy on which depends the salvation of human souls. That is the trouble with this whole business. So much of it does not matter! And there is one thing that does matter — more than anything else in all the world — that men in their personal lives and in their social relationships should know Jesus Christ.

Conversion — A Personal Revolution

Billy Graham

The enemies and oppressors of Fosdick's liberalism, instead of fading away, as he had hoped, have grown in numbers, influence, and vigor. But they no longer call themselves fundamentalists. By the 1950s, those who distinguished themselves from the liberals and who located their theology to the right of center adopted new names and labels, such as "Bible-believing Christians" and "evangelicals." The latter designation seems to have caught on, in spite of its ambiguity. (In Europe, "evangelical" means Protestant; in Barth's last book, *Evangelical Theology*, it simply refers to the "gospel").

Evangelicals are to be found in all denominations, in many different kinds of churches, and in every area of the country. They are loosely bound together through the National Association of Evangelicals (NAE), which stands over against the older and more ecumenical National and World Councils of Churches (NCC, WCC).

Evangelicals stand for the Bible as the authoritative, inspired, and infallible Word of God; they stress conversion and personal salvation; they accept Jesus Christ as Lord and Savior; they are committed to evangelism and the world-wide spread of the gospel.

By the 1970s, the evangelical movement had gathered strength and self-assurance. Social and political shifts in the country moved to the right. Permissiveness was rejected, the cry went up for law and order, and conservatism at all levels was in style.

Without question, the popular spokesman for the evangelical movement over the years has been Billy Graham. A southern Baptist minister with rural, conservative associations, Billy Graham projected his evangelistic crusades onto a world-wide screen of astonishing proportions, and over a period of more than 30 years.

Invoking the straightforward authority of the Scriptures ("the Bible says") and pleading for personal decision to accept Christ, Graham combined old-time evangelism with modern methods of mass communication.

Unlike many in his own conservative camp, Billy Graham has always been on good speaking terms with the whole ecumenical movement. In various study sessions sponsored by the World Council of Churches, the theme of conversion has been widely discussed. In 1966, the World Conference on Church and Society, held in Geneva, provoked the question of conversion in connection with the current controversy over "revolution." At the fourth assembly of the WCC in Uppsala, Sweden, in 1968, one of the major sections dealt with "renewal in mission."

Invited to contribute to a symposium on the relation of religious conversion to social and political revolution, Billy Graham prepared an essay which was published in *The Ecumenical Review* (July, 1967). A digest of that article is reprinted here.

The word on the lips of the peoples of the world today is "revolution." Every few days we read in our newspapers of another revolution somewhere in the world; an old regime has been overthrown and a new regime has taken over. Conversion is a revolution in the life of an individual. The old forces of sin, self-centredness, and evil are overthrown from their place of supreme power. Jesus Christ is put on the throne . . . .

When I began my ministry of evangelism over twenty-five

years ago I had not read a single book on the subject of conversion. However, I had experienced conversion myself when but a young rebellious student of sixteen. Now, over thirty years later, the brilliance and wonder of that encounter with Jesus Christ remains unabated by time or maturity . . . .

No one can read the New Testament without recognizing that its message calls for a verdict. It was Jesus who said: "Except a man be converted" (Matt. 18:3), and Paul who said: "Be reconciled to God" (2 Cor. 5:20) and insisted that God now "commands all men everywhere to repent" (Acts 17:30). Paul viewed his office as that of an ambassador for Christ "as though God were beseeching you" (2 Cor. 5:20). It was James who said: "Let him know that he which converteth the sinner from the error of his way shall save a soul from death and shall hide a multitude of sins" (James 5:20), and Peter who taught that we are "born again not of corruptible seed by of incorruptible, by the Word of God which liveth and abideth forever (1 Peter 1:23).

In reading the New Testament we are confronted with many incidents of men and women who encountered Christ either personally or through hearing the message preached. Something happened to them! What was it? What terminology would we use to describe it? None of their experiences were identical but most of them experienced a change of mind and attitude and many of them entered an entirely new dimension of living. There was Matthew, who apparently had no intellectual problems when he met Jesus (Matt. 9:9). Certainly this original encounter began a chain of events that transformed and changed Matthew's entire life. There was the woman at the well, with her sense of guilt, alienation and questions. What was the experience that transpired in this woman's life that turned her within a few hours into an enthusiastic follower of Christ? What was this rescuing, renewing, transforming and elevating experience that she had? What word could we use to describe the experience of Zaccheus who encountered Christ and within the space of a few hours was willing to say, "Behold, Lord, the half of my goods I give to the poor, and if I have wrongfully exacted anything of any man I restore fourfold" (Luke 19:8). How could you describe the experience of the Philippian jailor? Here we are dealing with a case in which alarm and terror seems to have been the determining factor. When he asked the question, "What must I do to be saved?" most of us would have answered, "You are in no emotional state to make a permanent decision." Many of us would have sent him to see a psychiatrist; but Paul did not do that. He said: "Believe on the Lord Jesus Christ and thou shalt be saved" (Acts 16:31). What a simple proclamation! Just believe! The Apostle Paul did not even wait to see if his decision was permanent or sincere. He baptized him that very night! What one word could we use to describe such a transforming experience? Or, there was the Ethiopian treasurer who was reading the 53rd chapter of Isaiah but could not understand what he was reading: "And Philip opened his mouth, and began at this same scripture, and preached unto him Jesus . . ." — he believed and was baptized — ". . . and he went on his way rejoicing" (Acts 8:26-39). What one word could you use to describe this experience? . . .

Out of any simple survey of the language of conversion emerges one profound fact. Conversion is the turning of the whole man to God; it is commitment to Christ as the first loyalty in life. Conversion is concerned with the attitude and relationship of men to God. The need of conversion is grounded not merely in acts of sin but in the rebelliousness of man against God . . . .

The whole response to the Gospel can be summed up as repentance toward God and faith in the Lord Jesus Christ (Acts 20:21). Faith in Jesus Christ means turning away from sin (Acts 3:26; 8:20) and turning to God (Acts 20:21; 26:20).

I am often questioned why I ask people to "come forward" and make a public commitment! Certainly this act is not necessary for conversion. However, it has a sound psychological and biblical basis. I have had many psychologists and psychiatrists study my methods. They have criticized certain aspects of it, but one aspect that most of them commend is the "invitation." Many of them have publicly written that this method is psychologically sound. Certainly when such churches as the Roman Church or the Anglican Church invite people to come forward to receive the bread and the wine this too is an act of public commitment. However, there is also a sound biblical basis. There are invitations throughout the Bible. Moses gave an invitation in Exodus 32:26, when after the destruction of the golden calf he stood in the gate of the camp and said: "Who is on the Lord's side? Let him come unto me." Joshua appealed to Israel to make a definite decision and commitment, and said: "Choose you this day whom you will serve (Joshua 24:15). When the people said they would choose and serve the Lord, Joshua put it down in writing and had a great stone set up under an oak as a witness to their decision. Joshua called for a public declaration of loyalty to Jehovah and had it recorded and memorialized so they could never forget. King Josiah gave a public invitation when he called an assembly of the people after the Book of the Law had been found, and read to them and called upon them to stand in assent to a covenant to keep the law of God (2 Chronicles 34:30-32). Ezra called upon the people to swear publicly to carry out his reformations (Ezra 10:5), and there are other instances in the Old Testament!

In the New Testament Jesus gave invitations. He said to Peter and Andrew: "Follow me" (Matthew 4:19). He said to Matthew: "Follow me, and he arose and followed Him" (Matthew 9:9). These invitations clearly imply a call for action. Jesus invited Zaccheus down out of the tree. Jesus gave the parable of the slighted dinner invitation when the lord said to his servants: "Go out into the highways and hedges and compel them to come in, that my house may be filled" (Luke 14:23). This word implies strong persuasion. The apostles often used persuasion to an intense degree. In Acts 2:40 we read that on the day of Pentecost Peter "with many other words did . . . testify and exhort saying, Save yourselves from this untoward generation." These words imply strong persuasion. On several occasions Paul is spoken of as having "persuaded" people (Acts 19:8; 19:26; 26:28; 28:23). Paul uses strong language and emotion when he recites to the Ephesian elders how "that by the space of three years he ceased not to warn everyone night and day with tears" (Acts 20:31). We could go on with many thoughts and illustrations from both the Old and the New Testament to indicate that the early preachers of the Gospel, while not using high-pressure emotional methods, did persuade people to make a definite commitment to Christ. We are told that on the day of Pentecost 3,000 made a commitment in one day! Certainly most of these were instantaneous.

We live in a day of skilful and high-pressure advertising. People are accustomed to all kinds of appeals from television, radio, newspapers, magazines and billboards. They are bringing a flood of solicitations to see and buy. Salesmen ask us to sign on the dotted line when their sales appeal ends. Our generation is perhaps more invitation minded in this respect than any other has ever been. It seems to me that we as a Church today could use this invitation consciousness at every favorable evangelistic opportunity . . . .

Conversion can be as sudden and dramatic as the conversion of pagans who transfer their affection and faith from idols carved of stone and wood to the person of Christ. We may call this a crisis conversion. There are many others, however, who experience conversion only after a long and difficult conflict with their inner motives. With others, conversion comes as the climactic moment of a longer period of gradual conviction of their need and revelation of what God has done through Christ. This prolonged process results in a conscious acceptance of Christ as personal Saviour and in the yielding of life to him. We may say, therefore, that conversion can be an instantaneous event, a crisis in which the person receives the clear revelation of the love of God, or it can be a gradual unfoldment.

No two conversions are exactly alike! My wife, for example, cannot remember the exact day or hour when she became a

Christian, but she is certain that there was such a moment in her life — a moment when she actually crossed the line. I find many Christians who have grown up in Christian homes, been baptized or confirmed and had the benefit of Christian training, who are unaware of the time when they committed their lives to Christ, yet their faith and lives clearly testify that they know Christ. Others remember very clearly when they had their great encounter. There were people in the New Testament who had a dramatic conversion, such as Saul of Tarsus, and there were others who quietly opened their hearts to the Lord, as did Lydia . . . .

In the interests of clarification, it should be pointed out that although thousands of persons have responded to our simple invitation to receive Christ as Saviour and Lord, they cannot by any means all be considered to be genuinely converted persons. This is why we call them "inquirers." True biblical conversion did not necessarily take place in many of them, but I am convinced that for the majority of them it did, and there are today transformed lives and personalities throughout the world who are willing to stand up and testify to this fact. A sampling of these inquirers has revealed some significant and sometimes thrilling after effects of these crusades. When the results are finally tabulated it becomes a modern day fulfilment of Jesus's parable of the sower. The seed has sometimes fallen by the wayside and for many inquirers no lasting effects can be observed. They are not converted. For some the seed fell and sprang quickly up but could not withstand when difficulties arose, and withered. But it cannot be denied that an impressive majority reveals a clear and lasting change that can be called conversion . . . .

I am . . . convinced that the preaching of the gospel and the call for conversion would do more to remedy the social ills of our time than anything we could possibly do. There is no doubt that the social gospel has directed its energies toward the release of many of the problems of suffering humanity. I am for it and I believe that it is biblical! However, I am convinced that we do not have a personal gospel and a social gospel. There is one gospel and one gospel only, and that gospel is the dynamic of God to change the individual and, through the individual, society. The gospel has the power to redeem the individual and also the power to redeem the social order. In the ministry of our Lord it was said that "He went about doing good," never separating the forgiving from the healing ministry. The same truth was expressed by Isaiah in prophetic vision: "He was wounded for our transgressions . . . and by His stripes we are healed" (53:5). In fact, it appears that evangelism and biblical conversion have consistently been the inspiration for social work . . . .

The first century message works twentieth century wonders. Another remarkable aspect is the fact that the same gospel proclaimed through the lips of an interpreter in Spanish, Japanese, Tamil or an African dialect will penetrate the darkened mind and flood it with the light of the gospel. There seems to be no such thing as a language barrier when the gospel is proclaimed. Even the voice of the interpreter does not hinder or limit its power. That is why we can go to any country, no matter what their language or their culture may be, and proclaim Christ crucified and risen, the only Saviour from sin and the hope of the world, and they will respond! There is something in this message of the gospel when proclaimed in the power of the Holy Spirit that touches the human heart, whatever the cultural, ethnic or religious background.

I would suggest three elements which in combination I have found most effective in conversion. The first is the use of the Bible. The Bible needs more proclaiming than defending, and when proclaimed, its message can be relied upon to bring men to conversion. But it must be preached with a sense of authority. This is not anthoritarianism or even dogmatism; it is preaching with utter confidence in the reliability of the gospel . . . . I know of no great forward movements of the Church that have not been closely bound up with the message of the Bible . . . .

Second, there needs to be a clearly defined theology of

evangelism. This is not so much a new theology but a special emphasis upon certain aspects of the theology that focuses attention upon the person and work of Christ on behalf of the alienated in every generation. It is the theology that involves beseeching men to be reconciled to God . . . .

Third, there must be an awareness that conversion is a supernatural change brought about by the Holy Spirit who himself communicates the truth. At every evangelistic conference we hear discussion on "how can we communicate the gospel to our age." We must always remember that the Holy Spirit is the communicating agent. Without the work of the Holy Spirit there would be no such thing as conversion. The Scriptures teach that this is a supernatural work of God. It is the Holy Spirit who convicts men of sin. Jesus said: "And when He is come He will reprove the world of sin and of righteousness and of judgment" (John 16:8). It is the Holy Spirit who gives new life. "Not by works of righteousness which we have done, but according to His mercy He saved us, by the washing of regeneration, and renewing of the Holy Ghost" (Titus 3:5). There is a mystery in one aspect of conversion that I have never been able to fathom and I have never read a book of theology that satisfies me at this point — the relationship between the sovereignty of God and man's free will. It seems to be that they are both taught in the Scriptures and both are involved. Certainly we are ordered to proclaim the gospel and man is besought to respond by repentance and faith. However, it must not be concluded that this one act is the end of the matter! It is only the beginning! The Scriptures teach that the Holy Spirit comes to indwell each believing heart (1 Corinthians 3:16). The missionary expansion of the Church in the early centuries was a result of the great commission (Matthew 28:19-20) and no less of the joyful constraint created in believers' hearts on and following Pentecost. They had been filled with the Spirit. This great event was such a transforming experience that believers did not need to refer to a prior command for their missionary activities. They were spontaneously moved to proclaim the gospel. While there is no doubt that certain individuals have a charismatic endowment by the Holy Spirit for evangelism (Ephesians 4:11), yet in a sense every Christian is to be an evangelist.

Conversion then is the impact of the gospel upon the whole man, convincing his intellect, warming his emotions, and causing his will to act with decision! I have no doubt that if every Christian in the world would suddenly begin proclaiming the gospel and winning others to an encounter with Jesus Christ, we would have a different world over night. This is the revolution that the world needs!

The Dilemma Of
Love And Justice

Reinhold Niebuhr

Schooled in Protestant liberalism, Reinhold Niebuhr became in the mid-twentieth century the recognized prophet for a new biblical-dialectical theology.

As a young man, Niebuhr served as minister of a church in Detroit (1915-1928), and the agony of dealing with religious problems in the midst of an industrial society made a lasting impression on him. In 1928 he became professor of applied Christianity at Union Theological Seminary, New York.

A vigorous and explosive lecturer, Niebuhr attracted a generation of students and many from social and political positions of power. Speaking, lecturing, and writing, he was also directly involved in dozens of social action groups. In politics, he became more liberal; in theology, more conservative.

In a steady succession of books, Niebuhr developed a dialectical method which allowed him to overarch the conventional disputes between liberals and conservatives. The Bible, he said, takes a higher view of human nature than either naturalism or materialism (because of the doctrine that God created humanity in the divine image); but it takes a lower view of human possibilities than either idealism or romanticism (because of the doctrine of sin).

Combining biblical interpretation, theological perception, and social conscience, Reinhold Niebuhr steered a path between a too optimistic and a too pessimistic perspective. To expect too much of human nature or of the Christian ethic of love is an unrealistic as to despair completely.

In an often-quoted chapel prayer, he once summed up his whole theology: "God, give us grace to accept with serenity the things that cannot be changed, courage to change the things that should be changed, and the wisdom to distinguish the one from the other."

Toward the end of his active literary life, Niebuhr prepared an appraisal of current problems from a Christian perspective for "The Church in the World" section of the religious quarterly *Theology Today* (January, 1959). It sums up his views and is reprinted here.

We are living in a tragic age in which all international relations are conducted under the Damocles sword of possible nuclear war, and in which the world is divided between two blocs of nations: the one led by our own nation, and comprising the so-called "free world"; and the other a bloc of nations, informed by a fanatic communist creed and under the hegemony, and possibly the actual authority, of communist Russia.

The situation tortures the conscience of all sensitive spirits, and it naturally engages the conscience of Christians. The question is what general and what unique insight the Christian church and the Christian gospel can contribute to the possible solution of this dilemma, that displays a dimension which former ages did not expect or were incapable of imagining. No one can give a confident answer to this question. I believe that one of the requirements of the hour is that Christians should cease to present the gospel as a simple panacea for all the world's ills, insisting, for instance, that if only people loved each other, all these evils would disappear.

We are certainly beyond those simple precepts of the "social gospel" which assumed that it was necessary only to apply the love ethic to collective, as well as to individual, man. The whole Christian apprehension of the human situation includes the Pauline conviction that there is a "law in my members which wars against the law that is in my mind." And we all know that this is the law of self-love, warring against the law of love. We also know that it is more difficult for collective man, as distinguished from the individual, to obey the law of love. We must take the self-interest of nations and even of whole civilizations for granted, and ask the question whether it is possible to achieve standards of justice and accommodation within the limits of this ineradicable self-interest.

If this generalization be correct, we ought to make a sharp distinction between the Christian solutions of the problems of the nuclear dilemma and insights of gospel origin which might assuage the severity of the cold war. The distinction must be made because there is literally no definitive Christian or any solution for the nuclear dilemma. The World Council of Churches' statement on this subject, presented by the executive committee in 1958, admitted as much, in a slightly confused way, because it entertained the possibility of a unilateral disavowal of nuclear weapons on the one hand, and on the other called attention to the responsibility of statesmen in preserving the defenses of the West. This means that it is acknowledged that our security depends upon the horrible "balance of terror," in which, in Churchill's eloquent phrase, "security is the child of terror and annihilation the twin brother of survival." It is always possible for individuals to bow out of such a terrible situation and disavow any reliance on nuclear weapons. That is a new version of the pacifist solution, and the question is whether it does not merely illustrate the hiatus between individual solutions of the moral problem and solutions which are applicable to nations and civilizations.

Surely the fact that it is necessary for Christian nations to preserve their defenses against nuclear attack by the power of nuclear retaliation, hoping that in this way a nuclear war may be avoided, is merely the old problem of the difference between individual and collective morality in a new dimension. The one allows and enjoins an ethic of self-sacrifice, while the other transmutes love into justice; and justice enjoins both concern for the other and a discriminate judgment which gives "each man his due." Ages of experience have proved that an adequate justice requires not only discriminate judgments, apportioning the due of each man, but an equilibrium of forces, preventing one group from taking advantage of another. In a nuclear age this equilibrium means a balance of nuclear weapons. Christians, like other sensitive spirits, may well call attention to the fact that we ought not put our sole reliance on military force; and, in estimating military power, not put our complete reliance on weapons which have the single purpose of preventing a nuclear war by preserving a balance of forces. But there is obviously no "Christian" way of avoiding the dilemma in which the whole world is caught. Escaping it by "self-sacrifice" means escaping it by the capitulation of the democratic world.

If there is little chance, either by Christian or other means, of abolishing the nuclear dimension of modern warfare and of escaping the nuclear terror which hangs over the world, there is a great deal of opportunity of harnessing the inspiration and insights of the Christian faith in cooling off the cold war and making coexistence with a system, which we abhor, sufferable. One of the reasons it seems insufferable is that it is informed by a fanatic creed, which makes absolute distinctions between the "righteous" nations, who are all on the other side of the revolution, and the "unrighteous," that is, the "capitalistic" nations. But we are not sufficiently conscious of the fact that we are in danger of developing an even more vexatious self-righteousness of our own because we represent the "free world" or because we are "God-fearing" nations rather than "atheistic" ones. This self-righteousness is not only a moral hazard in our relations to the uncommitted nations, but it violates the basic principles and insights of our faith, which recognizes the fragmentary character of all human virtues and the ambiguity of all human achievements. If the Christian faith is to be effective in moderating the arrogance of nations and the pride of civilizations, it must emphasize both the biblical faith of the majesty of God, before whom the nations are "as a drop in the bucket," and the insights of political common sense, which must recognize that while our democratic society seems to us the ultimate in political virtue, it will appear as a luxury from the perspective of the dark continents. We have made freedom compatible with both justice and stability in the Western world. But we have accomplished this through centuries of tortuous experience, in which social power has been balanced by competing social power to prevent injustice, and in which various forms of unity have prevented the fluid and pluralistic structure of democratic society from degenerating into anarchy.

Even so the achievement of justice and stability is unique in Western society. Only the Western European nations and the Anglo-Saxon nations, including the British Dominions, have established stable democracies, and it is still a question whether either France or Italy can boast of a stable democracy. In part of the so-called "free world," more particularly in Latin America, the usual form of government is military dictatorship. The division between the virtuous and the unrighteous nations is, in short, not as clear as we think or pretend. As for our own nation we combine the virtues of freedom with complacently high living standards which seem either odious or irrelevant to the Asian and African nations. They are impressed, on the other hand, with the Russian ability to climb from agrarian backwardness to modern technical civilization in four decades. Its despotism is no doubt an evil, but it will not appear so to nations which have never known freedom. Whether we think of our own nation or of the so-called "free world," we are not the paragons of virtue we pretend to be and which decades of polemics against the foe have prompted us to believe that we are.

Nor is the Russian venture pure evil, however dangerous its

despotism. It is idle to say that it is more evil than Tsarist despotism, for it contains the possibilities of development through its free and equal education, which the traditional despotism of the Tsars never achieved. These educational advantages will not result in democratic life immediately and perhaps not for a long time. But they are more generous than those offered by many of the nations of the free world. In other words common sense reinforces the precepts of our faith and emphasizes the warning not to think of ourselves more highly than we ought to think. A more generous appreciation of the "virtues and good intentions" of the foe and more modesty in estimating our own achievements is the best application of the injunction to "love our enemies." It is, moreover, the only way of making long decades of competitive coexistence sufferable to us, and of preventing the cold war from resulting in the ultimate war of nuclear annihilation. Certainly Christians are bound to offer any relevant insights of their faith for guiding the generation in accomplishing the most difficult task which any generation has been called upon to fulfill.

The most important insight deals with the problem of living together tolerably with an acknowledged foe for decades and perhaps for centuries. But one other insight of the Christian faith must be added as relevant to the present hour. It deals not only with the fragmentary quality of all our virtues, but with the inconclusive character of all historic tasks and responsibilities. Modern culture, whether liberal or Marxist, has always sought the final fulfillment of history within history, and thus a utopian color has been imparted to the whole of our culture. This utopianism prevents us from giving ourselves wholeheartedly to the responsibilities which have no chance of being crowned with fulfillment. We must live, probably for centuries, in a state partly of peace and partly of war. We cannot live in such a state unless we observe the injunction of our Lord: "Sufficient unto the day are the evils thereof." This can only mean that an act or task in God's sight has its virtue not in any immediate historical consequences but in the fulfillment of the divine intention in the present moment.

While the tragic international situation is uppermost in the mind and conscience of our generation, it does not exhaust the meaning of the "world" to which we must be related. The world includes all levels of human community to which we must have a responsible relation, and in which we must strive for the largest measure of justice and community, within the limits set for such a task by the sin of man, particularly the ineradicable self-regard of individuals, families, and nations. The task of relating ourselves to the world therefore includes the organization of national communities as well as the relation of these communities to each other. Primarily the task is to apply the law "thou shalt love thy neighbor as thyself" in such a way as to make it relevant to collective relations. Love always has the task of perfecting the rough justice of communities by personal attitudes of trust and respect for the "thou" which no impersonal system of justice can guarantee . . . .

This problem becomes more and more serious as technical civilization dissolves the organic relations of traditional communities and constructs systems of justice in which the principle that each man is to have his due is roughly fulfilled. It was certainly the mistake of Christian liberalism to believe that the law of love could and would be applied neatly to the collective as well as to the personal relations of men. It was a mistake because every system of justice must take account not only of the imperatives of love but of the persistence of the power of self-love. In view of the persistence of this power, order requires a preponderant power in the community, a fact which Luther, with his Augustinian realism, saw so clearly. But justice requires an equilibrium among subordinate vitalities in the community, a fact which no one saw clearly, not even the Christian radicals of the seventeenth century and the rational idealists of the eighteenth century. It is a truth of justice which was forced upon men providentially through the fact that it was impossible to achieve justice in any other way. One must recall that in our own nation, the fact that the collective power of the industrial worker was a necessary counterpoise to the power of management if rough justice was to be achieved, was not recognized until recent decades. Significantly, it is now accepted by enlightened managers, despite the revelations of the abuse of power in the ranks of "big labor" which have recently come to light.

Naturally not only Christian insights contributed to the acceptance of this truth about the anatomy of justice. But it is significant that the Christian, rather than the modern, estimate of human nature would have hastened the discovery of the unwelcome truth, if Christians had not tried to outdo modern secularists in their optimistic view of human nature. Not so much by human wisdom as by the providence of God, the Western world now has achieved forms of community in which liberty has been made compatible with both justice and stability. It is our business to perfect those organs of community which preserve this heritage.

But the motive of love must be applied not only through the instrument of justice but through the instrument of respect. Justice deals with the impersonal institutions of the social order. Respect applies love where relations are personal but not intimate. It may seem irrelevant to ask men to "love" people of another race, though the gospel particularly enjoins love beyond one's own group. Had not our Lord said, "If ye love them which love you, what thank have ye?" Universal love is the cornerstone of the Christian ethical system, which simply means that the Christian is enjoined to accept responsibilities for his fellows beyond the circles of mutuality. Hannah Arendt, in an interesting book, *The Human Condition* (1958), has recently challenged the universal love ethic on the ground that it demands the impossible. But that is only true if the concept of love is made to mean attachment to the object of love. To give it this connotation is to confuse *eros* with *agape* (self-seeking love with self-giving love. *Agape* must be transmuted into respect for the person, respect for his common humanity, if the injunction is to become relevant.

The race situation in America, occasioned by the Supreme Court decision that equality before the law means common education, offers the supreme test of the vitality of the Christian life in meeting the requirement of the love commandment. Those of us who do not live in the South ought not to underestimate the validity of the honest scruples of southerners about common education for races with different cultural inheritances. But we also dare not defy the commandment which enjoins that we give the other person the basic respect due to his common humanity.

We must humbly confess that the Catholic version of our common faith has been more successful than the Protestant versions in insisting on this respect for all men of all races. The race issue thus remains for Protestantism the primary challenge to prove our faith according to the scriptural test "by their fruits shall ye know them."

Religious Symbols And God

Paul Tillich

Theology can be defined as intellectual reflection on religious experience. Part of the theological task is to *understand* the content of faith, and another part is to *communicate* in terms that make sense. But this is not simple, because religious truth is unlike other truth, and we must use human, rather than divine, language.

The problem of communication is especially irksome in theology since we are trying to express the inexpressible. We can remain silent but uncommunicative, or we can make the best possible use of the means at our disposal.

Unfortunately, in modern times language itself becomes increasingly suspect as a medium of communication. Bombarded on all sides with words, clichés, slogans, and rhetoric, we have become skeptical about all verbal statements.

That is why there is a revival of interest, Paul Tillich would argue, in symbols. When we are frustrated by the limitations of descriptive language, we grope after alternative ways of articulating reality, such as are provided in art, films, and music. Our country's flag is a political symbol; the cross is a Christian symbol.

But language itself is symbolical, and especially religious language. What we say about God, for example, is a symbolic expression of what we believe. But the forms we use are not, of course, identical with the reality of God. Symbols point to eternal truth, they open up new levels of reality, and they widen our perspective and understanding.

This way of thinking about theology was characteristic of Paul Tillich. Deeply philosophical, he was also interested in art, and he enlisted both in his attempt to interpret, explain, and apply the eternal truths of biblical and Christian faith.

Born in Germany, Paul Tillich came to America in 1933 and soon became known as an original and creative thinker. He was a prolific writer on all phases of theology and a frequent lecturer on college campuses. He taught at Union Theological Seminary in New York and at the Universities of Harvard and Chicago.

On several occasions, Tillich applied himself to the examination of religious symbols. The passage presented here is taken from the transcript of a lecture, "Religious Symbols and Our Knowledge of God," delivered at Shimer College, Mt. Carroll, Illinois. It first appeared in print in *The Christian Scholar,* (September, 1955).

The fact that there is so much discussion about the meaning of symbols going on in this country as well as in Europe is a symptom of something deeper. I believe it is a symptom of two things: something negative and something positive. It is a symptom of the fact that we are in a confusion of language in theology and philosophy and related subjects which has hardly been surpassed in any time in history. Words do not communicate to us anymore what they originally did and what they were invented to communicate. This has something to do with the fact that our present culture has no clearing house such as medieval Scholasticism was, and Protestant scholasticism in the seventeenth century at least tried to be . . . .

The second point which I want to make is that we are in a process in which a very important thing is being rediscovered: namely, that there are levels of reality of great difference, and that these different levels demand different approaches and different languages: that not everything in reality can be grasped by the language which is most adequate for mathematical sciences; the insight into this situation is the most positive side of the fact that the problem of symbols is taken seriously again.

I want to proceed in my own presentation with the intention of clearing concepts as far as I am able. And in order to do this I want to make five steps, the first of which is the discussion of "symbols and signs." Symbols are similar to signs in one decisive respect: both symbols and signs point beyond themselves to something else. The typical sign, for instance the red light on the corner of the street, does not point to itself but it points to the necessity of cars stopping. And every symbol points beyond itself to a reality for which it stands. In this, symbols and signs have an essential identity — they point beyond themselves. And this is the reason that the confusion of language . . . has also conquered the discussion about symbols for centuries and has produced confusion between signs and symbols. The first step in any clearing up of the meaning of symbols is to distinguish it from the meaning of signs.

The difference which I see as a fundamental difference between them is that signs do not participate in any way in the reality and power of that to which they point. Symbols, although they are not the same as that which they symbolize, participate in its meaning and power. The difference between symbol and sign is the participation in the symbolized reality which characterizes the symbols, and the nonparticipation in the "pointed to" reality which characterizes a sign. For example, letters of the alphabet as they are written, an "A" or an "R" do not participate in the sound to which they point; on the other hand, the flag participates in the power of the king or the nation for which it stands and which it symbolizes . . . .

Now I come to my second consideration dealing with the functions of symbols . . . . Every symbol opens up a level of reality for which nonsymbolic speaking is inadequate. Let me interpret this or explain this in terms of artistic symbols . . . . In poetry, in visual art, and in music, levels of reality are opened up which can be opened up in no other way. Now if this is the function of art, then certainly artistic creations have symbolic character. You can take that which a landscape of Rubens, for instance, mediates to you. You can not have this experience in any other way than through this painting made by Rubens. This landscape has some heroic character; it has character of balance, of colors, of weights, of values, and so on. All this is very external. What this mediates to you cannot be expressed in any other way than through the painting itself . . . .

This example may show what I mean by the phrase "opening up of levels of reality." But in order to do this, something else must be opened up — namely, levels of the soul, levels of our interior reality. And they must correspond to the levels in exterior reality which are opened up by a symbol. So every symbol is two-edged. It opens up reality and it opens up the soul. Here I could give the same example — namely, the artistic experience. There are people who are not opened up by music, or who are not opened up by poetry, or more of them (mostly in Protestant America) who are not opened up at all by visual arts. The "opening up" is a two-sided function — namely, reality in deeper levels and the human soul in special levels.

If this is the function of symbols then it is obvious that symbols cannot be replaced by other symbols. Every symbol has a special function which is just *it* and cannot be replaced by more or less adequate symbols. This is different from signs, for signs can always be replaced. If one finds that a green light is not so expedient as perhaps a blue light (this is not true, but could be true), then we simply put on a blue light, and nothing is changed. But a symbolic word (such as the word "god") cannot be replaced. No symbol can be replaced when used in its special function. So one asks rightly, "How do symbols arise, and how do they come to an end?" As different from signs, symbols are born and die. Signs are consciously invented and removed. This is a fundamental difference. "Out of which womb are symbols born?" I would say out of the womb which is usually called today the "group unconscious" or "collective unconscious," or whatever you want to call it — out of a group which acknowledges, in this thing, this word, this flag, or whatever it may be, its own being. It is not invented intentionally; and even if somebody would try to invent a symbol, as sometimes happens, then it becomes a symbol only if the unconscious of a group says "yes" to it. It means that something is opened up by it in the sense which I have just described. Now this implies further that in the moment in which this inner situation of the human group to a symbol has ceased to exist, then the symbol dies. The symbol does not "say" anything any more. In this way, all of the polytheistic gods have died; the situation in which they were born has changed or does not exist any more, and so the symbols died. But these are events which cannot be described in terms of intention and invention.

Now I come to my third consideration — namely, the nature of religious symbols. Religious symbols do exactly the same thing as all symbols do — namely, they open up a level of reality, which otherwise is not opened at all, which is hidden. I would call this the depth dimension of reality itself, the dimension of reality which is the ground of every other dimension and every other depth, and which therefore, is not one level beside the others but is the fundamental level, the level below all other levels, the level of being itself, or the ultimate power of being. Religious symbols open up the experience of the dimension of this depth in the human soul. If a religious symbol has ceased to have this function, then it dies. And if new symbols are born, they are born out of a changed relationship to the ultimate ground of being, i.e., to the holy.

The dimension of ultimate reality is the dimension of the holy. And so we can also say, religious symbols are symbols of the holy. As such they participate in the holiness of the holy according to our basic definition of a symbol. But participation is not identity; they are not themselves the holy. The wholly transcendent transcends every symbol of the holy . . . .

Religion, as everything in life, stands under the law of ambiguity, "ambiguity" meaning that it is creative and destructive at the same time. Religion has its holiness and its unholiness, and the reason for this is obvious from what I have said about religious symbolism. Religious symbols point symbolically to that which transcends all of them. But since, as symbols, they participate in that to which they point, they always have the tendency (in the human mind, of course) to replace that to which they are supposed to point, and to become ultimate in themselves. And in the moment in which they do this, they become idols. All idolatry is nothing else than the absolutizing of symbols of the holy, and making them identical with the holy itself. In this way, for instance, holy persons can become god. Ritual acts can take on unconditional validity, although they are only expressions of a special situation. In all sacramental activities of religion, in all holy objects, holy books, holy doctrines, holy rites, you find this danger which I like to call demonization. They become demonic in the moment in which they become elevated to the unconditional and ultimate character of the holy itself.

Now I come to my fourth consideration — namely the levels of religious symbols. I distinguish two fundamental levels in all religious symbols: the transcendent level, the level which goes *beyond* the empirical reality we encounter, and the immanent level, the level which we find *within* the encounter with reality. Let us first look at the first level, the transcendent level. The basic symbol on the transcendent level would be God himself. But we cannot simply say that God is a symbol. We must always say two things about him: we must say that there is a nonsymbolic element in our image of God — namely that he is ultimate reality, being itself, ground of being, power of being; and the other, that he is the highest being in which everything that we have does exist in the most perfect way. If we say this we have in our mind the image of a highest being, a being with the characteristics of highest perfection. That means we have a symbol for that which is not symbolic in the idea of God — namely "being itself."...

We could not be in communication with God if he were only "ultimate being." But in our relationship to him we encounter him with the highest of what we ourselves are, *person*. And so in the symbolic form of speaking about him, we have both that which transcends infinitely our experience of ourselves as persons, and that which is so adequate to our being persons that we can say, "thou" to God, and can pray to him. And these two elements must be preserved. If we preserve only the element of the unconditional, then no relationship to God is possible. If we preserve only the element of the ego-thou relationship, as it is called today, we lose the element of the divine — namely, the unconditional which transcends subject and object and all other polarities. This is the first point on the transcendent level.

The second is the qualities, the attributes of God, whatever you say about him: that he is love, that he is mercy, that he is power, that he is omniscient, that he is omnipresent, that he is almighty and all this. These attributes of God are taken from experienced qualities we have ourselves. They cannot be applied to God in the literal sense. If this is done, it leads to an infinite amount of absurdities. This again is one of the reasons for the destruction of religion through wrong communicative interpretation of it. And again the symbolic character of these qualities must be maintained consistently. Otherwise, every speaking about the divine becomes absurd.

A third element on the transcendent level is the acts of God. For instance, when we say, "He has created the world," "He has sent his son," "He will fulfill the world." In all these temporal, causal, and other expressions we speak symbolically of God. And I would like here to give an example in which the four main categories of our finitude are combined in *one* small sentence: *"God has sent his son."* Here we have in the word "has" temporality. But God is beyond *our* temporality, though not beyond every temporality. Here is space; "sending somebody" means moving him from one place to another place. This certainly is speaking symbolically, although spatiality is in God as an element in his creative ground. We say that he "has sent," that means that he has caused something. In this way God is subject to the category of causality. And when we speak of him and his Son, we have two different substances and apply the category of substance to him. Now all this, if taken literally, is absurd. If it is taken symbolically, it is a profound expression, the ultimate Christian expression, of the relationship between God and man in the Christian experience. But to distinguish these two kinds of speech, the nonsymbolic and the symbolic, in such a point is so important that if we are not able to make understandable to our contemporaries that we speak symbolically when we use such language, they will rightly turn away from us, as from people who live still in absurdities and superstitions.

Now consider the immanent level, the level of the appearances of the divine in time and space. Here we have first of all the incarnations of the divine, different beings in time and space, divine beings transmuted into animals or men or any kinds of other beings as they appear in time and space. This is often forgotten by those within Christianity who like to use in every second theological proposition the word, "incarnation." They forget that this is not an especially Christian characteristic, because incarnation is something which happens in paganism all the time. The divine beings always incarnate in different forms. That is very easy in paganism. This is not the real distinction between Christianity and other religions. Let me say something here, about the relationships of the transcendent to the immanent level just in connection with the incarnation idea. Historically, one must say that preceding both of them was the situation in which the transcendent and immanent were not distinguished. In the Indonesian doctrine of "Mana," that divine mystical power which permeates all reality, we have some divine presence which is both immanent in everything as a hidden power, and at the same time transcendent, something which can be grasped only through very difficult ritual activities known to the priest. Out of this identity of the immanent and the transcendent the gods of the great mythologies have developed in Greece and in the Semitic nations and in India. There we find incarnations as the immanent element of the divine. The more transcendent the gods become, the more incarnations of personal or sacramental character are needed in order to overcome the remoteness of the divine which develops with the strengthening of the transcendent element . . . .

And now I come to my last consideration — namely, the truth of religious symbols. Here I must distinguish a negative, a positive, and an absolute statement. First the negative statement. Symbols are independent of any empirical criticism.You cannot kill a symbol by criticism in terms of natural sciences or in terms of historical research. As I said, symbols can only die if the situation in which they have been created has passed. Symbols are not on a level on which empirical criticism can dismiss them. I will give you two examples, both connected with Mary, the mother of Jesus, as Holy Virgin. Here you have first of all a symbol which has died in Protestantism by the changed situation of the relation to God. The special, direct, immediate relationship to God, makes an mediating power impossible. Another reason which has made this symbol disappear is the negation of the ascetic element which is implied in the glorification of virginity. And as long as the Protestant religious situation lasts it cannot be reestablished. It has not died because Protestant scholars have said, "Now there is no empirical reason for saying all this about the Holy Virgin." There certainly is not, but this the Roman Church also knows. But the Roman Church sticks to it on the basis of its tremendous symbolic power which step by step brings her nearer to Trinity itself, especially in the development of the last decade. If this should ever be completed as is now discussed in groups of the Roman Church, Mary would become co-Saviour with Jesus. Then, whether this is admitted or not, she is actually taken into the divinity itself. Another example is the story of the virginal birth of Jesus. This is from the point of view of historical research a most obviously legendary story, unknown to Paul and to John. It is a late creation, trying to make understandable the full possession of the divine Spirit of Jesus of Nazareth. But again its legendary character is not the reason why this symbol will die or has died in many groups of people, in even quite conservative groups within the Protestant churches. The reason is different. The reason is that it is theologically quasi-heretical. It takes away one of the fundamental doctrines . . . . that the full humanity of Jesus must be maintained beside his whole divinity. A human being who has no human father has no full humanity. This story, then has to be criticized on inner-symbolic grounds, but not on historical grounds. This is the negative statement about the truth of religious symbols. Their truth is their adequacy to the religious situation in which they are created, and their inadequacy to another situation is their untruth. In the last sentence both the positive and the negative statement about symbols are contained . . . .

I believe that if Christianity claims to have a truth superior to any other truth in its symbolism, then it is the symbol of the cross in which this is expressed, the cross of the Christ. He who himself embodies the fullness of the divine's presence sacrifices himself in order not to became an idol, another god beside God, a god into whom the disciples wanted to make him. And therefore the decisive story is the story in which he accepts the title "Christ" when Peter offers it to him (Matt. 16:13-23). He accepts it under the one condition that he has to go to Jerusalem to suffer and to die; that means to deny the idolatrous tendency even with respect to himself. This is at the same time the criterion of all other symbols, and it is the criterion to which every Christian church should subject itself.

Contemporary Creeds

Most Protestant churches, in their worship services, make use of the Apostles' Creed or the Nicene Creed from the early church era. A creed (from the Latin *credo* meaning "I believe") is a formula of basic doctrines. It can be long or short, theological or liturgical, optional or binding like a "loyalty oath."

Some Protestant churches, such as Presbyterians and Lutherans, have a long history of creedal formulation; others, such as Methodists and Baptists, have always regarded creeds as restrictive and unnecessary. All Protestant churches regard creeds as having secondary authority to the Scriptures and the person of Jesus Christ.

Now and then a new creed is proposed, and three such are presented here: a short *Statement of Faith* (1975) for the United Church of Christ; a longer *Confession of 1967* for the United Presbyterian Church U.S.A.; and an ecumenical consensus know as *The Living Faith* (1970).

The United Church of Christ came into being in 1957 as the result of a merger of four previously distinct denominations: the Reformed Church in the U.S. (which stemmed from the Palatinate region in Germany); the Evangelical Synod of North America (which traced its roots to a Lutheran-Reformed coalition, the "Prussian Union of 1817"); the Congregational Church (with early New England background); and the Christian Church (which emerged out of a nineteenth century American revival). The significance of this four-way merger can be seen in the combination of very different doctrinal and ecclesiastical traditions. On the occasion of the union in 1957, the brief Statement of Faith was approved to be "used when Christians want to use it."

The Confession of 1967 is a Presbyterian attempt to update the seventeenth century Westminster Confession of Faith. But the new creed is intended as a supplement to, rather than a substitute for, the earlier confession. Some introductory and strictly ecclesiastical paragraphs have been deleted in the form printed here.

The ecumenical creed, The Living Faith, is a cooperative product of the Consultation on Church Union, otherwise known as COCU. Inaugurated in 1962 as an interdenominational conversation, looking toward ultimate church union, COCU issued in 1970 "A Plan of Union." The creedal statement, reproduced here with a few paragraphs deleted, is a part of this Plan. Until the churches approve the Plan, the creed of course has no official status. The member churches of COCU at the time when the Plan was distributed were: The African Methodist Episcopal Church, African Methodist Episcopal Zion Church, Christian Church (Disciples of Christ), Christian Methodist Episcopal Church, Episcopal Church, Presbyterian Church in the U.S., United Church of Christ, United Methodist Church, United Presbyterian Church U.S.A.

Statement of Faith

We believe in God, the Eternal Spirit, Father of our Lord Jesus Christ and our Father, and to his deeds we testify:

> He calls the worlds into being,
>   creates man in his own image
>   and sets before him the ways of life and death.

He seeks in holy love to save all people from aimlessness
   and sin.

He judges men and nations by his righteous will
   declared through prophets and apostles.

In Jesus Christ, the man of Nazareth, our crucified and
      risen Lord,
   he has come to us
   and shared our common lot,
   conquering sin and death
   and reconciling the world to himself.

He bestows upon us his Holy Spirit,
   creating and renewing the church of Jesus Christ,
   binding in covenant faithful people of all ages, tongues,
      and races.

He calls us into his church
   to accept the cost and joy of discipleship,
   to be his servants in the service of men
   to proclaim the gospel to all the world
      and resist the powers of evil,
   to share in Christ's baptism and eat at his table,
   to join him in his passion and victory.

He promises to all who trust him
   forgiveness of sins and fullness of grace,
   courage in the struggle for justice and peace,
   his presence in trial and rejoicing,
   and eternal life in his kingdom which has no end.

Blessing and honor, glory and power be unto him. Amen.

The Confession of 1967

PART I

GOD'S WORK OF RECONCILIATION

The Grace of Our Lord Jesus Christ

Jesus Christ

In Jesus of Nazareth true humanity was realized once for all. Jesus, a Palestinian Jew, lived among his own people and shared their needs, temptations, joys, and sorrows. He expressed the love of God in word and deed and became a brother to all kinds of sinful men. But his complete obedience led him into conflict with his people. His life and teaching judged their goodness, religious aspirations, and national hopes. Many rejected him and demanded his death. In giving himself freely for them he took upon himself the judgment under which all men stand convicted. God raised him from the dead, vindicating him as Messiah and Lord. The victim of sin became victor, and won the victory over sin and death for all men.

God's reconciling act in Jesus Christ is a mystery which the Scriptures describe in various ways. It is called the sacrifice of a lamb, a shepherd's life given for his sheep, atonement by a priest; again it is ransom of a slave, payment of debt, vicarious satisfaction of a legal penalty, and victory over the powers of evil. These are expressions of a truth which remains beyond the reach of all theory in the depths of God's love for man. They reveal the gravity, cost, and sure achievement of God's reconciling work.

The risen Christ is the savior for all men. Those joined to him by faith are set right with God and commissioned to serve as his reconciling community. Christ is head of this community, the church, which began with the apostles and continues through all generations.

The same Jesus Christ is the judge of all men. His judgment discloses the ultimate seriousness of life and gives promise of God's final victory over the power of sin and death. To receive life from the risen Lord is to have life eternal; to refuse life from him is to choose the death which is separation from God. All who put their trust in Christ face divine judgment without fear, for the judge is their redeemer.

The Sin of Man

The reconciling act of God in Jesus Christ exposes the evil in men as sin in the sight of God. In sin men claim mastery of their own lives, turn against God and their fellow men, and become exploiters and despoilers of the wold. They lose their humanity in futile striving and are left in rebellion, despair, and isolation.

Wise and virtuous men through the ages have sought the highest good in devotion to freedom, justice, peace, truth, and beauty. Yet all human virtue, when seen in the light of God's love in Jesus Christ, is found to be infected by self-interest and hostility. All men, good and bad alike, are in the wrong before God and helpless without his forgiveness. Thus all men fall under God's judgment. No one is more subject to that judgment than the man who assumes that he is guiltless before God or morally superior to others.

God's love never changes. Against all who oppose him, God expresses his love in wrath. In the same love God took on himself judgment and shameful death in Jesus Christ, to bring men to repentance and new life.

The Love of God

God's sovereign love is a mystery beyond the reach of man's mind. Human thought ascribes to God superlatives of power, wisdom, and goodness. But God reveals his love in Jesus Christ by showing power in the form of a servant, wisdom in the folly of the cross, and goodness in receiving sinful men. The power of God's love in Christ to transform the world discloses that the Redeemer is the Lord and Creator who made all things to serve the purpose of his love.

God has created the world of space and time to be the sphere of his dealings with men. In its beauty and vastness, sublimity and awfulness, order and disorder, the world reflects to the eye of faith the majesty and mystery of its Creator.

God has created man in a personal relation with himself that man may respond to the love of the Creator. He has created male and female and given them a life which proceeds from birth to death in a succession of generations and in a wide complex of social relations. He has endowed man with capacities to make the world serve his needs and to enjoy its good things. Life is a gift to be received with gratitude and a task to be pursued with courage. Man is free to seek his life within the purpose of God: to develop and protect the resources of nature for the common welfare, to work for justice and peace in society, and in other ways to use his creative powers for the fulfillment of human life.

God expressed his love for all mankind through Israel, whom he chose to be his covenant people to serve him in love and faithfulness. When Israel was unfaithful, he disciplined the nation with his judgments and maintained his cause through prophets, priests, teachers, and true believers. These witnesses called all Israelites to a destiny in which they would serve God faithfully and become a light to the nations. The same witnesses proclaimed the coming of a new age, and a true servant of God in whom God's purpose for Israel and for mankind would be realized.

Out of Israel God in due time raised up Jesus. His faith and obedience were the response of the perfect child of God. He was the fulfillment of God's promise to Israel, the beginning of the new creation, and the pioneer of the new humanity. He gave history its meaning and direction and called the church to be his servant for the reconciliation of the world.

The Communion of the Holy Spirit

God the Holy Spirit fulfills the work of reconciliation in man. The Holy Spirit creates and renews the church as the community in which men are reconciled to God and to one another. He enables them to receive forgiveness as they forgive one another and to enjoy the peace of God as they make peace among themselves. In spite of their sin, he gives them power to become representatives of Jesus Christ and his gospel of reconciliation to all men.

The New Life

The reconciling work of Jesus was the supreme crisis in the life of mankind. His cross and resurrection become personal crisis and present hope for men when the gospel is proclaimed and believed. In this experience the Spirit brings God's forgiveness to men, moves them to respond in faith, repentance, and obedience, and initiates the new life in Christ.

The new life takes shape in a community in which men know that God loves and accepts them in spite of what they are. They therefore accept themselves and love others, knowing that no man has any ground on which to stand except God's grace.

The new life does not release a man from conflict with unbelief, pride, lust, fear. He still has to struggle with disheartening difficulties and problems. Nevertheless, as he matures in love and faithfulness in his life with Christ, he lives in freedom and good cheer, bearing witness on good days and evil days, confident that the new life is pleasing to God and helpful to others.

The new life finds its direction in the life of Jesus, his deeds and words, his struggles against temptation, his compassion, his anger, and his willingness to suffer death. The teaching of apostles and prophets guides men in living this life, and the Christian community nurtures and equips them for their ministries.

The members of the church are emissaries of peace and seek the good of man in cooperation with powers and authorities in politics, culture, and economics. But they have to fight against pretensions and injustices when these same powers endanger human welfare. Their strength is in their confidence that God's purpose rather than the man's schemes will finally prevail.

Life in Christ is life eternal. The resurrection of Jesus is God's sign that he will consummate his work of creation and reconciliation beyond death and bring to fulfillment the new life begun in Christ.

The Bible

The one sufficient revelation of God is Jesus Christ, the Word of God incarnate, to whom the Holy Spirit bears unique and authoritative witness through the Holy Scriptues, which are received and obeyed as the word of God written. The Scriptures are not a witness among others, but the witness without parallel. The church has received the books of the Old and New Testament as prophetic and apostolic testimony in which it hears the word of God and by which its faith and obedience are nourished and regulated.

The New Testament is the recorded testimony of apostles to the coming of the Messiah Jesus of Nazareth, and the sending of the Holy Spirit to the Church. The Old Testament bears witness to God's faithfulness in his covenant with Israel and points the way to the fulfillment of his purpose in Christ. The Old Testmanet is indispensable to understanding the New, and is not itself fully understood without the New.

The Bible is to be interpreted in the light of its witness to God's work of reconciliation in Christ. The Scriptures, given under the guidance of the Holy Spirit, are nevertheless the words of men, conditioned by the language, thought forms, and literary fashions of the places and times at which they were written. They reflect views of life, history, and the cosmos which were then current. The church, therefore, has an obligation to approach the Scriptures with literary and historical understanding. As God has spoken his word in diverse cultural situations, the church is confident that he will continue to speak through the Scriptures in a changing world and in every form of human culture.

God's word is spoken to his church today where the Scriptures are faithfully preached and attentively read in dependence on the illumination of the Holy Spirit and with readiness to receive their truth and direction.

PART II

THE MINISTRY OF RECONCILIATION

The Mission of the Church

To be reconciled to God is to be sent into the world as his reconciling community. This community, the church universal, is entrusted with God's message of reconciliation and shares his labor of healing the enmities which separate men from God and from each other. Christ has called the church to this mission and given it the gift of the Holy Spirit. The church maintains continuity with the apostles and with Israel by faithful obedience to his call.

The life, death, resurrection, and promised coming of Jesus Christ has set the pattern for the church's mission. His life as man involves the church in the common life of men. His service to men commits the church to work for every form of human well-being. His suffering makes the church sensitive to all the sufferings of mankind so that it sees the face of Christ in the faces of men in every kind of need. His crucifixion discloses to the church God's judgment on man's inhumanity to man and the awful consequences of its own complicity in injustice. In the power of the risen Christ and the hope of his coming the church sees the promise of God's renewal of man's life in society and of God's victory over all wrong.

The church follows this pattern in the form of its life and in the method of its action. To live and serve is to confess Christ as Lord . . . .

Reconciliation in Society

In each time and place there are particular problems and crises through which God calls the church to act. The church, guided by the Spirit, humbled by its own complicity and instructed by all attainable knowledge, seeks to discern the will of God and learn how to obey in these concrete situations. The following are particularly urgent at the present time.

a. God has created the peoples of the earth to be one universal family. In his reconciling love he overcomes the barriers between brothers and breaks down every form of discrimination based on racial or ethnic difference, real or imaginary. The church is called to bring all men to receive and uphold one another as persons in all relationships of life: in employment, housing, education, leisure, marriage, family, church, and the exercise of political rights. Therefore the church labors for the abolition of all racial discrimination and ministers to those injured by it. Congregations, individuals, or groups of Christians who exclude, dominate, or patronize their fellowmen, however subtly, resist the Spirit of God and bring contempt on the faith which they profess.

b. God's reconciliation in Jesus Christ is the ground of the peace, justice, and freedom among nations which all powers of government are called to serve and defend. The church, in its own life, is called to practice the forgiveness of enemies and to commend to the nations as practical politics the search for cooperation and peace. This search requires that the nations pursue fresh and responsible relations across every line of conflict, even at risk to national security, to reduce areas of strife and to broaden international understanding. Reconciliation among nations become peculiarly urgent as countries develop nuclear, chemical, and biological weapons, diverting their manpower and resources from constructive uses and risking the annihilation of mankind. Although nations may serve God's purposes in history, the church which identifies the sovereignty of any one nation or any one way of life with the cause of God denies the Lordship of Christ and betrays its calling.

c. The reconciliation of man through Jesus Christ makes it plain that enslaving poverty in a world of abundance is an intolerable violation of God's good creation. Because Jesus identified himself with the needy and exploited, the cause of the world's poor is the cause of his disciples. The church cannot condone poverty, whether it is the product of unjust social structures, exploitation of the defenseless, lack of national resources, absence of technological understanding, or rapid expansion of populations. The church calls every man to use his abilities, his possessions, and the fruits of technology as gifts entrusted to him by God for the maintenance of his family and the advancement of the common welfare. It encourages those forces in human society that raise men's hopes for better conditions and provide them with opportunity for a decent living. A church that is indifferent to poverty, or evades responsibility in economic affairs, or is open to one social class only, or expects gratitude for its beneficence makes a mockery of reconciliation and offers no acceptable worship to God.

d. The relationship between man and woman exemplifies in a basic way God's ordering of the interpersonal life for which he created mankind. Anarchy in sexual relationships is a symptom of man's alienation from God, his neighbor, and himself. Man's perennial confusion about the meaning of sex has been aggravated in our day by the availability of new means of birth control and the treatment of infection, by the pressures of urbanization, by the exploitation of sexual symbols in mass communication, and by world overpopulation. The church, as the household of God, is called to lead men out of this alienation into the responsible freedom of the new life in Christ. Reconciled to God, each person has joy in and respect for his own humanity and that of other persons; a man and woman are enabled to marry, to commit themselves to a mutually shared life, and to respond to each other in sensitive and lifelong concern; parents receive the grace to care for children in love and to nurture their individuality. The church comes under the judgment of God and invites rejection by man when it fails to lead men and women into the full meaning of life together, or withholds the compassion of Christ from those caught in the moral confusion of our time . . . .

PART III

THE FULFILLMENT OF RECONCILIATION

God's redeeming work in Jesus Christ embraces the whole of man's life: social and cultural, economic and political, scientific and technological, individual and corporate. It includes man's natural environment as exploited and despoiled by sin. It is the will of God that his purpose for human life shall be fulfilled under the rule of Christ and all evil be banished from his creation.

Biblical visions and images of the rule of Christ such as a heavenly city, a father's house, a new heaven and earth, a marriage feast, and an unending day culminate in the image of the kingdom. The kingdom represents the triumph of God over all that resists his will and disrupts his creation. Already God's reign is present as a ferment in the world, stirring hope in men and preparing the world to receive its ultimate judgment and redemption.

With an urgency born of this hope the church applies itself to present tasks and strives for a better world. It does not identify limited progress with the kingdom of God on earth, nor does it despair in the face of disappointment and defeat. In steadfast hope the church looks beyond all partial achievement to the final triumph of God.

"Now to him who by the power at work within us is able to do far more abundantly than all we ask or think, to him be, glory in the church and in Christ Jesus to all generations, forever and ever. Amen."

The Living Faith

The Church of Christ Uniting confesses Jesus Christ as Lord and Savior. In glad celebration we worship the one God: Father, Son, and Holy Spirit.

We confess that man's hope is in Jesus Christ, the savior of each person and the redeemer of the whole world. Through Christ, the Word made flesh, we are saved by grace being justified by faith. "He is the image of the invisible God, the first-born of all creation; for in him all things were created, in heaven and on earth, visible and invisible, whether thrones or dominions or principalities or authorities — all things were created through him and for him. He is before all things, and in him all things hold together. He is the head of the body, the church; he is the beginning, the first-born from the dead, that in everything he might be preeminent. For in him all the fulness of God was pleased to dwell, and through him to reconcile to himself all things, whether on earth or in heaven, making peace by the blood of his cross" (Colossians 1:15-20).

Through the Holy Spirit we are led to repentance, made members of the new creation, and united with one another in Christ. This apostolic faith is continuously believed and expressed anew by the church. The faith of the united church is expressed in Scripture, Tradition, creeds, confessions, preaching, liturgies, baptism and the Lord's Supper, and in action in obedience to our Lord.

Scripture

The united church acknowledges the unique and normative authority of the Holy Scripture of the Old and New Testaments. The Scripture witnesses to God's revelation, fulfilled in Christ, and to man's response to that revelation. It proclaims the Gospel which is the power of God for salvation. It testifies to God's mighty acts of creation and re-creation, his judgment on our sinfulness and his never-failing mercy; it points to the glorious consummation of his Kingdom which will have no end. It is the inspired writing bearing witness to

God's acts in history by which he has called into being and sustained his people, and by which he calls all men to unite in his service and to share in his reconciliation of the world to himself. The Scripture is the supreme norm of the church's life, worship, witness, teaching, and mission. It is the fundamental guardian, since it is the source of new life and light as the Holy Spirit illuminates and makes Scripture alive and fruitful in the church.

Jesus Christ, crucified and risen, the living Lord and head of the church, is the center of Holy Scripture. In him the promises of God are fulfilled; to him the apostolic writings bear witness. Christ summons the church to that continuing reformation it always needs because it is on earth a community of sinful people.

Tradition

The united church recognizes that there is a historic Christian Tradition. Each of the uniting churches inevitably appeals to that Tradition in matters of faith and practice. By Tradition (with a capital "T"), we understand the whole life of the church insofar as it is guided and nourished by the Holy Spirit. This uniting Tradition is expressed in its teaching, worship, witness, sacraments, way of life, and its order. Tradition includes both the act of delivery by which the good news is made known and transmitted from one generation to another, and the teaching and practice handed on. Living Tradition is a continually flexible reality . . .

Creeds

The united church accepts the Apostles' and Nicene Creeds as witnesses of Tradition to the might acts of God recorded in Scripture. They are classic expressions of the Chirstian faith. The Apostles' Creed developed as a short summary of the Church's teaching and has been used for instruction and confession of faith in baptism. The Nicene Creed developed in the context of the early councils to guard the truth of the gospel against current distortions and has often been used in the celebration of the Lord's Supper. Conditioned, as all formulations are, by the patterns of language and thought of their time, these symbols (creeds) have to a remarkable degree transcended such limitations by their continuing power to set forth the reality and mystery of the Incarnation and to lead to deeper understanding of God's reconciling work in Jesus Christ. These ancient creeds, therefore, have a wider acceptance than the more recent formulations or confessions by separated parts of the church . . .

Contemporary Affirmations

The uniting churches have from time to time expressed particular understandings of the faith in their corporate covenants and confessions. The united church agrees to the continued use of these as enrichments of its own understanding of the Gospel. It will not, however, use any of these confessions as an exclusive requirement for all, nor permit them to become a basis for divisions in the new community. As we unite, we agree to listen attentively to the truths embodied in all these confessions which are accepted by the uniting churches, and to seek renewal and revitalizing of our corporate faith through sharing these covenants in the light of Scripture and the Holy Spirit . . . .

The united church recognizes the necessity for continuous development in the understanding of truth. It will, therefore, from time to time confess and communicate its faith in contemporary language and in new forms under the authority of Scripture and with the guidance of the Holy Spirit. The same church that celebrates God's mighty acts in history is concerned to perceive his action in the world today and to be a co-worker with him. After the united church is formed and shares a common life, it may prepare affirmations of its faith. The united church will constantly remind itself of the divisive dangers in verbal confessions and intellectual formulations, and of the need to keep open and continuous the theological dialogue within which the church grasps the riches that are in Jesus Christ.

Inclusiveness

Because the united church confesses Jesus Christ as Lord and Savior, it acknowledges the Fatherhood of God and the brotherhood of man. No one can truly call him Lord without binding himself to his brother. Thus the united church will not only recall the judgments of God upon the sins and evils of the past, but will address itself to contemporary wrongs which alienate man from himself, from his brother, from creation, and from God.

To be faithful to the Lord the united church takes its stand against all forms of prejudice, hatred, and discrimination based on supposed racial superiorities or purity. The united church believes that racism is the denial of the demands of the Fatherhood of God, that it negates the concept of one Lord and one humanity, that in inflicts upon the helpless poverty, ignorance, despair, and hopelessness. Congregations, individuals, or groups of Christians who exclude, exploit, or patronize any of their fellowmen, however subtly, offend God and place the profession of their faith in doubt.

The united church believes in the equality and dignity of men of every race. It accepts as rightful the concerted resistance of those for whom justice has been thwarted. Rectification of past inequities is urgently needed. Thus the united church will insist upon freedom from racial discrimination within its own life and will work for the abolition of injustice in society at large. In this effort to express love for all men and to eliminate the idolatry of race, the educational program and total witness of the church will stress continually the wholeness of the people of God, as given in the Gospel of Jesus Christ.

Worship and Action

The united church will confess its faith not only through Scripture, creeds, and confessions, but also through liturgies. These not only define faith but demand action. The united church will confess its faith through pastoral, prophetic, and reconciling acts toward persons and toward power structures of the world. It will seek to assess the needs of the world and involve itself in the issues of economics, politics, international relations, and culture. Accepting the cost in Christ's name and example, the united church will seek to translate its faith into action as it gives itself in suffering love for the world. The people of God will express their faith through concerned witness and action, particularly as they explore and risk new approaches in their areas of daily responsibility and special competence. Only in such translation of faith into deeds will the church participate in the suffering and glory of the crucified and risen Lord.

The Sun And
The Umbrella

Nels F. S. Ferré

A temptation of theologians is to equate complexity with profundity. Of course, many other people fall into the same temptation. It would seem that the construction of abstractions holds peculiar fascination for all kinds of theorists.

Sometimes a specialized vocabulary is necesseary, and we should not expect life's highest riddles to be translated into conversational chitchat. The theologian's problem is not just convoluted language but the possibility that divine truth may actually be obscured through human ambiguity. Whenever that happens, protest and reform in the name of common sense are in order. Protestantism was itself such a protest in the sixteenth century, and its reform was undertaken to simplify what had become too complex.

One way to communicate simple truth is to tell a story. The parables of Jesus are classic religious examples. The narrative format, as in the prodigal son or the good samaritan, appeals to everyone, even if different interpretations emerge. If the light of

God's sunshine is clouded by those of us who go around hiding under our umbrellas, then we need to be jolted out of our timidity. Perhaps all we really need is to walk out into the sunshine which is there waiting for us.

This at least is the daring suggestion of Nels F. S. Ferré in his little parable, "The Sun and the Umbrella." Originally used as a preface to a series of lectures on college and seminary campuses, the parable was later published as a book under the same title (1953). The author was for many years professor of Christian theology at the Andover Newton Theological School. He also taught at Vanderbilt University and was a regular speaker to college students and ministerial groups.

Once upon a time there were some people who lived under an Umbrella. The amusing thing about them was that they called themselves *sunworshipers*. They had not always lived there. Their former domicile was the House of Legality. This was an old barn, very wide but of low ceiling, and with no windows in it. The Lamps of the Law kept the people busy lighting them, for they smoked and went out easily. Therefore the light in the old bar was very dim. And so the people sighed, waiting for new and brighter Light to appear, but while century after century went by the people went to their graves in disappointment.

Then one day came a prophet with a new light on his face. He told them there was bright sunshine outside. All they needed to do to test his truth was to step out and see for themselves. But they feared to do so. He said: "I come from the Light; I know the Light. I am of the Light. Trust me. Follow me into the Light." Many listened. Many marveled. But as he kept pleading with them to leave the dark barn for the light of the Sun, they became angry and hated him. They said he spoke ill of their great dwelling place, reared at untold expense by their former prophets and forefathers. After all, how could anyone now living know more about the Light than did the wisest scholars and noblest prophets of old? The more they thought on this obvious truth, the more they resented his claim. Finally they decided to kill this impostor, who, after all, would only lead their young ones away from the Light secured for them at so great cost. And they killed him.

But some among them had trusted the young prophet and some had even ventured out into the sunshine with him to find it real. They had not gone very far, to be sure, because the bright sunshine had hurt their eyes, unused to it as they were. They had kept themselves mostly inside the House of Legality. When the prophet was dead, however, they could not deny that there actually was sunshine outside and that the sunshine was a stronger Light than even that of the Lamps of the Law. As they then studied the writings about the Light to come which were written by their own prophets, they became convinced that the young prophet was the bringer of that Light and they worshiped him as their Lord and Leader. He had delivered them from darkness and made a way for them into the Light. Yet they could now neither be happy inside the House nor dared they yet to out into the strong Sun. Therefore they built themselves an Umbrella, large and strong, under which they all walked out into the Sun. Inside the Umbrella they wrote: "We are the *Sunworshipers*. We believe in him who said that we ought to leave the House of Legality to live in the Sun. All who want to live in the Sun must now come under our Umbrella. Leave the dark House of Legality, even with its Lamps of the Law, and dare to venture out into the Sun under our Umbrella." And many did.

Soon, however, wise men among them said: "We may shortly forget what our Prophet told us about the Sun and how to live in its light. He alone comes from the Sunshine and knows about it. Let us therefore now make for ourselves writings which shall preserve for us and for our children the truths about the Sun." Thereupon they built themselves another Umbrella under the Large One, inside which they recorded the holy testimony of those who themselves knew the Prophet who alone knew the Sun. The holy words recorded, as carefully as possible, what the first followers into the Sun knew about the Prophet, what He had told them about the Sun, and how all who followed Him should live unafraid in its light.

But even their wisest men disputed among themselves concerning what the words which were written inside the new Umbrella meant and who had the right to interpret them, whereupon they set about gradually to construct a third Umbrella, inside the second, which they called the Church. On the under side of this new Umbrella they wrote: "Gather here all who want to accept the Prophet who came from the Sun and taught us to live in the Sun. We are the true *Sunworshipers*. Outside this Umbrella no one can be sure of the Sun, nor that it truly lights, warms and heals us. We know only Him and what the writings tell of Him as these are authoritatively interpreted for us by those under this Umbrella called the Church. Come under this Umbrella all ye who want to live in the light of the Sun. We are the true *Sunworshipers*."

Nevertheless fear arose. Some did not trust even the teachings of the savants under the Church. Even the large Umbrella plus both the others could not make them feel secure about the Sun. They said: "Let us now interpret the writings for ourselves to arrive at the original words of our Lord and Leader. Let us accept Him only and what He did for us and taught us." Some of these made themselves smaller Umbrellas inside which they wrote formulas, called creeds, concerning that which was really important in the original writings and kept repeating these formulas about the Prophet who came from the Sun and told them to come out to live in the light of the Sun. Others picked out this saying or that for their little Umbrellas as the most important clue to understanding and the most obedient way of accepting the Prophet and His message concerning their living in the Sun.

It happened, however, that one of their number began to wonder about the Umbrellas. He read over and over again the words of the Prophet to the effect that they should *live* in the Sun; that to honor him was to follow him into the sunshine. And so he went forth into the sunshine. At first, to be sure, the Light hurt his eyes and for a while he longed to return under the Umbrellas. As he grew used to living in the light of day, however, he grew happier and happier about it. At last he could no longer bear not to tell his friends under the Ubmrellas about his new life in the Sun. He returned with great joy to let his friends know that the Prophet was right. Not only could they leave the dark, old barn with the Lamps of the Law, but they could even leave the Umbrellas — all of them — to live in the Sunlight itself!

They looked at him with mingled feelings of hope and fear, of temptation and resistance, of near-belief and hurt. At last they cried out, however, "You dishonor our Prophet! You scorn our Umbrellas! Apart from him and apart from these we know no Sun, whether it can help us and whether we can live in its light." The young man who had himself tried the words of the Prophet and who knew for himself that in the Light was the best place to live tried to tell his friends that in order to honor the Prophet they must not merely call him their Lord and Leader but take him at his word and move out into the Sunlight. And some listened and came out, at first with pain but then with unbelievable joy; and they would not again return under the Umbrellas to find the Sun. But others preferred the way of faith in the Umbrellas and heeded not his word. Instead they went on praising the Prophet of the Sun while living under the Umbrellas. "After all," they said, "we know that we have been freed from the darkness of the House of Legality." And they went on so believing.

Those who now were in the Light, however, could not forbear to go everywhere to tell about that Light. Not only did they return to those who worshiped the Sun under the Umbrellas while averring to live fully in its Light, but they also went into the House of Legality to share their good news with the people there, and they ventured into all the earth, into Houses of strange religions, and into all Houses where in sundry fashions men tried to find and to live in the Light. As they kept telling the good news of the Light their joy increased, and the time being ready, there was a great and joyful exodus from all Umbrellas and Houses into the Light.

Whither American Protestantism?

James I. McCord

It is always easier to write about the past than to describe what is happening or what will happen in the future. As one of the well-known graffiti put it: "Today is the tomorrow we worried about yesterday." The trouble is that today and tomorrow won't stand still long enough for careful analysis. That, of course, doesn't prevent seers and sages, prophets and futurologists, from "discerning the signs of the times" (Matt. 16:1-3).

Religion has a vested interest in trying to interpret history. And Protestantism in particular has always been acutely aware of its historical roots, its current crises, and its prospects for tomorrow. Catholics have sometimes twitted Protestants that their history only began in the sixteenth century. But neither Luther nor Calvin would have agreed to that; the Reformation, they insisted, was the reformation of the church according to the models of the New Testament and the Apostolic Church. That is why the Bible and the

213

early Apostles' and Nicene Creeds were given such prominence within Protestant doctrinal systems.

Today, in America, the historic forms of Protestant faith and life have been undergoing swift and radical change. Gradually over the years, but with greatly increasing tempo in mid-twentieth century, we have moved from the simplicities of unity and conformity to an age of pluralistic multiformity which some would describe as confusion. New voices are being raised as old conventions fade away; the securities of a former age are shaken with the emergence of daring, even reckless, innovations; and, with all the radical critiques of conventional religion, we witness a searching and questing, especially among young people, for the transcendent, the ineffable, the mysterious, and the all-encompassing.

In this expansive commentary on the "whither" of Protestantism, we can catch the nuances of the contemporary agony. What are the challenges to Protestantism and how will they be faced?

A revised and updated version of an editorial that appeared originally in the religious quarterly, *Theology Today* (October, 1967), this present analysis serves to introduce the series of items included in Part IV, "Current Problems and Issues." James I. McCord, president of Princeton Theological Seminary and professor of theology, has had a wide, ecumenical association with all branches of Christendom. For many years he has served in executive roles with the World Alliance of Reformed Churches; with conversations among Reformed, Lutheran, and Catholic leaders; with the World Council of Churches; and with theological exchanges between Eastern and Western churches. Standing firmly on Protestant turf, he surveys the religious landscape. This is the stance required for today if Protestantism is to have a tomorrow.

The church, like all institutions today, is caught up in a global revolution that has many dimensions and that will transform the existence of the majority of mankind. Structurally and theologically Protestantism is ill-equipped for mission and ministry in such an age. It has had nothing like the Second Vatican Council to help it confront the possibilities inherent in this new situation. The flood of renewal literature which it has produced has been for the most part barren, bereft of new ideas, and repetitive. It seems caught in a tension between the need of new forms of ministry to meet new conditions and a stubborn desire to hang on to old forms that are familiar and comfortable.

Moreover, there are signs that Protestantism is guilt ridden by its economic affluence. The new polarities, between North and South, white and nonwhite, rich nations and poor nations, all point to the necessity for radical change in order to deal with these . . . dislocations and inequities, but no clear alternatives present themselves. Protestantism has always regarded the gospel as culture-transforming, but now it finds itself accused at the same time of acculturation and irrelevance. Identified with the West, caught in the vise of global unrest, burdened with its institutions and riches, it talks endlessly of mission, while the word has been steadily drained of meaning, and openly wonders what will make a difference during the last third of this century.

In American Protestantism this situation has produced a crisis that is reflected in at least five dimensions. The word "crisis" has been deliberately selected, for in each dimension change is indicated and with it the possibility of new and more authentic responses to the gospel. But such change will require more than a mere reshuffling of parts within the context of given structures. In each circumstance something qualitatively new is demanded, a response that will involve a fresh apprehension of the center of the faith and a commensurate witness and style. On this basis it can be argued that, just as a new world is coming into being, a new and transformed Protestantism can emerge from the present crisis, one that will no longer be paralyzed by the cultural situation but that will be a responsible partner in the new emergent. It is in this sense that the spirit of Protestantism is revived from age to age, as the Reformation principle is grasped and becomes operative in the life of the church. Such a position, of course, is based on the theological nature of the church and takes seriously the promise of Christ, "Upon this rock I will build my church; and the gates of hell shall not prevail against it."

An implication of this promise is that the church is renewable from above, that the Spirit of God, like a rushing mighty wind, can blow through it and re-make it into a revolutionary movement.

The *first dimension* of today's crisis is that of place, the place of Protestantism in American culture and, beyond this, in a world where the old balance is being rapidly revised. Just as it is possible to maintain that a Protestant ethos was reflected in American life from the earliest days of colonization along the Atlantic, with the New England village the symbol of this society, so today it seems equally clear that this ethos is in the process of being disestablished and disavowed. If by ethos we understand "the character, sentiment, or disposition of a community of people," then we are reflecting on a tradition that has lost its power to motivate and inspire, to capture the imagination and loyalty of a given communal entity. This is a condition that has been brought about not simply by the presence of Catholic, Jew, and humanist in the American scene, or by the changed and diminished sensibilities of a people saturated with the values of a secularized society, but it involves the conscious rejection of a mode of life long identified with Protestantism.

It has been said that in previous generations the old Protestant theological system was largely abandoned, but that only in this generation has there been a repudiation of Protestant morality. While this is a generalization too glib to be defended, it does point to a significant characteristic of the contemporary scene. The narrowness and negativism, the oppressive moralism long associated with one type of religious behavior, are now being increasingly rejected as a human style of life and are recognized as the products of a limited and parochial culture and a desiccated view of life and of creation. James Baldwin in one of his essays describes this way of life, the context in which he himself grew up, as having "the air of an endless winter," and it is this wintry style that is being cast aside. To dismiss it as bourgeois is not enough. It is a religious phenomenon that has missed completely the rich and full potential of a humanity created by God and set on this good earth to share in the divine purpose.

Alternative responses to the loss of place or position, to cultural disestablishment at home and abroad, are always possible. One is to assume a ghetto stance and to wait for the storm to blow itself out. This, of course, is essentially defeatist and world-denying. Another is to accept the new conditions as evidence of God's judgment and mercy, to give up all claims to triumphalism, and to re-enter today's world purged and purified to perform a new role. Signs that the church is willing to do this constitute the greatest human reason for hope in our time. The role of the servant has become one of its most gripping symbols, informing the nature of its mission. Dialogue is becoming a reality as Christians are entering into the new age, eager to listen and to struggle alongside neighbors in order to learn the questions which haunt and goad us in our quest for maturity and meaning. And the sheltered morality of a narrow and bucolic culture is being replaced by a new freedom of persons who have experienced the reality of justification by faith and who have learned what it means to be established in the context of grace.

But it is precisely here, in the area of theology, that the *second dimension* of the current crisis appears. Protestantism has always taken its theological responsibility seriously. Its close association with the university since the inception of the Reformation movement has enabled it to be influenced by and to influence the major currents of thought. Today, however, we are at the end of a theological era, with the old theological systems a shambles. The generation of the theological giants, the "modern church fathers," has closed, and the dominant position of this generation is now under attack.

Perhaps the most telling judgment comes in the charge that an overemphasis on the second article of the Apostles' Creed has produced a theology which is parochial — that has cut off dialogue with the world of culture, science, and philosophy, as also with the great world religions — just at the time when we have been drawn into a single history and western culture is undergoing a massive cultural revolution.

One result of this theological shift is a deliberate return to the nineteenth century and a fresh attempt to understand its theological writings. This is an effort to lay hold of the problems which were central when theology was in dialogue with the world, when the frontiers of human inquiry and discovery were essential posts to be manned in order to ascertain the spiritual nature of the age. This does not mean that the criticisms of this period have been forgotten or that the gains registered by the past generations have been ignored. It does mean, though, that there is a feeling of solidarity with the theology tradition that was willing to engage the world and to deal with the issues it considered significant.

Today's theological task is one of reconstruction on a much wider foundation. Protestants will accomplish it no longer in isolation but in cooperation with their Roman Catholic colleagues, and it is evident that it will include dimensions that were squeezed out during the age of ideology, when historical circumstance forced the church into withdrawal and introversion. Already the work of reconstruction is under way, in the new biblical studies which reveal the rich variety of New Testament thought, in the various theologies of creation that are widening the old categories of redemption, and in the remarkable new energy that is being brought to the study of world religions.

This new movement in theology and the radical new demands for political, social, and economic injustices to be rectified have produced the *third dimension* of the crisis, that of role. American Protestantism's role up to the present has been strikingly simple. It has had evangelism at its center and has followed migrations of its people in their transcontinental trek, converting and reviving them and through programs of church extension providing places of worship wherever their travels have taken them, even in their last migration from the city. While there have been notable exceptions to this pattern in every period of the church's life, the general emphasis has always been highly individualistic. The role of the church has been to convert individuals. Relations, structures, powers, society, all these belong to another realm.

There is a large segment of American Protestantism that is still dominated by this point of view, and it is not limited to fundamentalist or spiritualist bodies. It cuts across virtually every major communion, with neither Catholic nor Quaker exempt. On the other hand, this is the position that has been rejected by the vast majority of responsible church leaders because of the narrowness of its concern, its ahistorical and unbiblical character, and its aloofness from the great overarching issues threatening us today. The future, they argue, will be determined by whether peace can be established, the races can live together harmoniously, population can be controlled, and economic justice can be achieved. The church, in an attempt to accomplish these goals, has taken a New Testament theme that scholars tell us is central to understanding the work of Christ, namely, reconciliation, as descriptive of its mission today. Long criticized for irrelevance, it is now involved as an agent of reconciliation in areas of tension and strife. Evangelism is redefined in terms of community action or even by a new theological reference which points to what is going on in history as evidence that God is involved in creating a new balance through the current revolutionary movements.

These two groups with their differing emphases have begun to polarize, as nearly every pastor knows. The former tends to accuse the other of neglecting the gospel, of becoming involved in politics, and of substituting practical programs of social reform for conversion, while the latter retorts by describing the first as attempting to limit or even to deny the Lordship of the Lord and to forget that the God of the Bible is the God of politics.

Surely it is at this very point, where the church's conception of the gospel and faithfulness in mission are at stake, that a fresh apprehension of the fullness of the faith is required. To perpetuate a false dualism of spirit and world, of sacred and profane, or of "two kingdoms," in the face of the pressing needs of this generation is indefensible. But it is equally fallacious to attempt to transform the Christian mission into a mere programmatic agency, thus eliminating the whole dimension of the prophetic and transcendent, of judgment and grace, of ultimate concern and ultimate meaning.

American Protestantism's *fourth* confusion is most obvious in its *crisis of identity*, a confusion that is shared by Protestant bodies throughout the world. Creation of and participation in the ecumenical movement have not resolved this situation; rather, it has been recognized that the denominational pattern is an inadequate response to the ecumenical imperative and that it is hardly an accurate reflection of religious differences in this country. Any major denomination is as variegated and heterogeneous as the Democratic Party. As denominational loyalties have diminished, the percentage of church members who cross and recross communal lines has grown in proportion to the growth of the independent voters.

The denominational response in early America was an inevitable by-product of a cultural situation that had been produced by waves of immigrants from different ethnic backgrounds and different religious traditions. From the first decade of this century an effort to temper denominationalism has been made through the conciliar movement. It has emphasized practical unity and has produced at best cooperative Christianity. While acknowledging the contributions of this movement, the establishment of councils at every level from local to world, joint action on many fronts, a common forum for discussion and better understanding, and success in drawing churches out of isolation and into dialogue with each other, it is clear by this date that the churches will not assign to the councils more than minimal ecclesiological significance and no ecclesiastical character or power. To put it candidly, the historic Protestant churches have resolved to remain the centers of power, a resolution that has been implemented by retaining for themselves resources and personnel as well as their own discipline.

Accentuating and underscoring the other dimensions of Protestantism's crisis is another, the *fifth*, that it shares with all other institutions today. This is the chasm between generations. It is a truism that this student generation is separated from its parents by perhaps the widest span in history. For those seeking comfort it should be noted that the oncoming generation will be separated from the next by an even wider cultural abyss, so accelerated is the pace of technological achievement. Further comfort may also come from numerous reports emanating from Russia that the youth there have taken to religion as their form of protest against the older generation.

It is difficult to generalize about any generation beyond conceding that it is immensely complex and usually misunderstood, noting perhaps that the father-son relationship is the essence of many of literature's great tragedies. Nonetheless, any survey of the new Protestant generation, including those who are enrolled in theological schools, will suggest certain common characteristics.

The first is a strong idealism and an urgent quest for spiritual values. It is generally recognized that the motivation of the counterculture is primarily religious. Spiritual movements have sprung up all around us, and, while some are bizarre and exotic, they bear witness to an eternal religious impulse. Augustine's prayer remains a constant reminder of this dimension of human nature: "Thou has made us for Thyself, and restless is our heart until it comes to rest in Thee."

The youth generation of the 1970s is less prone to accept the idea of a *post*-Christian age, or even of an *ex*-Christian era. Modern scholars have shown the limitations of the old concept of Christendom and its parochialism, and there is a fresh awareness that much of the world remains *pre*-Christian.

In many nations today, the church is experiencing remarkable growth, notably in Korea, Indonesia, and East Africa. In the secular societies of eastern, socialist Europe, the church is far from extinct. Congregational life there remains strong, and the witness of the church has been purified and strengthened. Evidence of vitality in the life of the church in the Third World, and the Second World, has not been lost on the youth of the First World.

Perhaps the future of the church, whether Protestant or Catholic, has, from a human standpoint, always stood under the sign of a question mark. But there are indications that the question will be answered in the affirmative. Robert Bellah and Andrew Greeley, both sociologists of religion, contend that today is as much an age of faith as we have ever known.

Anyone associated with this younger generation of seminarians has experienced a fresh wind blowing through the church that is undoubtedly the movement of the Spirit. Its effect can be seen in renewed lives, awakened communities, and in certain trends that are easily discernible. Among these new impulses are the recovery of transcendence; the reestablished centrality of worship; the discovery of a Christ who is more human and, therefore, more divine; and a new evangelism that seeks to change persons, relations, and structures, and to minister to the whole of life.

It would be a mistake to interpret this turn of events as a "back to God and Adam Smith" movement. The lessons learned in the crisis of the 1960s must not be lost by a new generation. The Church cannot return to a life of introversion and introspection. In returning to the center, the Church will find a mandate to follow the living Christ into the world, with new authority and new credibility.

From The Mountaintop

Martin Luther King, Jr.

It could be that Martin Luther King, Jr., will be remembered primarily as a Protestant preacher. No one could equal him in eloquence, and to reread his speeches, or listen again to the tapes of his public addresses, is to realize the unique power of his rhythmic refrains and his oratorical cadences. History will record his dreams and achievements in the early and continuing struggle for civil rights and social justice. But Martin Luther King, Jr., was also an ordained Baptist minsiter, a devout and committed Christian, and a persistent gadfly among the churches and the clergy. He often noted that his concern for black justice was based on his Christian convictions, rooted in the biblical tradition.

Martin Luther King, Jr., was a graduate in theological studies and a pastor. He was better known as the initiator and leading spirit of the civil rights movement of the 1960s. President of the Southern Christian Leadership Conference and of the Montgomery Improvement Association, he was also the author of several books and the recipient, in 1964, of the Nobel Peace Prize. Always in the forefront of the emerging black protest, he consistently advocated a nonviolent strategy.

The day before he was assassinated, April 4, 1968, he gave an informal talk at the Mason Temple in Memphis, Tennessee, entitled, "A View from the Mountaintop." This text is adapted from a report in *Renewal,* (April 1969).

In Memphis to support striking sanitation workers, this was his final word to America. The next day, just a week before Good Friday, he was shot and his voice silenced. Silenced? His truth goes marching on; and, like Moses on the mountaintop, he saw not only for himself for but anyone who could recognize the signs, the promised land stretching out beyond.

If I were standing at the beginning of time with the pulse of energy ticking, with a panoramic view of the whole of human history up to now, and the Almighty said to me, "Martin Luther King, which age would you like to live in?" I would take a mental flight to Egypt, and I would watch God's children on their magnificent trek from the dark dungeons of Egypt, across the Red Sea, through the wilderness, on toward the Promised Land. But in spite of its magnificence, I wouldn't stop there.

I would move on to Greece and take my mind up to Mount Olympus. I would see Plato, Aristotle, Socrates, Euripides, and Aristophenes assembled around the Parthenon. And I would watch them as they discussed the great and eternal issues of reality. But I wouldn't stop there.

I would go on to the great heyday of the Roman Empire. And I would see what developed through the various emperors and leaders. But I wouldn't stop there.

I would come up to the day of the Renaissance and get a good picture of the cultural and aesthetic life of those times. But I wouldn't stop there.

I would go by the place where the man for whom I'm named had his home, and I would watch Martin Luther as he tacked his Ninety-five Theses on the church door in Wittenberg. But I wouldn't stop there.

I would come up to 1863 and watch a vacillating president by the name of Abraham Lincoln finally come to the conclusion that he had to sign an Emancipation Proclamation. But I wouldn't stop there.

I would come up to the 1930s and see a man grappling with the problems of a bankrupt nation, announcing in an eloquent cry that we have "nothing to fear but fear itself." But I wouldn't stop there.

Strangely enough, I would turn to the Almightly and say, "If you allow me to live just a few years in the second half of the twentieth century, I will be happy." Now that's a strange statement to make because the world is all messed up, the nation is sick, trouble is in the land, confusion all around . . . that's a strange statement. But I know somehow that only when it is dark enough can you see the stars. And I see God working in this period of the twentieth century in a way that men in some strange way are responding to. Something is happening in our world. The masses of people are rising up — whether they are in Johannesburg, South Africa; Nairobi, Kenya; Ghana; New York City; Atlanta, Georgia; Jackson, Mississippi; or Memphis, Tennessee — the cry is always the same "we want to be free."

I'm happy to live in this period in which we're going to have to grapple with the problems that men have been trying to grapple with through history. Survival demands that we grapple with them. Men for years now have been talking about war and peace. But now, no longer can they just talk about it. It is no longer a choice between violence and nonviolence in this world. It's nonviolence or nonexistence. That is where we are today.

Now, I'm just happy that God has allowed me to live in this period, to see what is unfolding. And I'm happy that he's allowed me to be in Memphis. I can remember when Negroes were just going around, as Ralph (Abernathy) has said so often, "scratchin' heavy to the ditch and laughin' when they were not tearful." But that day is all over. We mean business now and we are determined to gain our rightful place in God's world.

That's what this whole thing's all about; we aren't engaged in any negative protest and in any negative arguments with anybody. We are saying that we are determined to be men, we are determined to be people. We are saying that we are God's children, and if we are God's children, we are going to have to live like we are supposed to live. Now what does all this mean in this great period of history? It means that we've got to stay together and maintain unity.

You know, whenever Pharaoh wanted to prolong the period of slavery in Egypt, he had a favorite formula for doing it. What was that? He kept the slaves fighting among themselves. But whenever the slaves get together, something happens in Pharaoh's court, and he cannot hold the slaves in slavery; when the slaves get together, that's the beginning of the end of slavery. Now let's maintain *our* unity.

We've got to go on in Memphis just like that. I call upon you to be with us when we go out Monday. We'll have an injunction but we'll go on into court tomorrow morning to fight this illegal, unconstitutional injunction. All we'll say to "massa" is "be true to what you said on paper." If I live in China, or even Russia, or in any totalitarian country, maybe I could understand some of these illegal injunctions. Maybe I could understand the denial of certain basic First Amendment privileges. But somewhere I read of the freedom of assembly; somehwere I read of the freedom of speech; somewhere I read of the freedom of press; somewhere I read that the greatness of America is the right to protest for right.

What is beautiful to me is to see all these ministers of the gospel here tonight. And I want you to thank them. Because so often preachers aren't concerned about anything but themselves. And I'm always happy to see a relevant minister. It's all right to talk about long white robes over yonder in all of its symbolism. But all too many people need some suits and dresses and shoes to wear down here. It's all right to talk about streets flowing with milk and honey. But God has commanded us to be concerned about the slums down here and the children who can't eat three square meals a day. It's all right to talk about the New Jerusalem, but one day God's creatures must talk about the new New York, the new Atlanta, the new Philadelphia, the new Los Angeles, the new Memphis, Tennessee.

This is what we have to do. Always anchor our eternal direction with the power of economic control. Now we're poor people. Individually we're poor, when you compare us with white society in America. We're poor. But collectively, that means all of us together, collectively we are richer than most of the nations in the world. Did you ever think about that?

After the United States, Soviet Russia, Great Britain, West Germany, France, I could name others, the American Negro collectively is richer than most nations in the world. We have an annual income of more than 30 billion dollars a year, which is more than all of exports of the United States and more than the national budget of Canada. Did you know that?

That's power right there if we know how to pool it. We don't have to argue with anybody. We don't need any bricks and bottles; we don't need any molotov cocktails. We just need to go around to these stores and massive industries in our country and say, "God sent us by here, to say to you that you're not treating his children right. And we come by here to ask you to make the first item on your agenda fair treatment where God's children are concerned. Now if you are not prepared to do that, we do have an agenda that we must follow. And our agenda calls for withdrawing, economic support from you." Up to now, only the garbage men have been feeling pain. Now we must kind of redistribute the pain.

Now let me say as I move to my conclusion, that we've got to give ourselves to this struggle until the end. Nothing will be more tragic than to stop at this point in Memphis. We've got to see it through. When we go on our march, you need to be there. If it means leaving work, if it means leaving school, be there! Be concerned about your brother. You may not be on strike, but either we go up together or we go down together.

I remember when Mrs. King and I were first in Jerusalem. We rented a car to go from Jerusalem down to Jericho. And as soon as we got on that road, I said to my wife, "I can see why Jesus used this as the setting for the parable of the good samaritan." It's a winding, meandering road. It's really conducive for ambushing. You start out in Jerusalem which is about 1200 feet above sea level. And by the time you get down to Jericho, 15 or 20 minutes later, you're about 2200 feet below sea level. That's a dangerous road. In the days of Jesus it came to be known as the Bloody Pass.

And you know it's possible that the priest and the Levite looked over that man on the ground and wondered if the robbers were still around. It's possible that they felt the man on the ground was merely faking — acting like he had been robbed and beaten in order to lure them there for quick and easy seizure. And so the first question that the priest asked, the first question that the Levite asked was, "If I stop to help this man, what will happen to me?" But then the good samaritan came by. And he reversed the question. "If I do not stop to help this man, what will happen to him?" That's the question before you tonight. Not if I stop to help the sanitation workers what will happen to my job; not if I stop to help the sanitation workers what will happen to all of the hours that I usually spend in my office every day of every week as a pastor. The question is not if I stop to help this man in need, what will hapen to me. The question is, if I do not stop to help the sanitation workers, what will happen to them. That's the question.

Let us rise up tonight with a greater readiness. Let us stand with a greater determination. And let us move on, in these powerful days, these days of challenge, to make America what it ought to be. We have an opportunity to make America a better nation. And I want to praise God once more for allowing me to be here with you.

You know, several years ago I was in New York City, autographing the first book that I had written. While sitting, autographing books, a demented woman came up. The only question I heard from her was. "Are you Martin Luther King?" And I was looking down writing. I said "yes." The next minute I felt something beating on my chest. Before I knew it, I had been stabbed by this demented woman. I was rushed to Harlem Hospital. It was a dark Saturday afternoon. X-rays revealed that the tip of the blade was on the edge of my aorta, the main artery. And once that's punctured, you drown in your own blood. That's the end of you. It came out in the *New York Times* the next morning that if I would have sneezed, I would have died.

Well, about four days later, they allowed me to read some of the mail that came in from all over the States and the world. Kind letters came in. I read a few, but one of them I will never forget. I had received one from the president and the vice president: I've forgotten what those telegrams said. I had received a visit and a letter from the governor of New York, but I've forgotten what that letter said. But there was another letter. It came from a young girl. I looked at that letter, and I'll never forget it. It said simply: "Dear Dr. King, I am a 9th grade student at the White Plains High School." She said, "While it should not matter I'd like to mention that I'm a white girl. I read in the paper of your misfortune and of your suffering. And I read that if you had sneezed, you would have died. I'm simply writing you to say that I'm so happy that you didn't sneeze."

And I want to say tonight that I, too, am happy that I didn't sneeze. Because if I had sneezed, I wouldn't have been around here till 1960 when students all over the South started sitting-in at lunch counters. And I knew that if they were sitting-in, they were really standing up for the best in the American dream, and taking the whole nation back to those great wells of democracy which were dug deep by the Founding Fathers in the Declaration of Independence and the Constitution. If I had sneezed, I wouldn't have been down here in 1961 when we decided to take a ride for freedom and ended segregation in interstate travel. If I had sneezed, I wouldn't have been around here in 1962 when Negroes in

Albany, Georgia, decided to straighten their backs up. And whenever men and women straighten their backs up, they are going somewhere; because a man can't ride your back unless it is bent. If I had sneezed I wouldn't have been here in 1963; black people down in Birmingham, Alabama aroused the conscience of this nation and brought into being the Civil Rights bill. If I had sneezed, I wouldn't have had a chance later that year to try to tell America about a tune that I had heard. If I had sneezed, I wouldn't have been down in Selma, Alabama to start a movement there. If I had sneezed, I wouldn't have been in Memphis to see a community rally around those brothers and sisters who were suffering. I'm so happy that I didn't sneeze.

It really doesn't matter what happens now. I left Atlanta this mroning, and as we got started on the plane, there was trouble. The pilot said, over the public address system, "We're sorry for the delay. But we have Dr. Martin Luther King on the plane and to be sure that all of the bags were checked and to be sure that nothing would be wrong on the plane, we had to check out everything carefully and we've had the plane protected and guarded all night." Then I got into Memphis and some began to talk of threats or talk about the threats that were out, and what would happen to me from some of our sick white brothers.

Well, I don't know what will happen now. We've got some difficult days ahead, but it really doesn't matter with me now because I've been to the mountaintop. And I don't mind. Like anybody, I would like to live a long life. Longevity has its place. But I'm not concerned about that now. I just want to do God's will. And He has allowed me to go up to the mountain. And I've looked over, and I've seen the promised land. I may not get there with you, but I want you to know tongiht that we as a people will get to the promised land. So I'm happy tonight. I'm not worried about anything. I'm not fearing any man. Mine eyes have seen the glory of the coming of the Lord.

The Story Context Of
Black Theology

James H. Cone

While many, in and out of the civil rights movement, bypassed the nonviolent strategy, others were quietly but deliberately putting together new forms and credos of black self-consciousness. "Burn, Baby, Burn," "Black Power," "Black Is Beautiful" — these and other marching slogans inspired, for a time, and brought fear and apprehension to others. Often the churches were in the midst of the emerging black awareness, as when James Forman unexpectedly confronted the congregation of the Riverside Church in New York, May 4, 1969, with a "Black Manifesto," demanding five hundred million dollars in "reparations" from the white churches.

With less spectacular attention, but possibly with more durable effect, some black church leaders were beginning to "do" theology in a new way. One of the most articulate of these was James H. Cone, professor of theology at New York's Union Theological Seminary. Mainly through his books, *Black Theology and Black Power* (1969), *A Black Theology of Liberation* (1970), *The Spirituals and the Blues* (1972), and *God of the Oppressed* (1975), Dr. Cone was widely acclaimed as a responsible and aggressive spokesman for the new trend.

Combining critical appreciation for the old religious overtones of the spirituals with fresh approaches to current problems, the new Black theology of thinkers such as James Cone emerged as a powerful and creative alternative to traditional ways of doing theology.

This essay is a shortened version of an address, "The Social Context of Theology," presented by Dr. Cone to the 1974 meeting of the American Theological Society. The full text appears in *God of the Oppressed* (1975).

Because Christian theology is human speech about God, it is always related to historical situations, and thus all of its assertions are culturally limited. Although God, the subject of theology, is eternal, theology itself is — like those who articulate it — limited by history and time. It is not universal language; it is interested language, always reflecting the values and aspirations of a particular people in a particular time and place. In North America it is evident that white theology was formed in accordance with the needs of a people dependent upon the slave labor of blacks. Therefore, despite certain variations, theological issues have been shaped in such a way that slavery and other structures of oppression could either be justified or else omitted altogether from the realm of moral discourse.

Like white American theology, black thought on Christianity has been influenced by its social context. But unlike white theologians, who spoke to and for the culture of the ruling class, black people's religious ideas were shaped by the cultural and political existence of the victims in North America. Unlike Europeans who immigrated to this land to escape from tyranny, Africans came in chains to serve a nation of tyrants. It was the slave experience that shaped our idea of this land. And this difference in social existence between Europeans and Africans must be recognized if we are to understand correctly the contrast in the form and content of black and white theology.

The form of black religious thought is expressed in the style of story, and its content is liberation. Black theology is the story of black people's struggle for liberation in an extreme situation of oppression. Consequently, there is no sharp distinction between thought and practice, worship and theology, because black theological reflections about God occurred in the black struggle of freedom.

White theologians built logical systems; black folks told tales. Whites debated the validity of infant baptism or the issue of predestination and free will; blacks recited biblical stories about God leading the Israelites from Egyptian bondage, Joshua and the battle of Jericho, and the Hebrew children in the fiery furnace. While theologians argued about the general status of religious assertions in view of the development of science generally and Darwin's *Origin of Species* in particular; blacks were more concerned about their status in American society and its relation to the biblical claim that Jesus came to set the captives free. White thought on the Christian view of salvation was largely "spiritual" and sometimes "rational," but usually separated from the concrete struggle of freedom in this world. Black thought was largely eschatological and never abstract but usually related to their struggle against earthly oppression.

The difference in the form of black and white religious thought is on the one hand sociological. Since blacks were slaves and had to work from sunup to nightfall, they did not have time for the art of philosophical and theological discourse. They, therefore, did not know about the systems of Augustine, Calvin, or Edwards. And if Ernst Bloch is correct in his contention that "need is the mother of thought,"[1] then it can be said that black slaves did not *need* to know about Anselm's ontological argument, Descartes' *Cogito, ergo sum*, and Kant's *Ding an sich*. Such were not their philosophical and theological problems as defined by their social reality. Blacks did not ask whether God existed or whether divine existence can be rationally demonstrated. Divine existence was taken for granted, because God was the point of departure for their faith. The divine question which they addressed was whether God was with them in their struggle for liberation. Neither did blacks ask about the general status of their personal existence or that of the physical world. The brutal presence of white people did not allow that sort of philosophical skepticism to enter their consciousness. Therefore the classical philosophical debate about the priority of concepts versus things, which motivated Kant and his predecessors' reflective endeavors, did not interest black people. What was "real" was the presence of oppression and the historical need to strive against it. They perhaps intuitively perceived that the problem of the auction block and slave drivers would not be solved through philosophical debate. The problem had to be handled at the level of concrete history as that history was defined by the presence of slavemasters. Slaves, therefore, had to devise a language commensurate with their social situation. That was why they told stories. Through the medium of stories, black slaves created concrete and vivid pictures of their past and present existence, using the historical images of God's dealings with his people and thus breaking open a future for the oppressed not known to ordinary historical observation.

The difference between black and white thought is also theological. Black people did not devise various philosophical arguments for God's existence, because the God of black experience was not a metaphysical idea. He was the God of history, the liberator of the oppressed from bondage. Jesus was not an abstract Word of God, but God's Word made flesh who came to set the prisoner free. He was the "Lamb of God" that was born in Bethlehem and was slain on Golgotha's hill. He was also "the Risen Lord" and "the King of Kings." He was their Alpha and Omega, the One who had come to make the first last and the last first.

While white preachers and theologians often defined Jesus Christ as a spiritual savior, the deliverer of people from sin and guilt, black preachers were unquestioningly historical.

They viewed God as the liberator in history. That was why the black church was involved in the abolitionist movement in the nineteenth century and the Civil Rights movement in the twentieth. Black preachers reasoned that if God delivered Israel from Pharoah's army and Daniel from the lion's den, then he will deliver black people from American slavery and oppression. So the content of their thought was liberation and they communicated that message through preaching, singing and praying, telling the story of how "We shall overcome."

Consider the song about that "Old Ship of Zion" and how "she had landed many a thousand . . . and will land as many a more. O glory, Hallelu!" They say "she is loaded down with angels . . . and King Jesus is the Captain." The presence of Jesus as the Captain was black people's assurance that the ship would "carry [them] all home." The "Old Ship of Zion" was a symbol that their life had meaning despite the condition of servitude. It was their guarantee that their future was in the hands of the One who died on Calvary. That was why they proclaimed: "Glory hallelujah!" It was an affirmation of faith that black slaves would triumph over life's contradictions, because they had met the Captain of that "Old Ship of Zion" and were already on board.

At other times, the salvation story was described as "the gospel train." Blacks described this reality with eschatological and future expectation: "The gospel train is coming." And they also saw it as already realized in their present: "I hear it just at hand" and "the car wheels moving and rumbling thro' the land." One can "hear the bell and the whistle" and it's "coming round the curve." Of course, this is not a normal train, not one created by white society. This is an eschatological train, the train of salvation, and it will carry the oppressed to glory. If you miss this train, "you're left behind." That partly accounts for the urgency of the call to:

> Get on board, Children,
> Get on board, Children,
> Get on board, Children,
> There's room for many a more.

There is no excuse for not making the existential decision to "Get on board" because:

> The fare is cheap and all can go,
> The rich and the poor are there
> No second class on board the train,
> No difference in the fare.

Salvation is not only a train and a ship but also a sweet chariot, swinging low, "coming for to carry me home." It is that "Old time religion" that brought the slaves out of bondage and "good when you're in trouble." It's that "rock in a weary land" and the "shelter in the time of storm." It is the divine presence in their situation that holds their humanity together in the midst of the brokenness of black existence. It is the power to endure in struggle and the patience to remain calm when surrounded by inexplicable evil. That was why black people sang "Been down in the valley so long, and I ain't got weary yet." They did not give up in despair during slavery and subsequent oppression, because of the presence of the One who controls life and who can overcome its contradictions. This is the time of black religion, and it was expressed in concrete images derived from their social situation.

The relation between the form and the content of black thought was dialectical. The story was both the medium through which truth was communicated and also a constituent of truth itself. In the telling of a truthful story, the reality of liberation to which the story pointed was also revealed in the actual *telling* of the story itself. That was why an equal, and often greater emphasis, was placed on the storyteller.

In black churches, the one who preaches the Word is primarily a storyteller. And thus when the black church community invites a minister as pastor, their chief question is: "Can the Reverend tell the story?" This question refers both to the theme of black religion and also to the act of storytelling itself. It refers to a person's ability to recite God's historical dealings with his people from Abraham to Jesus, from St. Paul to John on the island of Patmos, and to the preacher's ability to relate these biblical stories to contemporary black stories. The past and present are joined dialectically, creating a black vision of the future.

Black churches usually do not emphasize academic degrees as a criterion for preaching, because they do not associate a learned discourse with storytelling. Indeed many blacks are suspicious of "intellectuals" in the pulpit, because they identify that term with white people. Black church people contend that one needs more than "book learning" in order to tell God's story. One needs to be *converted* to the faith and *called* to the ministry of Jesus Christ. When these two events happen, then one is ready to be used by God as the instrument of his story, of his dealings with his people.

In the black church, little emphasis is placed on the modern distinction between liberals and fundamentalists as found in white churches. Blacks show little concern about the abstract status of the Bible, whether fallible or infallible. Their concern is with Scripture as a living reality in the concreteness of their existence. Since the biblical story of God's dealings with people can be told in various ways, the chief concern of the people is not the information the preacher includes in his message but rather *how* he arranges that information into a story and how re relates it all to the daily lives of the people. The preacher may begin with Adam and Eve in the Garden of Eden or with John on the island of Patmos. The concern is not *where* he begins because the people already know the various scenes in God's drama with his people. They are concerned with how the preacher takes the bare facts of God's story and weaves them into the structure of their lives, giving his unique touch as a storyteller.

Consider the sermon "Behold the Rib!" The preacher begins by emphasizing the power of God. He is "High-riding and strong armed God" who "walk[s] across his globe creation . . . wid de blue elements for a helmet . . . and a wall of fire round his feet." "He wakes the sun every morning from its fiery bed wid de breath of his smile and commands de moon wid his eyes." Then the preacher moves to the essence of the story as suggested by his subject:

> So God put Adam into a deep sleep
> And took out a bone, ah hah!
> And it is said that it was a rib.
> Behold de rib!
> A bone out of man's side.
> He put de man to sleep and made wo-man,
> And men and women been sleeping together ever since.
> Behold de rib!
> Brothers, if God
> Had taken dat bone out of man's head
> He would have meant for women to rule, hah!
> If he had taken a bone out of his foot,
> He would have meant for us to dominize and rule,
> He could have made her out of back-bone
> And then she would have been behind us.
> But, no, God Almighty, he took de bone out of his side
> So dat places de woman beside us.
> Hah! God knowed his own mind.
> Behold de rib![2]

This sermon stresses not only the power of God but the equality of man and woman in God's creation. The rib, rather than symbolizing the woman's inferiority, actually stands for equal status, the right to be fully human. That is why the preacher placed so much emphasis on the phrase "Behold de rib!" The rib is not a "foot-bone" or a "back-bone," both of which represent inferiority. It is a "side-bone," thereby making woman equal to man.

Sometimes it was difficult to understand the exact verbal point the black preacher was making. But because the power of the story was embedded in the *act* of telling itself, it did not always matter. One could hear the message in the passion and mood which was created by the rising and falling of the voice as the preacher moved in bodily rhythm across the pulpit and in the aisle, describing rapidly the different scenes of God's salvation drama. The message was in the feeling of the Spirit that moved "from heart to heart and from breast to breast" throughout the congregation as the preacher hummed and moaned the story. The truth of the story was dependent upon whether the people received that extra strength to go one more mile in their struggle to survive and whether they received the courage to strive one more time to right the wrongs in this world. The message was the passion for affirming the truth of their lives, a truth not recognized in the white world. And this "knowledge" was received everytime the biblical story was preached as it was meant to be. That was why the people inquired of every minister: "Can the Reverend tell the story?"

The theme of liberation expressed in story form is the essence of black religion. Both the content and form were essentially determined by black people's social existence. Because black people were oppressed but not destroyed by it, they intuitively knew that servitude was a denial of their essential worth. They therefore looked for religious and secular themes in their social existence that promised release from the pain of slavery and oppression. It was not simply through an exegetical study of the Bible that blacks decided to center their preaching on the Exodus and not Paul's letter to Philemon; neither was it through exegesis that they centered their spirituals on the cross and resurrection of Jesus and not his birth in Bethlehem. In view of their social situation of oppression, black people needed liberating visions so that they would not let historical limitations determine their perception of black being. Therefore, when Christianity was taught to them and they began to read the Bible, blacks simply appropriated those biblical stories that met their historical need. That was why some themes are stressed and others are overlooked. The one theme that stood out above all other themes was *liberation,* and that was because of the social conditions of slavery. Such traditional Calvinistic problems as unconditional election and limited atonement did not occur to them. They did not debate religion on an abstract theological level but lived their religion concretely in history.

Like the theme of liberation, the *form* of black religion in story was chosen for similar sociological reasons. The easiest way for the oppressed to defy conceptual definitions that justify their existence in servitude is to tell stories about another reality where they are accepted as human beings. Story is not only easy to understand and to remember, it is often deceptive to those who stand outside the community where it was created. This is the meaning behind the black comment:

> The white man is always trying to know into some-
> body else's business. All right, I'll set something outside
> the door of my mind for him to play with and handle.
> He can read my writing but he sho' can't read my mind.
> I'll put this play toy in his hand, and he will seize it and
> go away. Then I'll say my say and sing my song.[3]

What white slave masters would have recognized that the tales of Brer Rabbit and his triumphs over the stronger animals actually expressed black slaves' conscious hopes and dreams of overcoming the slavemasters themselves? Who among the white community would have perceived that in the singing and preaching about "crossing the river Jordan and entering the New Jerusalem" that black slaves were some-times talking about Canada, Africa, and America north of the Mason Dixon line? White slave masters were no brighter than our contemporary white theologians who can only see in black religion what their axiological presuppositions permit them to see. And that vision usually extends no further than some notion of black "otherworldliness" leading to passivity. But there is something much deeper than that simplistic idea in black religion. Nat Turner's spirit is buried beneath the shouts and the cries. And that spirit will soon rise and claim the eschatological future promised in God's encounter with his community.

It is difficult to express this liberating truth in rational discourse alone; it must be told in story. And when this truth is told as it was meant to be, the oppressed are transformed, taken into another world and given a glimpse of the promised land. And when they leave the church, they often say to one another what the disciples said after having experienced the Risen Lord: "Did not our hearts burn within us while he talked to us on the road, while he opened to us the scriptures?" (Luke 24:32).

Notes

1. Ernst Bloch, *A Philosophy of the Future,* trans. J. Cumming (New York: Seabury Press, 1970), pp. 2f.

2. Cited in Langston Hughes and Arna Bontemps, *Book of Negro Folklore* (New York: Dodd, Mead & Co., Inc., 1969) p. 234.

3. Zora Neale Hurston, *Mules and Men* (New York: Perennial Library, Harper and Row, 1970), pp. 18-19.

Toward A Feminist Theology

Sheila D. Collins

The aims and goals of the women's movement should hardly require any descriptive explanation. That is not to say that every expectation has been fulfilled or that everyone now knows about, let alone rejoices in, the ideals and programs of the women's movement. It is undoubtedly true, as many women have noted, that the churches are still reluctant to move forward into a sex-inclusive age, with some denominations denying ordination to women and others relegating them to minor or subordinate roles.

As a matter of fact, the Judeo-Christian tradition and especially the Old and New Testaments appear so masculine-oriented as to preclude the possibility of anything like a religious equal rights amendment. For some women, "the tradition" is so male-dominated as to discourage any significant reformation, and they have dropped out of the churches, repudiating the "Fatherhood of God and the brotherhood of man." Others have chosen to work within the religious establishment as witnesses to the new age, much as "foreign missionaries" in the nineteenth century circled the globe to bring the gospel to the heathen.

In the early 1970s, women were beginning to find the strength of their voices, and their numbers, and in no uncertain terms they asserted their own personhood, their newly raised consciousness, their special concerns for an inclusive church, and their burgeoning theological sophistication.

An early expression of these and other trademarks of the women's movement in religious thought is the comprehensive survey by Sheila D. Collins, "Toward a Feminist Theology," which appeared first in *The Christian Century* (August 1972). In a few years, the word "feminist" would itself be rejected by most women because of its cultural fixations. But the article pinpoints the main issues and grievances of many church-related women, and it alerted many in the churches to even more radical proposals yet to come.

Sheila D. Collins is a member of the Joint Strategy and Action Committee of the National Council of Churches. She has written several articles on the women's movement in religious circles and is the author of *A Different Heaven and Earth* (1974).

What has been dismaying church women of late is the failure of male theologians even today to distinguish between the essence of the faith and some of its most blatant cultural accretions. Just as the theory of the divine right of kings served to legitimize a feudal system which kept a vast majority of the people in subjection and poverty, so the system of male-oriented symbols, doctrines and taboos in the Judeo-Christian tradition has served to keep females in subjection to men and in spiritual, if not always physical, poverty.

The women's liberation movement has awakened women theologians, seminary students and churchwomen to the need to rethink theology in radical terms. Starting with an analysis of the patriarchal society out of which Judaism and, later, Christianity developed, these women are developing new models of Christian consciousness, based on an egalitarian ethic of liberation, and are attempting to replace outmoded symbols with fresh, dynamic, more humane symbols which give meaning and vision to the experiences of all people. They are not attempting to appropriate male religious symbols for themselves, but to right an imbalance in the system which has shaped religious consciousness since the time of the patriarchs. But in order to right this imbalance they must first upset the applecart; which is to say that the feminist theologians are not reformers but revolutionaries, who attack even the theology of hope as being tied to old patriarchal symbols. . . .

The feminist theologians see in the religion of the Scriptures as it has been transmitted by the church a reflection of the male experience of the world. In both Old and New Testament times women were regarded as an inferior species to be owned like cattle, as unclean creatures incapable of participating in the mysteries of the worship of Yahweh. For whatever historical reason — perhaps out of violent reaction to the excesses of the more female-oriented Canaanite fertility cults — ancient Hebrew society was blatantly misogynist and male dominated. No wonder that in such a society God became male — "King," "Father," "Lord," "Master." "So God created man in his own image, in the image of God *he* created *him*." Or was it the other way around?

Of course, sophisticated thinkers have never identified God with an elderly male parent in heaven. We like to think we are beyond such anthropomorphism. But what happens to us when we change the words around? God created *woman* in *her* own image, in the image of God *she* created *her*. As linguist Benjamin Lee Whorf has observed: "The limits of my language are the limits of my thought." Theological language was fixed in the era of the early patriarchy and has never shaken itself loose, in spite of our changing conceptions of reality. Images, solidified in language, have a way of surviving in the imagination so that a person can function on two different and often contradictory levels. One can speak of the abstract conceptualization of God as spirit and still imagine "him" as male.

When God was identified as male, a hierarchy of values was established. Since man was made in God's image and God was male, females were excluded from participation in that image. We may express what happened in an equation: Man is to God as woman is to *not God*. Paul puts it plainly in 1 Corinthians: "For a man ought not to cover his head since he is the image and glory of God; but woman is the glory of man. For man is not made from woman, but woman from *man*." Since all that was not God was sinful, woman became identified with sin; and this identification was reinforced by the myth of Adam and Eve.

With the incorporation of Hellenistic dualism into Christian theology, a further dimension was added to the growing alienation of man from woman and of woman from God in the Christian imagination. Hellenism brought with it an identification of sin with the body. And since in Hebrew culture woman was already identified (because of childbearing and menstruation) with unclean bodily functions, it was but a natural extension to identify her with this new dimension of sin. Thus woman became the temptress, the devouring earth mother, the witch whose very existence threatened the spirituality of theocratic man. The patristic commentators on Genesis interpret the Fall as a succumbing to bodiliness, to femaleness, to sexuality. It is no historical accident that Ann Hutchinson, who dared to counsel self-determination for women in spiritual matters, was banished from the Massachusetts Bay Colony as a witch.

The effect of elevating patriarchal structures to the realm of belief was to put those beliefs in the service of the hierarchical, inegalitarian infrastructures of the society. Thus St. Paul could counsel women to be quiet in church and to obey their husbands because this was ordained by God, this was the nature of creation (Eph. 5:24; 1 Cor. 11:13). Despite his insight that we are all one in Christ Jesus, Paul was very much a man of his times.

So was Thomas Aquinas, who declared in the *Summa Theologica:* "Woman was made to be a help to man. But she was not fitted to be a help to man except in generation, because another man would prove a more effective help in anything else." The Roman church's veneration of Mary as virgin and mother can be seen as an attempt to make sense out of a theological system which had become alienated from existential reality. To reconcile the fact of and the necessity for procreation with a theology which declared that everything having to do with the body — therefore sexual/procreative activity — was unclean and evil, the church simply asserted that God incarnate was not conceived in a "natural" way and sentimentalized the role of mother so that it no longer needed to be tied to natural bodily functions.

Centuries after Aquinas, Martin Luther held to the old patriarchal view. His "priesthood of all believers" challenged the hierarchy of the Roman church, but he did nothing to reform the hierarchical relationship between men and women. Indeed he declared: "Women are on earth to bear children. If they die in child-bearing, it matters not; that is all they are here to do." Even in our own day a theologian of the stature of Karl Barth holds to the same revelatory religion which has always excluded the existential experience of women. "Women," he wrote, "are ontologically inferior to men."

As Rosemary Ruether points out, modern psychoanalysis sees such theological formulations as the result of an alienation within the human psyche, as projections onto another of the fear in one's own unconscious. Man, fearing his own sexuality, passivity and emotinality, projects them onto woman, thus doing away with the need to deal with that part of his nature. (Just so white society projected similar attributes onto the black population it held inferior.)

The results of such psychic alienation are widely visible today. Thus the Roman Catholic and Episcopal churches refuse to ordain women; the Protestant churches fail to take women's intellectual and moral gifts seriously; many congregations insist that female ministers would be sexually distracting or would lack the image the ministry needs if it is to be an effective interpreter for God. But perhaps the worst result is the internalization by many women of their own inferiority to men. This limits their life options and their potential, so that they can see themselves as baking cakes for the women's society but not as head of the board of trustees or the council on ministries.

Having torn down the symbols which have kept them oppressed, what would the feminist theologians substitute?

The first step is to go back to the roots of the faith to see what is meaningful in them once they are shorn of their cultural outgrowths. One of the most important contributions to this stage of inquiry has been the reexamination of Jesus' life in terms of his relationships with people. In the gospels Jesus appears as a man at odds with his time and culture — so much at odds that even his disciples (and much less his later followers) did not often understand what he was doing.

Leonard Swidler (a Catholic theologian) offers evidence that, flouting the social and religious mores of his time which kept women strictly cloistered and in bondage to their husbands, Jesus went out of his way to treat women (and the other pariahs of his time) as complete human beings, equal to men and capable of being spokeswomen for God. In view of the fact that the gospels must be seen through the lens of first century Christian communities which, obviously, shared the antiwoman culture then prevailing, it is all the more extraordinary that the gospels reveal no negative attitude toward women on the part of Jesus. As Dorothy Sayers has so beautifully said it: "There is no act, no sermon, no parable in the whole Gospel that borrows its pungency from female perversity; nobody could possibly guess from the words and deeds of Jesus that there was anything 'funny' about woman's nature."

Seen in this light, Jesus' life and its meaning take on new dimensions and bring us to a clearer understanding of Paul's truly prophetic passage:

> Now before faith came, we were confined under the law, kept under restraint until faith should be revealed. But now that faith has come we are no longer under a custodian; for in Christ Jesus you are all sons of God, through faith. There is neither Jew nor Greek, there is neither slave nor free, there is neither male nor female; for you are all one in Christ Jesus [Gal. 3:23-28].

Though but fleetingly, Paul saw that the Hebrew laws regarding the ordering of persons — among them laws which stipulated that women were ritually unclean, that they could not be seen or talked with in public, that in adultery they were more guilty than their male partners, and that they were the property of their husbands — were all made irrelevant by Jesus and were ignored by ·him in his relationships with people. It is a sad commentary on the history of Christian thought that scarcely a single theologian, beginning with Paul, picked up this unique aspect of Jesus ministry. . . .

Many Christians have written at length about the "new man," the "new humanity," that Christ came to bring about. Few, however, have explained what it means to be "new." Feminists see the man/woman relationship as the key to the new humanity. The alienation between man and woman, they say, is the primordial one from which all other false or unjust relationships derive. Lest any accuse us of exaggerating the man/woman thing out of all proportion, let them recall Gunnar Myrdal's discovery that when, 200 years ago, laws were needed to justify the enslavement of black Africans, the slaveholders took as their models the English laws of the time which restricted the rights of women. How can we hope to be for reconciliation with our black or poor brothers and sisters if we cannot achieve reconciliation with that other half of ourselves?

For the feminists, salvation is that discovery and celebration of the "other" in ourselves. When men discover their femininity and women their masculinity, then perhaps we can form a truly liberating and mutually enriching partnership. And then perhaps we can discover our own "blackness" and "whiteness," our own poverty and affluence, which we have so long kept hidden from ourselves. The new humanity is a humanity which is becoming, impelled by a revelation that is not located in the distant past but is only now becoming manifest in the clamor for dignity and liberation on the part of underdeveloped peoples.

Women And Liberation

Letty M. Russell

Evidence that the religious women's movement has come of age can be found in the increasing quantity and quality of books and articles being written. Especially in biblical studies and in theology an extensive bibliography could be assembled.

Much of this literature leaps across old denominational boundaries, and the insistence that religious language must be sex-inclusive (or at least not sex-exclusive) demands new ways of writing, thinking, and articulating the faith. If it is no longer permissible to talk about "God and *his* purpose for *man*kind that all *men* be *brothers*,"then the change in syntax requires a radical readjustment in conventional ways of thinking about God.

Though male chauvinists may scoff, many women are expressing their joy and exhilaration over their new sense of freedom and liberation. They identify easily with all oppressed peoples, classes, and groups — blacks, ethnic minorities and Third World nations. With a new self-consciousness and a new freedom to be themselves, they also sense their responsibility to spread the word of liberation and to rehumanize the world.

Letty Russell's book, *Human Liberation in a Feminist Perspective — A Theology* (1974), illustrates these emphases. The passages cited come from the introduction and the conclusion (which she calls "Prologue," since women's theological work has only just begun). Letty M. Russell is an ordained minister and teaches theology at Yale Divinity School. She has also worked in an ecumenical parish in East Harlem, for the World Council of Churches, and for the YWCA.

These are especially exciting and challenging times for women. Exciting, because so many new ideas, life-styles, and ways of service are opening up. Challenging, because women are often moving away from old securities along new paths where there are many questions and few answers. Every field of learning, every skill, every life-style, becomes a new arena of experiment as women seek out their own perspectives, the contribution that they would make in building a new house of freedom.

Certainly, theology is no exception to this excitement and challenge. Women are voicing their search for liberation by rejecting oppressive and sexist religious traditions that declare that they are socially, ecclesiastically, and personally inferior because of their sex. They are digging deeper into their traditions, raising questions about the authority of the church "fathers," and searching out the hidden evidence of the contributions of the church "mothers" to the life and mission of the church. They are looking for truly authentic and liberating roots as they search for a *usable past*. At the same time, women are joining other oppressed groups in seeking out a clear vision of a new society of justice and *shalom,* so that they can join the global struggle for a *usable future*.

These women are *feminists* because they advocate changes that will establish political, economic, and social equality of the sexes. In a Christian context they reflect on the way in which theology can become more complete, as all people are encouraged to contribute to the meaning of faith from their own perspective. Such action and theory form the basis of *feminist theology*. It is "feminist" because the women involved are actively engaged in advocating the equality and partnership of women and men in church and society.

It is not *feminine theology* because femininity refers to a culturally defined set of roles and personal characteristics that elaborate the biological ability of women to bear children. According to the stereotypes of Western culture, some theology is masculine and some is feminine. One theology might contain elements of aggression, assertion, and analytical thinking; another might have elements of wholistic and contextual sensitivity and a concern for interrelationships of persons and of human nurture. But, as Mary Daly has stated, all theology must be "concerned with the problems of persons in relation to others" and not with preconceived notions about the nature of women around which an isolated theology is developed. For this reason feminist theology strives to be *human* and not just *feminine,* as other forms of theology should strive to be *human* and not just *masculine*.

Feminist theology today is, by definition, *liberation theology* because it is concerned with the liberation of all people to become full participants in human society. . . .

Feminist theology has common roots with many types of, so-called, Third World liberation theologies. *Third World* is used here to refer to people living outside the United States and Western Europe *(First World),* and of the Communist bloc countries in Eastern Europe *(Second World),* and includes their descendants living in racial oppression in any country. Third World has economic as well as racial overtones pointing toward experiences of economic exploitation and colonialism. The term is presently used by groups in North America as a way of emphasizing that nonwhite groups are a majority of the world's population. They make up two-thirds of the world's population, although they are a minority among those who hold political, social, and economic power. Women belong to all these various "worlds," and as such they are numbered among the oppressed and oppressors. Yet in relation to the male domination of the social structures of most societies women have a growing consciousness of their own oppression. . . .

Like Third World liberation theology, feminist theology is written out of an experience of oppression in society. It interprets the search for salvation as a journey toward freedom, as a process of self-liberation in community with others in the light of hope in God's promise. Together with other people searching for freedom, women wish to speak of the hope that is in them. They want to tell the world that they are part of God's plan of human liberation. . . .

We have only just begun the search for human liberation in a feminist perspective. No one knows what it would be like "if they gave a revolution and everybody won." No one knows how it would be to live in a truly androgynous world where men and women were equal and each one could express his or her life-style in a variety of ways. No one knows how the oppressed peoples of the world can move together to eliminate barriers of sex, race, and class which deprive human beings of the praxis of freedom. And no one knows the variety of ways in which the renewal of the church for mission might take place. . . .

The things hoped for are not simply future events. They shape us, touch us, and hurt us *now*. Liberation theology is also rooted in *experience:* the act of trying things out by "putting our bodies on the line" (cf. Rom. 12:1). This praxis model helps us to proclaim the coming of God's liberation and blessing into the world now, and to celebrate the presence of new humanity in our midst.

Evangelical Social
Ethics

Winds of change appear to be blowing over even the evangelical movement. This conservative right-of-center consortium of "Bible-believing Christians" has had a long disinclination toward theological change of any kind. After all, if one believes that the Bible is infallible, that science is an unreliable guide, that personal conversion is more basic than social justice, that women were created subordinate, and that ecumenical programs only dilute the gospel — then there's little incentive to change things around. Apparently. But not necessarily so.

The major change in the evangelical movement has been the slow but inevitable passing of time. A whole generation of leaders, once prominent among evangelicals, is gradually fading away as a new and young generation begins to assert itself. Two illustrations: first, a widely read book by Richard A. Quebedeaux, *The Young Evangelicals* (1974), which goes beyond the old stalemate between liberals and fundamentalists over the Bible, advocating ecumenical

253

dialogue and social ethics; and second, a statement — prepared by a large group of evangelicals in Chicago on Thanksgiving 1973 — known as "A Declaration of Evangelical Social Concern." This latter, which is reprinted here, represents a distinct shift of emphasis among evangelicals. Often criticized as being long on doctrine but short on ethics, evangelicals (at least some of them) are now openly calling for a new program of social ethics based on the Bible and personal commitment to Jesus Christ. Some at the Chicago conference wanted an even stronger statement that would condemn Richard Nixon and American involvement in Vietnam. But the group as a whole settled for a statement of general principles rather than spelling out details.

Billy Graham, during his White House association, was often criticized for not speaking out against corruption in government and for remaining silent about the moral issues of the Vietnam war. His only reply was that he interpreted his mission in life to be an evangelist to bring individuals to Christ. The Chicago declaration on social ethics is a straw in the wind, showing the new direction some young evangelicals are taking.

As evangelical Christians committed to the Lord Jesus Christ and the full authority of the Word of God, we affirm that God lays total claim upon the lives of his people. We cannot, therefore, separate our lives in Christ from the situation in which God has placed us in the United States and the world.

We confess that we have not acknowledged the complete claims of God on our lives.

We acknowledge that God requires love. But we have not demonstrated the love of God to those suffering social abuses.

We acknowledge that God requires justice. But we have not proclaimed or demonstrated his justice to an unjust American society. Although the Lord calls us to defend the social and economic rights of the poor and the oppressed, we have mostly remained silent. We deplore the historic involvement of the church in America with racism and the conspicious responsibility of the evangelical community for perpetuating the personal attitudes and institutional structures that have divided the body of Christ along color lines. Further, we have failed to condemn the exploitation of racism at home and abroad by our economic system.

We affirm that God abounds in mercy and that he forgives all who repent and turn from their sins. So we call our fellow evangelical Christians to demonstrate repentance in a Christian discipleship that confronts the social and political injustice of our nation.

We must attack the materialism of our culture and the maldistribution of the nation's wealth and services. We recognize that as a nation we play a crucial role in the imbalance and injustice of international trade and development. Before God and a billion hungry neighbors, we must rethink our values regarding our present standard of living and promote more just acquisition and distribution of the world's resources.

We acknowledge our Christian responsibilities of citizenship. Therefore, we must challenge the misplaced trust of the nation in economic and military might — a proud trust that promotes a national pathology of war and violence which victimizes our neighbors at home and abroad. We must resist the temptation to make the nation and its institutions objects of near-religious loyalty.

We acknowledge that we have encouraged men to prideful domination and women to irresponsible passivity. So we call both men and women to mutual submission and active discipleship.

We proclaim no new gospel, but the gospel of our Lord Jesus Christ who, through the power of the Holy Spirit, frees people from sin so that they might praise God through works of righteousness.

By this declaration, we endorse no political ideology or party, but call our nation's leaders and people to that righteousness which exalts a nation.

We make this declaration in the biblical hope that Christ is coming to consummate the kingdom and we accept his claim on our total discipleship till he comes.

Church Growth And
Religious Meaning

Dean M. Kelley

Whether church membership statistics provide an accurate index as to the state of religious life in America is perhaps an open question. Many in the churches are there for ulterior purposes; and many Christians have nothing whatever to do with the churches. The annual volumes of the *Yearbook of American Churches,* published by the National Council of Churches, give the data on the various denominations. In the late 1960s and early 1970s some churches were going down — in membership, resources, and influence — while others were going up. The old-time, major denominations with their long history of ecumenical concern and social involvement were declining; the conservative and evangelical churches were growing by leaps and bounds.

In his interpretive report, *Why Conservative Churches Are Growing* (1972), Dean M. Kelley takes a sociological look at the whole religious situation in America. The conservative upswing among the churches coincides with a conservative trend in the country at large in almost every other area — politics, education, business, civil rights, ecology, and the law.

But there is another factor involved. Religion, in whatever form, appears to serve the purpose of giving a meaningful structure to people's lives. If they cannot find a meaning for living in one church, or even in one religion, they will turn to another. It is at this level that the interest of many today, especially among young people, in all kinds of Eastern and occult religious experiences is indicative of what is happening.

Dean M. Kelley is an ordained Methodist minister and a sociologist of religion. For several years he was director for Civil and Religious Liberty, National Council of Churches.

In the latter years of the 1960s something remarkable happened in the United States: for the first time in the nation's history most of the major church groups stopped growing and began to shrink. Though not one of the most dramatic developments of those years, it may prove to be one of the most significant, especially for students of man's social behavior. Certainly those concerned with religion, either as adherents or observers, have wondered what it means and what it portends for the future.

At least ten of the largest Christian denominations in the country, whose memberships totalled 77,666,223 in 1967, had fewer members the next year and fewer yet the year after. Most of these denominations had been growing uninterruptedly since colonial times. In the previous decade they had grown more slowly, some failing to keep pace with the increase in the nation's population. And now they have begun to diminish, reversing a trend of two centuries. . . .

While most of the mainline Protestant denominations are trying to survive what they hope will be but a temporary adversity, other denominations are overflowing with vitality, such as the Southern Baptist Convention, the Assemblies of God, the Churches of God, the Pentecostal and Holiness groups, the Evangelicals, the Mormons (Church of Jesus Christ of Latter-Day Saints), Jehovah's Witnesses, Seventh-day Adventists, Black Muslims, and many smaller groups hardly even visible to the large denominations. . . .

Figure 1 shows a comparison of growth rates between two long-time rivals, the Southern Baptist Convention and the Methodist Church. In 1967, the former overtook the latter and has continued to increase at a rate of 2.26% per year, while the latter has begun to diminish, despite its merger with the Evangelical United Brethren Church in 1968. But even with the addition of 737,000 former EUB members, the United Methodist Church is not as large as the Southern Baptist Convention, which (unlike the United Methodist Church) is still increasing.

The foreign missionary personnel of the Southern Baptist Convention more than doubled, from 1,186 in 1958 to 2,494 in 1971, while the United Methodist overseas task force decreased from 1,453 to 1,175 in the same period.

Figure 2 is a reminder of the membership trends of other large Protestant denominations. . . .

The three Lutheran churches are shown separately. It is evident that of the six shown only the Lutheran Church-Missouri Synod is still increasing, and this at a decreasing rate, no longer matching the rate of U.S. population increase.

Figure 3 includes the membership rates for five rapidly growing churches of 250,000-400,000 members: the Seventh-day Adventists (3.2% increase per year), the Church of the Nazarene (2.6% increase), the Jehovah's Witnesses (5% increase per year), the Salvation Army (average 2.9% increase per year) and the Christian Reformed Church (2.2% per year). They are designated as rapidly growing because their growth rates exceed the rate of population growth.

Others in this category (not shown because of scale differences) are: Free Methodist Church (1.6% increase — from 54,942 in 1958 to 64,394 in 1969); Assemblies of God (2.1% increase — from 505,552 in 1958 to 625,027 in 1969); Pentecostal Holiness Church (3.9% increase — from 49,594 in 1958 to 66,790 in 1969); and Church of Jesus Christ of Latter-day Saints (Mormons, Salt Lake City, Utah: 5.6%

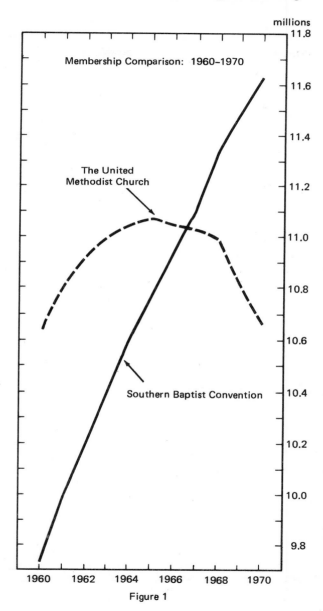

Figure 1

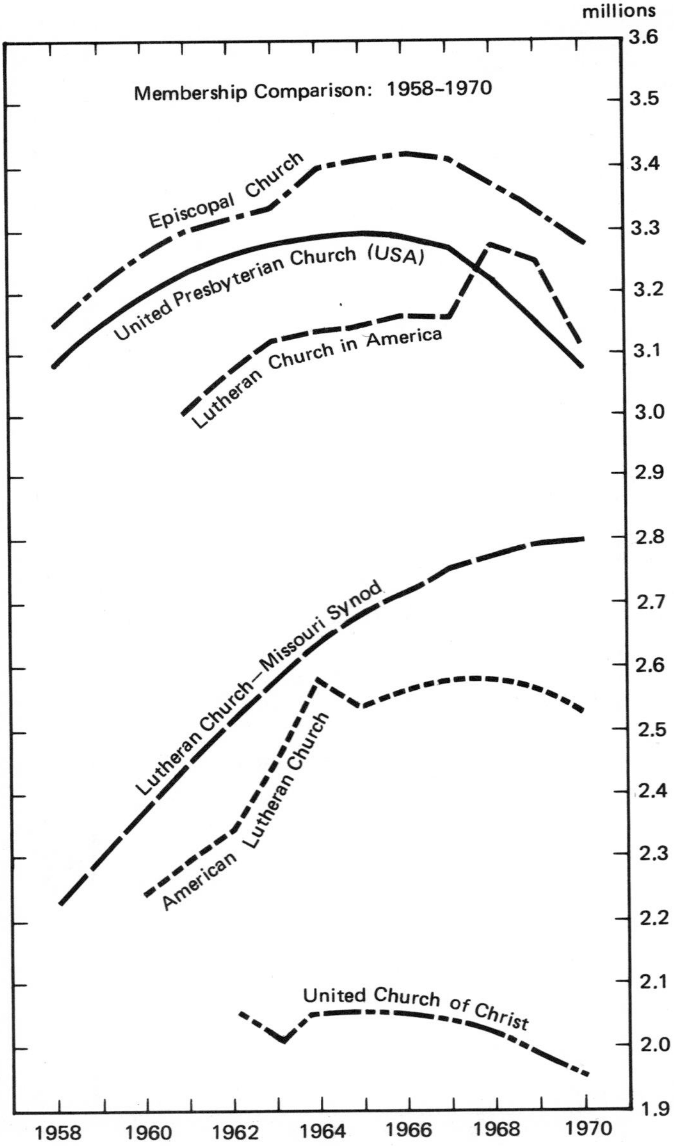
millions
Membership Comparison: 1958–1970
Episcopal Church
United Presbyterian Church (USA)
Lutheran Church in America
Lutheran Church—Missouri Synod
American Lutheran Church
United Church of Christ
3.6
3.5
3.4
3.3
3.2
3.1
3.0
2.9
2.8
2.7
2.6
2.5
2.4
2.3
2.2
2.1
2.0
1.9
1958
1960
1962
1964
1966
1968
1970

Figure 2

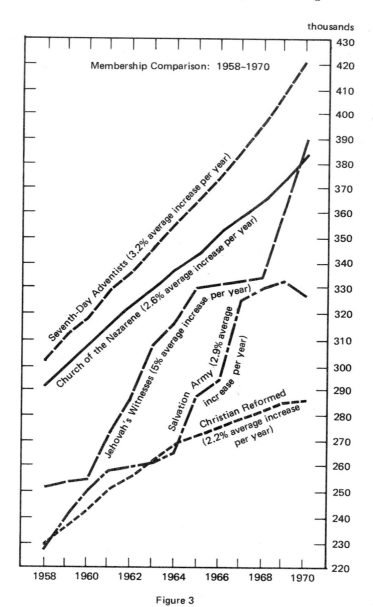

Figure 3

increase — from 1,394,729 in 1958 to 2,180,064 in 1968). No figures are available for the Churches of Christ; the Black Muslims; the Church of Christ, Scientist; and some others which may also be increasing rapidly. The rapidly growing bodies have also been increasing their missionary outreach while the mainline denominations have been cutting back. In 1958, the Evangelical Foreign Missions Association had 4,688 missionaries abroad and by 1971 this number had increased to 7,479, an increase of about 60%. The Wycliffe Bible Translators, beginning in 1935, reached 705 staff members abroad by 1958 and grew to 1762 in 1970! Dr. David Stowe, head of the United Church of Christ Board for World Ministries, observed that "the fundamentalists and pentecostals increased their numbers at about the same rate as the mainline churches' decreased." By this important index of spiritual vitality, the mainline churches are weakening while the rapidly growing churches are becoming stronger.

These groups not only give evidence that religion is not obsolete and churches not defunct, but they contradict the contemporary notion of an acceptable religion. They are not "reasonable," they are not "tolerant," they are not ecumenical, they are not "relevant." Quite the contrary!

They often refuse to recognize the validity of other churches' teachings, ordinations, sacraments. They observe unusual rituals and peculiar dietary customs, such as footwashing and vegetarianism among Seventh-day Adventists and abstention from stimulants among Mormons. They disregard the "decent opinions of mankind" by persisting in irrational behavior, such as the Jehovah's Witnesses' refusal of blood transfusions. They try to impose uniformity of belief and practice among members by censorship, heresy trials, and the like. For instance, the Southern Baptist Convention recently ordered the Boardman Press — its publishing house — to withdraw a biblical commentary which the Convention deemed too liberal; the president of the Lutheran Church — Missouri Synod, J. A. O. Preuss, undertook a personal investigation of Concordia Seminary to discover any faculty members whose teaching was not compatible with the faith of the church; the Salvation Army (in England) has expelled Major Fred Brown for publishing religious writings without first clearing them with his superiors. Some of these various bodies display the highest incidence of anti-Semitism among major religious organizations (cf. Glock & Stark, *Christian Beliefs and Anti-Semitism*).

It is ironic that the religious groups which persist in such "unreasonable" and "unsociable" behavior should be flourishing, while the more "reasonable" and "sociable" bodies are not. It is not only ironic, but it suggests that our understanding of what causes a religious group to flourish is inadequate. Some dynamic seems to be at work which contradicts prevailing expectations. . . .

Not only are some religious groups still thriving, but new ones are constantly coming into being, some of them quite unconventional and even bizarre in character. At the very moment when it begins to be accepted that religion is no longer needed and churches are expiring, new manifestations of religiousness appear where least expected — among adolescents and young adults — the very age groups which had most visibly abandoned the conventional religious bodies in seeming apathy and disillusionment.

On college campuses and in sophisticated urban circles, devotees of Zen Buddhism, yoga, and other exotic Eastern religions spring up, competing for adherents with neoastrology, satanism, witchcraft, hallucinogenic cults, and various free form mysticisms. Among the young men and women who have dropped out of college and the career rat race the same searching for something remarkably similar to religion is seen. Communes develop semisacramental rituals for the sharing of their macrobiotic diet, and vagrant elements of everything from voodoo to Vedanta are celebrated in a growing preoccupation with the irrational, the mystic, the mysterious. Popular magazines have discovered this new (or very old) phenomenon and gilded it with notoriety as deceptive as its former obscurity. . . .

No one knows what the full capacity of the human person is, especially for sustained, devoted, imaginative effort; it may never have been fully plumbed, let alone measured. But it is not likely that many of us are in danger of pressing the limits of human exertion or endurance. Physiologists tell us that normally only a small proportion of our physical and cerebral potential is utilized — how much less the more complex and exhausting creative and social proclivities of which we like to boast?

Suppose, to be charitable, that we are percolating along at about 20% of capacity most of the time. Sometimes, under the spur of ambition or stress, we may throw ourselves into a task with considerable energy and use as much as 40% for a little while. For the peripheral interests of our lives, which is what religion is for most people, we rarely expend more than a marginal 5% or 10% of our energy. And we never really get caught up fully and without reserve into anything above the 50% mark, if we can help it.

And all our lives we long to ease off from this arduous toil, this desperate exertion. We yearn to throttle down the old plant and lean back and take it easy — as though we ever took it hard. But on the rare occasions when we do relax more fully, we soon become restless and irritable. The vacationer may find himself after a while itching to get back to something "significant." The retired person may feel his long-awaited rest becoming empty and boring. The only thing man seems to be able to do all his life and remain sane and healthy is *work* (in the possibly idealized sense of sustained application of effort to purposive activity), even at the gently casual level on which we ordinarily operate.

But there are some energetic and irritating persons who are not satisfied with this easygoing arrangement. They not only drive themselves to ridiculous levels of activity, but they want to drive others too. They are the one-in-a-hundred or one-in-a-thousand who give more energy and time than anyone else is willing to give to keep the church going, or the lodge, or the union, or whatever cause or organization has won their loyalty. And by induction from their own devotion, they often stir the rest of us to a small additional percent of involvement. . . .

The greatest mobilizers, who are usually religious leaders, like John Wesley, are persons who live near their maximum capacity not just for a few moments, but for years — not just for fame or wealth or sport, but for meaning. Is it any wonder that these dedicated, dynamic men and women, intensely and continuously so much more alive than anyone else, draw to themselves little groups of followers who want to share that abundant life?

These little bands of committed men and women have an impact on history out of all proportion to their numbers or apparent abilities. In the main, they are usually recruited from the least promising ranks of society: they are not noble or wealthy or well educated or particularly talented. All they have to offer is themselves, but that is more than others give to anything. For when a handful of wholly committed human beings give themselves fully to a great cause or faith, they are virtually irresistible. They cut through the partial and fleeting commitments of the rest of society like a buzz saw through peanut brittle.

They are able to do this for several reasons: (1) They are willing to put in more time and effort for their cause than most people do for even their fondest personal ambitions. (2) They have an assurance, a conviction of rightness, of being on the side of God, that most people in most human endeavors cannot match. (3) They are linked together in a band of mutually supportive, like-minded, equally devoted fellow believers, who reinforce one another in times of weakness, persecution, and doubt. (4) They are willing to subordinate their personal desires and ambitions to the shared goals of the group.

The Charismatic Movement

William W. Menzies

Trying to catch the Holy Spirit long enough for descriptive analysis is like trying to capture the wind in a bottle. The analogy has ancient precedent: "The wind bloweth where it listeth, and thou hearest the sound thereof, but canst not tell whence it cometh, and whither it goeth: so is every one that is born of the Spirit" (John 3:8).

The "charismatic movement" is an umbrella term under which can be included faith healing, baptism with the Spirit, speaking in tongues, and other "gifts" of the Spirit *(charismata* is Greek for *gifts;* cf. 1 Cor. 12).

As with so many contemporary trends, we have to note that the charismatic movement cuts across denominational lines and is found within virtually all the established churches as well as in the specifically Pentecostal, Holiness, and Assemblies of God churches. It is a world-wide phenomenon, including Catholics as well as Protestants, and its rate of growth by mid-twentieth century was accelerating. The standard work on the subject is by Walter J. Hollenweger, *Handbuch der Pfingstbewegung*, in 10 volumes, 1965-67; a summary volume is his *The Pentecostals: The Charismatic Movement in the Churches,* 1972.

As a single, but representative, example of the charismatic movement, we include an address by William W. Menzies, chairman of the Department of Biblical Studies, Evangel College, Springfield, Missouri. Delivered in the chapel of the graduate school, this address entitled "Our Heritage" is reprinted from *Paraclete* magazine, (Winter 1975).

We are at the threshold of an awakening which may indeed surpass any awakening in the history of the Church. That the ministry of the Holy Spirit is being honored and coveted in a wide sweep of the Christian spectrum today has important origins in the Pentecostal movement.

Not since the Apostolic age has a charismatic movement survived long enough to gain the hearing of the main stream of the Church — that is, not until the twentieth century Pentecostal revival. And without question, that humble group of 300 ministers who gathered at Hot Springs, Arkansas, in 1914, to found the Assemblies of God, were an important part of this amazing story. Out of the scattered congregations that formed the Pentecostal movement, the Assemblies of God did a great deal to preserve the fruits of latter day Pentecost for two entire generations. . . .

It was a bizarre spectacle in the religious world of seven decades ago. Image! People speaking in tongues — and in the house of the Lord! What was this talk about a baptism in the Spirit? Gifts of the Spirit, you say? And, have you heard that they pray for the sick? These poor, uneducated folks talk excitedly about the soon return of Christ.

And I fear that they must be truly fanatical — without promise of adequate support, self-appointed missionaries are going to China, to India, and to Africa. No mission board approves of these zealots — they just go.

And the kind of people who preach! What a sight to behold! Listen, they do not wait for proper ordination — nor proper seminary education. There are women, mind you, women dressed in white and shrill of voice who campaign through the countryside as evangelists and even pastors! Many of their cottage prayer meetings are led by such women — and the amazing thing is that churches grow rapidly from such impossible beginnings.

If that were not shocking enough, most of these Pentecostal preachers are really just laymen. Fresh from the plow or the shop, in city after city, the deacons in the churches are thrust out to nearby hamlets to lead prayer meetings, which soon become churches. It seems that nearly all who receive this Pentecostal experience are seized with a compulsion to preach. You must admit that what they lack in polish they make up for in enthusiasm and conviction.

Why, these people act as if the Book of Acts was part of the morning mail. It is apparent that through their rough-formed speech there is a compelling and frightening authority. They call it the "anointing."

Women, laymen, and you might know — even the younger people are aflame! They call them "gospel bands." A whole group will drop their schooling, their employment, and leave family and friends to travel about the country holding meetings.

Sometimes with no more chaperonage than a single married couple, these people, some still in their late teens, will descend on a midwestern town. They seek out an empty store building or, failing that, will seek to use a lodge hall or a school building. Frequently a tattered tent is their cathedral. Sometimes these young zealots simply stand on the street, telling how their lives have been changed!

Most of them are such poor preachers that after a short time they move on, pitching their tent in another town. It's a pity that more of them do not stay to organize a church, for indeed their intensity and zeal have challenged many of the delinquents in the community. But, these early Pentecostals are a restless lot! . . .

Yes, it was a bizarre spectacle shortly after the turn of the new century! What were some of the important characteristics of this explosive and spectacular new movement that caused it to endure?

Reality

One cannot come away from perusal of early documents describing this charismatic awakening without being keenly aware of the sense of God's presence the people felt. Their services were "holy ground." Theirs were worshipping communities. Only later was the sense of the holy cheapened in some places by raucous music and whipped-up enthusiasm. Their lives were bathed in prayer — prayer which was genuine conversation with the living God. A word much used by these early saints was *reality*. The resurrected Christ had become intensely real and very much alive.

Expectancy

There was a sense of the manifest presence of God. Each service was freighted with the dramatic. Services were spontaneous, with a freshness born of experience. If they made room for God, He would come into their midst to bless, to heal, to convict, to save. Church was an exciting experience. What a stark contrast to the formal and stereotyped patterns in the older denominations from which they had been expelled!

There was another kind of expectancy. These early saints were fascinated by a keen sense of the imminence of the return of Jesus Christ. Premillennial expectation was already a major tenet among the fundamentalists by the beginning of the Topeka and Los angeles revivals. It is easy to see how the new Pentecostalists adopted this eschatology. Frequent utterances of the Holy Spirit reinforced the intensity of conviction that indeed a latter rain outpouring had begun. "Jesus is coming soon" was a frequent message from the lips of these early Pentecostal prophets.

Biblical Authority

Early Pentecostals sometimes abused by overemphasis some of the more spectacular features of experiential religion, but by 1905, beginning in the camp meetings in Texas, serious attempts were made to subordinate all emphases, practices, and teachings to the authority of God's Word. One of the important reasons for the formation of the General Council in 1914 was to facilitate doctrinal unity.

The Statement of Fundamental Truths, formulated two years later, contains this opening statement: "The Bible is our all-sufficient rule for faith and practice." All theology must stand under the judgment of the inspired, inerrant Word of God. At this point perhaps the most important single feature of stability emerged. *Interpretation of Biblical theology was defined in the terms of mainstream orthodox theology.* Donald Gee spoke profound words when he said, "We have added no new doctrines." This must be qualified in two ways:

1. All the great ecumenical creeds of the ancient church state in one form or another, "We believe in the Holy Spirit." It remained for the modern Pentecostal movement to give sharper definition to this brief creedal statement of the orthodox churches. Some woud say the baptism in the Holy Spirit with the initial physical evidence of speaking in tongues indeed is an addition to traditional theology. Others, like Donald Gee, would say, "No, we are just recalling the church to what was originally believed."

2. There is also this qualification. It has to do with biblical hermeneutics. The Book of Acts is generally viewed by evangelicals as operating on two levels: first, a history of the early Church; second, a stimulus to faith in the resurrected Christ. To these the Pentecostals would add a third: a normative pattern.

In the Apostolic Church the picture of faith and practice is accepted as a model for the church of today. So not only the pattern of methodology — notably the indigenous church — but also the pattern of religious experience becomes normativee. From this hermeneutic the Pentecostal draws his particular theology. He does not rely on proof-texts. He sees doctrine in the indicatives and in the imperatives of Scripture. But he also sees doctrine in the pictures painted in the Scriptures. Certainly the Pentecostal heritage is rich in biblical authority.

Simplicity

In the early Church ecclesiastical structures were added only as necessary. Authority rested in the local congregation. Only those things that directly profited the spiritual welfare of the people were considered important. There was a kind of "holy pragmatism." Only with reluctance in 1927 were the various General Council resolutions put into a constitution.

The genius of the rapid early growth of the fellowship was its heavy preoccupation with the grass roots, the cutting edge. There was more interest in local revival than in general resolutions.

Faith

Reality, expectancy, biblical authority, and *faith*. The early pioneers of Pentecost lived as if Jesus Christ were *real*. There is no natural way to explain the courage which drove Victor Plymire across Tibet — the first white man to make that journey — apart from his confidence in an abiding God! There is no way to account for the triumphs of grace in cities and villages across our land and around the world — the bold assault of simple believers on the citadels of hell — apart from *faith*.

A shining characteristic of Pentecostals from the early days has been this simple, utterly transparent confidence that God was against sin and suffering and anointed His servants who dared to move within that awareness. How many families were swept into the kingdom by a spectacular healing of an ill member! How many churches were born by the breaking into human need of God's awesome power! How do you account for all this? Donald Gee said it again: "The baptism in the Holy Spirit has made Jesus intensely real."

Joy

I suppose there is no better way to characterize the early Pentecostal revival than *joy*. In doing research some years ago, I ran into a modernist's description of a New York Pentecostal mission in the year 1924. The article was written from a supercilious perch in quite condescending tones. But at the very end of the article the writer with some wistfulness noted that on the faces of the humble people who worshiped there was a remarkable joy, a kind of countenance he did not detect on the faces of those who worshiped in the more respectable houses of the Lord.

The exuberance and gladness of Pentecostals, frequently disdained by offended fundamentalists and modernists alike, has somehow in more recent days become once again a cherished dimension of life for many. Ours is a day starved by the coldness of scientific rationalism. There is nothing so captivating as joy. And the Holy Spirit has come to lift the believer into a fuller realization that our Lord lives and that he has come to give us abundance of life. In his presence is fullness of joy!

Testimony

Pentecostals have often been accused of being man-centered, rather than God-centered. Our music is more frequently in the mood of testimony than of exaltation of God. This is likely true. But is not testimony an authentic expression of the transformed life? From the earliest days much of the proclamation of the good news was cast in the vein of "I know it is true, for it has happened to me."

The *personal* dimension of religion has been an important ingredient in the endurance of the Pentecostal revival. It may be true that theological formulation has not always received appropriate attention. Sometimes it has been true, too, that the behavioral dimensions of the Christ life have not always been given adequate scrutiny. But it has always been true that high priority has been placed on personal relationship with the living God. Great attention has been placed on the reality of crisis experiences of salvation through the blood of Jesus Christ; crisis encounters in the baptism in the Holy Spirit; a genuine concern for discerning a call from God; for "praying through" to specific answers to prayer.

Out of such specific transactions with God himself the testimonies of glowing reality flow. Deliverance from the dominion of sin; deliverance from sickness — these are tangible realities which issue in vocal and sometimes ecstatic praise to God! The Holy Spirit impelled these early people to give their testimony — at home and far afield. Evangelism and missions, the brilliant facets of our fellowship, are really to be seen as "anointed testimonies"!

These then are some of the core characteristics of our Pentecostal heritage. After sixty years they still have a pleasant and useful ring to them. We would do well to consider them today.

The Hartford Declaration

The Hartford Declaration, or more accurately, "An Appeal for Theological Affirmation," emerged out of a conference in January, 1975, at the Hartford Seminary Foundation in Connecticut. The two moving spirits behind the statement were Peter L. Berger, sociology professor at Rutgers University, and Richard John Neuhaus, Lutheran pastor of the Church of Saint John the Evangelist in Brooklyn. The text of the Declaration was circulated for about a year in advance to various kinds of interested people.

Since the cross-sectional and ecumenical character of the committee gives some clue as to the Declaration's sponsorship, the following people (in addition to Berger and Neuhaus) were involved: Elizabeth Ann Bettenhausen (Department of Church and Society, Lutheran Church in America); William Sloane Coffin, Jr., (Chaplain, Yale University); Avery Dulles (Catholic University of America); Neal Fisher (United Methodist Board of Global Ministries); George Forell (University of Iowa); James Gettemy (president, Hartford Seminary Foundation); George Lindbeck (Yale University); Ileana Marculescu (Union Theological Seminary, New York); Ralph

McInerny (University of Notre Dame); E. Kilmer Meyers (Episcopal Bishop, California); Richard J. Mouw (Calvin College); Carl Peter (Catholic University of America); Alexander Schmemann (Eastern Orthodox Seminary); Gerard Sloyan (Temple University); Lewis Smedes (Fuller Theological Seminary); George H. Tavard (Methodist Theological School); and Robert Wilken (University of Notre Dame). Several others were also involved in the preliminary stages of the Declaration.

The intent of the Declaration was not to make authoritative or binding pronouncements but to criticize the current Christian scene by isolating several widely held assumptions about faith and life. The thirteen "themes" try to express the kinds of overarching presuppositions many people today hold about Christianity, and the Declaration then goes on to repudiate and reject these pervasive notions.

Discussed and disputed on all sides, the controversy stirred up by the Declaration testifies to its vitality and cogency. Another group of theologians, led by Harvey G. Cox of the Harvard Divinity School, responded to the Hartford Appeal with a statement known as the "Boston Affirmations," dated January, 1976. Concerned that "much of contemporary piety ignores the social dimensions of the gospel," they drafted a plea to the churches to continue and extend the application of Christian faith to the social issues of the day. The next stage in religion for America may well depend on the creative responses made to the Hartford statement by theologians, ministers, church leaders, and all who work and pray for "a new heaven and a new earth" (Rev. 21:1).

An Appeal For Theological Affirmation

The renewal of Christian witness and mission requires constant examination of the assumptions shaping the Church's life. Today an apparent loss of a sense of the transcendent is undermining the Church's ability to address with clarity and courage the urgent tasks to which God calls it in the world. This loss is manifest in a number of pervasive themes. Many are superficially attractive, but upon closer examination we find these themes false and debilitating to the Church's life and work. Among such themes are:

Theme I: Modern thought is superior to all past forms of understanding reality, and is therefore normative for Christian faith and life.

In repudiating this theme we are protesting the captivity to the prevailing thought structures not only of the twentieth century but of any historical period. We favor using any helpful means of understanding, ancient or modern, and insist that the Christian proclamation must be related to the idiom of the culture. At the same time, we affirm the need for Christian thought to confront and be confronted by other world views, all of which are necessarily provisional.

Theme 2: Religious statements are totally independent of reasonable discourse.

The capitulation to the alleged primacy of modern thought takes two forms: one is the subordination of religious statements to the canons of scientific rationality; the other, equating reason with scientific rationality, would remove religious statements from the realm of reasonable discourse altogether. A religion of pure subjectivity and nonrationality results in treating faith statements as being, at best, statements about the believer. We repudiate both forms of capitulation.

Theme 3: Religious language refers to human experience and nothing else, God being humanity's noblest creation.

Religion is also a set of symbols and even of human projections. We repudiate the assumption that it is nothing but that. What is here at stake is nothing less than the reality of God: *We did not invent God; God invented us.*

Theme 4: Jesus can only be understood in terms of contemporary models of humanity.

This theme suggests a reversal of "the imitation of Christ"; that is, the image of Jesus is made to reflect cultural and countercultural notions of human excellence. We do not deny that all aspects of humanity are illumined by Jesus. Indeed, it is necessary to the universality of the Christ that he be perceived in relation to the particularities of the believers' world. We do repudiate the captivity to such metaphors, which are necessarily inadequate, relative, transitory, and frequently idolatrous. Jesus, together with the Scriptures and the whole of the Christian tradition, cannot be arbitrarily interpreted without reference to the history of which they are part. The danger is in the attempt to exploit the tradition without taking the tradition seriously.

Theme 5: All religions are equally valid; the choice among them is not a matter of conviction about truth but only of personal preference or life-style.

We affirm our common humanity. We affirm the importance of exploring and confronting all manifestations of the religious quest and of learning from the riches of other religions. But we repudiate this theme because it flattens diversities and ignores contradictions. In doing so, it not only obscures the meaning of Christian faith, but also fails to respect the integrity of other faiths. Truth matters; therefore differences among religions are deeply significant.

Theme 6: To realize one's potential and to be true to oneself is the whole meaning of salvation.

Salvation contains a promise of human fulfillment, but to identify salvation with human fulfillment can trivialize the promise. We affirm that salvation cannot be found apart from God.

Theme 7: Since what is human is good, evil can adequately be understood as failure to realize human potential.

This theme invites false understanding of the ambivalence of human existence and underestimates the pervasiveness of sin. Paradoxically, by minimizing the enormity of evil, it undermines serious and sustained attacks on particular social or individual evils.

Theme 8: The sole purpose of worship is to promote individual self-realization and human community.

Worship promotes individual and communal values, but it is above all a response to the reality of God and arises out of the fundamental need and desire to know, love, and adore God. We worship God because God is to be worshiped.

Theme 9: Institutions and historical traditions are oppressive and inimical to our being truly human; liberation from them is required for authentic existence and authentic religion.

Institutions and traditions are often oppressive. For this reason they must be subjected to relentless criticism. But human community inescapably requires institutions and traditions. Without them life would degenerate into chaos and new forms of bondage. The modern pursuit of liberation from all social and historical restraints is finally dehumanizing.

Theme 10: The world must set the agenda for the Church. Social, political and economic programs to improve the quality of life are ultimately normative for the Church's mission in the world.

This theme cuts across the political and ideological spectrum. Its form remains the same, no matter whether the content is defined as upholding the values of the American way of life, promoting socialism, or raising human consciousness. The Church must denounce oppressors, help liberate the oppressed and seek to heal human misery. Sometimes the Church's mission coincides with the world's programs. But the norms of the Church's activity derive from its own perception of God's will for the world.

Theme 11: An emphasis on God's transcendence is at least a hindrance to, and perhaps incompatible with, Christian social concern and action.

This supposition leads some to denigrate God's transcendence. Others, holding to a false transcendence, withdraw into religious privatism or individualism and neglect the personal and communal responsibility of Christians for the earthly city. From a biblical perspective, it is precisely because of confidence in God's reign over all aspects of life that Christians must participate fully in the struggle against oppressive and dehumanizing structures and their manifestations in racism, war, and economic exploitation.

Theme 12: The struggle for a better humanity will bring about the Kingdom of God.

The struggle for a better humanity is essential to Christian faith and can be informed and inspired by the biblical promise of the Kingdom of God. But imperfect human beings cannot create a perfect society. The Kingdom of God surpasses any conceivable utopia. God has his own designs which confront ours, surprising us with judgment and redemption.

Theme 13: The question of hope beyond death is irrelevant or at best marginal to the Christian understanding of human fulfillment.

This is the final capitulation to modern thought. If death is the last word, then Christianity has nothing to say to the final questions of life. We believe that God raised Jesus from the dead and are ". . . convinced that there is nothing in death or life, in the realm of spirits or superhuman powers, in the world, as it is or in the world as it shall be, in the forces of the universe, in heights or depths — nothing in all creation that can separate us from the love of God in Christ Jesus our Lord" (Romans 8:38 f.)

EPILOGUE

Religion In A Revolutionary Society

Peter L. Berger

The bicentennial celebrations before and after 1976 provided opportunity to reflect upon the changing as well as the constant qualities of American society. If *revolutionary society* implies rapid and far-reaching change, then today has much in common with yesterday, and this is as true of the religious scene as of anything. There is much to say about religion in America in both 1776 and 1976, even though great changes have taken place in the two-hundred-year span.

Using the bicentennial as a vantage point but restricting his perspective to the last 20 to 25 years, Peter L. Berger, in the essay that follows, surveys the religious terrain and comments on the continuing vitality of religion in America in the midst of a bewildering variety of fads and trends.

Alluding to many of the religious movements represented in the previous selections, this competent survey not only looks backward to the day before yesterday, but expertly analyzes the current religious situation, and dares to predict some likely trends for tomorrow. With special attention to Protestantism, the discussion also includes references to Catholicism and Judaism, and thus serves as an admirable summary epilogue for our volume.

Of major importance in any analysis of religion in America is the careful distinction between "denominational" and "civil" religion. The former relates to the faith and life of the churches and other religious institutions; the latter "refers to a somewhat vaguer entity, an amalgam of beliefs and norms that are deemed to be fundamental to the American way of life. The interplay between denominational and civil religion can be complex, but in the evaluation of a perceptive sociologist, who also happens to be a Christian believer, it can be instructive and illuminating.

Peter L. Berger is Professor of Sociology at Rutgers University. He is the author of several books dealing with religion and society, such as *The Noise of Solemn Assemblies* (1961), *A Rumor of Angels* (1969), and *Pyramids of Sacrifice* (1974). Born in Vienna, he later became a U.S. citizen. He has taught not only at Rutgers but at the New School for Social Research, the Universities of Georgia and North Carolina, and the Hartford Seminary Foundation.

The selection that follows is reprinted from Dr. Berger's chapter, "Religion in a Revolutionary Society," in the volume of bicentennial essays, *America's Continuing Revolution,* published by the American Enterprise Institute for Public Policy Research, Washington, D.C., 1976.

"Denominational" religion in America refers to what most people mean when they speak of religion — the bodies of Christian and Jewish tradition as these are enshrined in the major religious organizations in this country. Denominational religion is the religion of the churches. The plural, *churches,* is very important: there are many churches in America, and for a long time now they have existed side by side under conditions of legal equality. Indeed, Richard Niebuhr suggested that the very term "denomination" be defined on the basis of this pluralism.[1] A denomination is a church that, at least for all practical purposes, has come to accept coexistence with other churches. This coexistence was brought about in America by unique historical circumstances, which were not intended by anyone and which at first were only accepted with great reluctance. Later on, a virtue was made out of the necessity, as religious tolerance became part and parcel of the national ideology as well as of the basic laws of the American republic. . . .

"Civil" religion in America refers to a somewhat vaguer entity, an amalgam of beliefs and norms that are deemed to be fundamental to the American political order. In the last few years the idea of an American civil religion has been much discussed in terms proposed in an influential essay on the topic by Robert Bellah, but both the idea and the phrase antedate this essay.[2] Herberg, for instance, discussed very much the same idea using a slightly different terminology. The general assumption here is that the American polity not only bases itself on a set of commonly held values (this is true of any human society), but that these values add up to something that can plausibly be called a religion. The contents of this religion are some basic convictions about human destiny and human rights as expressed in American democratic institutions. Gunnar Myrdal, in his classic study of the Negro in America, aptly called all this "the American creed."[4] The proposition that all men are created equal is a first article of this creed.

An obvious question concerns the relationship between these two religious entities. Different answers have been given to this question, and I can claim no particular competence in the historical scholarship necessary to adjudicate between them. Thus, to take an example of recent scholarly debate, I cannot say whether the civil religion of the American republic should be seen in an essential continuity with the Puritan concept of the convenant,[5] or whether it should be understood as the result of a decisive rupture with Puritanism brought about by the Deist element among the Founding Fathers. Be this as it may, it is clear that the two religious entities have had profound relations with each other from the beginning. Nor is there any doubt that crucial ingredients of the civil religion derive directly from the Protestant mainstream of American church life, to the extent that to this day the civil religion carries an unmistakably Protestant flavor (a point always seen more clearly by non-Protestants than by Protestants, for people are always more likely to notice unfamiliar flavors). Thus, for instance, the codification of the rights of the individual conscience in the American political creed loudly betrays its Protestant roots, even when (perhaps especially when) it is couched in denominationally neutral language.

It is important to understand how the civil religion relates to the pluralism of denominations. Thus, in one sense, the civil religion is based on a principle of religious tolerance. Except for some isolated cases (Tom Paine was one),[6] the spokesmen of the civil religion were not only friendly to the major churches but insisted that the latter were vital to the moral health of the nation. In another sense, however, the civil religion marks the *limits* of tolerance and indeed of pluralism. While it accepts a broad diversity of religious beliefs in the society, it limits diversity when it comes to *its own* beliefs. The lines between acceptable and unacceptable diversity have frequently shifted in the course of time, but to this day the category "un-American" points to the fact that there are clearly unacceptable deviations from the common civil creed. Belief in the divine right of kings, for example, was as clearly beyond the lines of official acceptability in an earlier period of American history as belief in redemption through socialist revolution came to be later on.

Unlike some of the democratic ideologies of Europe and Latin America, democracy in the United States was not inimical to the churches. The separation between church and state in the American Constitution did not, until very recently, imply that the state must be antiseptically clean of all religious qualities — only that the state must not give unfair advantage to one denomination over another. In other words, the assumptions underlying the separation of church and state were pluralist rather than secularist. It is no accident that there is no adequate American translation of the French term *laique*,[7] and that (again, until very recently) there was no widespread demand that the American polity should become a "lay state" in the French sense. Indeed, a good case can be made that church/state relations in this country had the character of a "pluralistic establishment": officially accredited denominations were allowed to share equally in a variety of privileges bestowed by the state. Exemption from taxation and opportunity for chaplaincy in public institutions are cases in point. Just which groups were to be regarded as officially accredited, of course, was subject to redefinition.

To put it differently, the beneficiaries of the "pluralistic establishment" have been an expanding group ever since the system was inaugurated. First were added various less-than-respectable Protestant bodies (such as the Quakers), then Catholics and Jews, and finally groups completely outside what is commonly called the Judaeo-Christian tradition. The struggle of the Mormons to obtain "accreditation" marked an interesting case in this process. Recent court decisions on what (if my memory serves me correctly) were actually called "the religious rights of atheists," as well as recent litigation by Black Muslims, mark the degree of expansion of the system to date.

Historically, then, denominational religion and civil religion have not been antagonistic entities in America. Their relationship has rather been a symbiotic one. The denominations enjoyed a variety of benefits in a "pluralistic establishment," the existence of which was not only fostered by the state but solemnly legitimated by the civil religion to which the state adhered. Conversely, the civil religion drew specific contents and (in all likelihood) general credibility from the ongoing life of the denominations. Nevertheless, each entity has had a distinct history, with different forces impinging on the one or the other. Any assessment of the contemporary situation must allow for this distinction. . . .

Keeping this distinction in mind, then, let us go back to the period around 1955: what was the situation at that time?

As far as denominational religion was concerned, the market was bullish indeed. These were the years of what was then called a "religious revival." All the statistical indicators of organized religion were pointing up. Church membership reached historically unprecedented heights. Most significant (or so it seemed then), it was younger people, especially young married couples, who became active in the churches in large numbers. The offspring of these people crowded the Sunday schools, creating a veritable boom in religious education. Church attendance was up, and so was financial giving to the churches. Much of this money was very profitably invested, and the denominational coffers were full as never before. Understandably enough, the denominational functionaries thought in terms of expansion. "Church extension" was the phrase constantly on their lips. There was an impressive boom in church building, especially in the new middle-class suburbs. The seminaries were filled with young men getting ready to swell the ranks of the clergy. Perhaps they were not "the brightest and the best" among their peers, but they were competent enough to fulfill the increasingly complex tasks required of the clerical profession in this situation. In the bustling suburban "church plants" (a very common term at the time) this clerical profession often meant a bewildering agglomeration of roles, adding to the traditional religious ones such new roles as that of business administrator, educational supervisor, family counselor and public relations expert.

The "religious revival" affected most of the denominations in the Protestant camp, and it affected Catholics and Jews as well. It seemed as if everyone were becoming active in his respective "religious preference" . . . It was important, therefore, that all of this took place in a context of (apparently) solidifying ecumenism and interfaith amity. The Protestants within the mainline denominations were going through something of an ecumenical orgy. There were several church mergers, the most significance of these (long in preparation) being the union between the Congregationalists and the

Evangelical and Reformed Church to become the United Church of Christ. The formation of this body in 1957 was widely heralded as a landmark in the movement toward Christian unity.[8] Quite apart from these organizational mergers, there was a plethora of agencies concerned full time with interdenominational relations, ranging from the still quite young National Council of Churches to state and local councils. While some of these agencies engaged in theological discussion, most of their work was severely practical. An important task was the one formerly called "comity" and recently rebaptized as "church planning." Especially on the · local level this meant that church expansion was based on research and on agreements among the denominations not to engage in irrational competition with each other — and particularly not to steal each other's prospective members. The religious market, in other words, was increasingly parcelled out between cartel-like planning bodies (and no antitrust laws stood in the way of these conspiracies to restrain free competition). Beyond all these formal processes of collaboration, there was a broad variety of informal acts of *rapprochement* — intercommunion, exchange of pulpits, interdenominational ministries in special areas, and so on.

It should be emphasized that most of this occurred within the mainstream denominations, which had a predominantly middle-class constituency. The more fundamentalist groups, with their lower-middle-class and working-class members, stood apart, undergoing at the same time quite dramatic growth of their own. It seems that the apartness of these groups was not much noticed and even less regretted by the ecumenists: the presence of the Greek Orthodox in the National Council was noted with pleasure, the absence of the Pentecostalists was of little concern. More noticed was the new relationship to Catholics and Jews. While the Roman Catholic Church still moved slowly in those pre-Vatican II days, there was little doubt that the old hostility between the two major Christian confessions was a matter of the past. And both Protestants and Catholics habitually expressed goodwill toward Judaism and the Jewish community, not only through such organizations as the National Conference of Christians and Jews but, more important, in local churches and synagogues throughout the country. Significantly, the major Protestant denominations increasingly took for granted that practicing Catholics and Jews were not fair game for evangelistic activity, thus at least informally including them in ecumenical "comity."

In retrospect it has come to seem plausible that at least some of this religious boom was deceptive. Even then there were quite a few individuals who questioned how religious the "religious revival" really was. Several factors contributing to it had very little to do with religious motives proper — high social mobility, with large numbers of people moving into the middle class and believing that the old nexus between bourgeois respectability and church membership still held; high geographical mobility, with migrants finding in the churches a convenient symbol of continuity in their lives; the postwar baby boom, with parents feeling rather vaguely that Sunday schools could provide some sort of moral instruction that they themselves felt incompetent to give (there are data showing that frequently it was the children who dragged their parents after them into the churches, rather than the other way around). As a result of these factors, there was a good deal of what might be called *invisible secularization*. In the midst of all this boisterous activity the deepening erosion of religious content in the churches was widely overlooked.

The "religious revival" in the denominations was paralleled by an equally impresive flowering of the civil religion. These, after all, were the Eisenhower years, aptly characterized by William Lee Miller, in a famous article in *The Reporter* magazine, as "Piety along the Potomac." Indeed, it was Eisenhower himself who made statements that could be taken as crystalline expressions of the mid-1950s version of the civil religion, such as this one: "Our government makes no sense unless it is founded in a deeply felt religious faith — and I don't care what it is." The political relevance of this faith, deeply felt and at the same time seemingly devoid of content, was expressed in another Eisenhower statement: "America is great because she is good." One may call this patriotic religion or religious patriotism. Either way, the content was America — its political and social institutions, its history, its moral values, and not least its mission in the world.

The rhetoric of the national government during these years was full of such religio-political formulations. Except for a small minority of anti-Eisenhower intellectuals, the country found this rhetoric quite in accord with its mood. Despite some shocks (notably the McCarthyite hysteria and the less-than-victorious ending of the Korean conflict), the mood was still one of national self-confidence if not complacency. There was still the afterglow, as it were, of America's great victory in World War II — a most credible conjunction of greatness and goodness. The postwar American empire was going well, with American soldiers mounting the battlements of freedom from Korea to Berlin. The Cold War, if anything, deepened the affirmation of the virtues of the American way of life as against the Communist adversary. (Not the least of the latter's evils was its ideology of "godless materialism.") The economy was going well, the dollar was king, and American businessmen as well as tourists circled the globe as emissaries from "Eldorado." Indeed, many of its intellectuals were celebrating America (even if, as it later turned out, some of the celebration was subsidized by the CIA).

I do not want to exaggerate. I am not suggesting that there were no tensions, no doubts, in this mood. But compared to what happened later, this period impresses one in retrospect by the apparent unbrokenness — intactness — of the American creed. Just as the imperial cult of classical Rome was sustained by the unquestioned veneration of the familiar shrines in innumerable households, so the American civil religion drew its strength from the daily matter-of-course enactment of the virtues of the American way of life by innumerable individual citizens. I would not like to be misunderstood here: I am *not* saying that there was more morality in the 1950s than there is today; I *am* saying that such morality as was practiced was taken for granted in a different way. The American virtues, and the virtue of America as a society, were still upheld in the mind of the country as self-evident truths. I suppose that this assurance might well be characterized as innocence. To a remarkable degree, this rather grandiose self-image of Americans was reflected in the way they were viewed by foreigners — not least by the two major enemy nations of World War II. . . .

If that was the situation in 1955, what has happened since?

To summarize the change, I shall take the liberty of making reference to my first book, a sociological critique of American Protestantism published in 1961.[10] In this book, when describing the notion that the world is essentially what it is supposed to be, I used the phrase "the okay world." I argued that religion in middle-class America served to maintain this sense of the world being "okay." I still think this was a fair description. The change since then can be conveniently summed up by saying that more and more people have come to the conclusion that their world is *not* "okay," and religion has lost much of its ability to persuade them that it is.

In denominational religion, the changes have differed greatly by class. The Protestant groups drawing most of their membership from *below* the upper-middle class have continued to grow, some of them in a dramatic way.[11] They have largely remained untouched by the crises and self-doubts that have lacerated their higher-class brethren. Their theological fundamentalism has been modifed here and there and their organizational style has been modernized, but as far as an outside observer can judge, their self-confidence as upholders of Evangelical truth has remained largely unbroken. The picture is quite different in the mainstream denominations.

By the mid-1960s the "religious revival" was clearly over. All the statistical indicators started ebbing or even pointing down — membership, attendance, financial giving and (logically enough) church expansion. As budgets became leaner, the denominational and interdenominational organizations were forced to cut down on program as well as staff. Seminary enrollments stayed high, but there was widespread suspicion that the automatic exemption of seminary students from the draft had much to do with this (a suspicion that appears to be borne out in what is happening in the seminaries now). The market for denominational religion, in short, was becoming bearish. Not surprisingly, its amicable management through ecumenical cartels seemed less and less attractive. There appeared a marked reluctance to engage in further mergers, characterized by some observers (perhaps euphemistically) as "a resurgence of denominational spirit." The organizational mood became one of retrenchment.

More deeply, the 1960s were characterized in mainstream Protestantism by what can best be described in Gilbert Murray's phrase as a "failure of nerve."[12] The best-known theological movements seemed to vie with each other in the eagerness with which they sought to divest the churches of the traditional contents and to replace these with a variety of secular gospels — existentialism, psychoanalysis, revolutionary liberation, or *avant-garde* sensitivity. The "death-of-God" theology was the grotesque climax of this theological self-disembowelment. At the same time the church functionaries, increasingly panicky about the fate of their organizations, tended to jump on whatever cultural or political bandwagon was proclaimed by the so-called opinion leaders as the latest revelation of the *Zeitgeist*. As was to be expected, all these efforts "to make the church more relevant to modern society" had the effect of aggravating rather than alleviating the religious recession. Those church members who still felt loyalty to the traditional content of their faith were bewildered if not repelled by all this, and those whose membership was motivated by secular considerations to begin with often felt that such commodities as "personal growth" or "raised consciousness" could be obtained just as well (and less expensively) outside the churches. The major consequence (unintended, needless to say) of Vatican II seems to have been to spread the aforementioned Protestant miseries through the Catholic community: the "failure of nerve" has become ecumenical too. At the same time, American Judaism and the American Jewish community in general have been driven by a variety of causes into a much more particularistic and defensive posture than was the case when Herberg announced the arrival of a "tripartite" American faith.[13]

Just as there was good reason to doubt that the "religious revival" of the 1950s was caused by some sort of mass conversion, so it is unlikely that the subsequent decline is to be explained by sudden spiritual transformations. My own tendency is to think that secularization has been a long-lasting and fairly even process, and that nothing drastic happened to the American religious consciousness either after World War II or in the most recent decade. What happened, I think, is that the quite mundane social forces that made for the "religious revival" subsequently weakened. Most important, the linkage between middle-class status and church membership weakened (something that took place in England, by the way, in the wake of World War I). In consequence, the previously invisible secularization became much more visible. If you like, secularization came out of the closet. The inability of the churches to confront the emerging skeleton with a modicum of dignity almost certainly contributed to its devastating effect.

The changes that have taken place in the civil religion, I think, resulted partly from these changes in denominational religion (inevitable in view of the symbiotic relation between the two), and partly from extraneous developments in the society. To some degree, it can be said, the American polity has become more *laique* in recent years, and I suspect that this is largely due to the more openly acknowledged secularism of that portion of the college-educated upper middle class that finances what it considers good causes — in this instance, the cause of pushing secularist cases through the courts. The Supreme Court proscription of prayer in the public schools was the most spectacular of these cases. It was an exercise in extraordinary sociological blindness, though it appears that those who advocated it have learned absolutely nothing from the outcry that ensured. The same *laique* trend may be seen in the rigid resistance to any allocation of tax funds to church schools, in threats to the tax-exempt status of religious institutions, and in current discussion of various forms of chaplaincy. More important, a militant secularism today comes dangerously close to denying the right of the churches to attempt influencing public policy in accordance with religious morality. The abortion issue illustrates this most clearly. I doubt whether the tendency of the courts to go along with the secularists has profound reasons. Most likely it can be explained simply in terms of the parties attended by federal judges and the magazines read by their wives. (I assure you that I intend no disrespect to our judiciary — actually one of our more cheering institutions — but I am too much of a sociologist to believe that its decisions are made in some judicial heaven sublimely detached from the socio-cultural ambience of its members.)

There has thus come to be a threat to the old symbiosis between denominational and civil religion in America. And a more dramatic threat has come from much larger events in the society. It has often been said in the last few years that the legitimacy of the American political order faces the gravest crisis since the Civil War. Even after making proper allowance for the propensity of professional social critics to exaggerate, the diagnosis stands up under scrutiny. To be sure, there are important class and regional differences: what is perceived as doomsday by readers of the *New York Review of Books* may seem a less than overwhelming nuisance to the reader of a small-town newspaper in Kansas, and there is hard evidence to the effect that there continues to be large masses of people whose "okay world" has *not* been fundamentally shaken. Yet few people have remained untouched by the political and moral questioning induced by the headline events of the last decade — the continuing racial crisis, the seemingly endless fiasco of the imperial adventure in Indochina, the eruption of chaos on campus, and finally the shock of the Watergate revelations. I doubt if these events, singly or even in combination, are ultimately causes of the crisis of the American political creed: I think it is more plausible to see this crisis rooted in much more basic tensions and discontents of modern society, of "revolutionary" society, and to understand the events as *occasions* for the underlying difficulties to become manifest.

Obviously I cannot develop this point here. Suffice it to say that the survival in the twentieth century of a political order conceived in the eighteenth is not something about which I am sanguine (though, let me hasten to add, I fervently believe in the continuing effort to keep this eighteenth-century vision alive). Be this as it may, we have been passing through a process that sociologists rather ominously describe as *delegitimation* — that is, a weakening of the values and assumptions on which a political order is based. We have been lucky, I think, that this malaise of the political system has not so far been accompanied by severe dislocation in the economy: I can only express the hope that our luck continues to hold.

It may then be said that the civil religion has been affected by a double secularization. It has been affected by the secularizing processes in the proper sense of the word, the same processes that have come to the fore in the area of denominational religion. But it has also undergone a "secularization" — that is, a weakening in the plausibility of its own creed, quite apart from the relation of this creed to the several churches. Put simply, the phrase "under God," as lately introduced into the Oath of Allegiance, has become implausible to many people. But even without this phrase the propositions about America contained in the oath have come to sound hollow in many ears. *That* is the measure of our crisis. . . .

However prudent one may want to be with regard to the tricky business of prediction, it is almost inevitable in a consideration such as this to look toward the future. What are some plausible scenarios?

As we look at the future of denominational religion in America, a crucial consideration will be how one views the further course of secularization. In the last few years I have come to believe that many observers of the religious scene (I among them) have over-estimated both the degree and the irreversibility of secularization. There are a number of indications, to paraphrase Mark Twain, that the news about the demise of religion has been exaggerated. Also, there are signs of a vigorous resurgence of religion in quarters where one would have least expected it (as, for instance, among the college-age children of the most orthodox secularists). All this need not mean that we are on the brink of a new Reformation (though I doubt if anyone thought they were on the brink of a Reformation at the beginning of the sixteenth century either), but it seems increasingly likely to me that there are limits to secularization. I am not saying this because of any philosophical or theological beliefs about the truth of the religious view of reality, although I myself believe in this truth. Rather, I am impressed by the intrinsic inability of secularized world views to answer the deeper questions of the human condition, questions of *whence, whether,* and *why.* These seem to be ineradicable and they are answered only in the most banal ways by the *ersatz* religions of secularism. Perhaps, finally, the reversibility of the process of secularization is probable because of the pervasive boredom of a world without gods.

This does not necessarily mean, however, that a return to religion would also mean a return to the churches. It is perfectly possible that future religious resurgences will create new institutional forms and that the existing institutions will be left behind as museum pieces of a bygone era. There are two propositions, though, of which I am fairly certain. First, any important religious movements in America will emerge out of the Judaeo-Christian tradition rather than from esoterica imported from the Orient. And second, the likelihood that such revitalizing movements remain within the existing churches will increase as the churches return to the traditional contents of their faith and give up self-defeating attempts to transform their traditions in accordance with the myth of "modern man."

The scenarios for the American civil religion hinge most obviously on one's prognoses for American society at large. Only the most foolhardy would pretend to certainty on this score. But one thing is reasonably certain: No political order can stand a long process of delegitimation such as the one we have been going through of late. There is only a limited number of possible outcomes to such a crisis of legitimacy. One, perhaps the most obvious one, is that the society will move into a period of general decline, marked both by intensifying disturbance within and a shrinkage of its power in the world outside. Not much imagination is required to see what such a decline would mean internationally. A second possible outcome is a termination of the crisis by force, by the imposition of the traditional virtues by the power of the state. It hardly needs stressing that democracy and freedom, as we have known them, would not survive such an "Augustan age" in America. The third possibility is a revitalization of the American creed from within, a new effort to breathe the spirit of conviction into the fragile edifice of our political institutions. This possibility depends above all on political and intellectual leadership, of which there is little evidence at the moment. The future of the American experiment depends upon a quick end to this particular scarcity and upon the emergence of an altogether new unity of political will, moral conviction, and historical imagination — in order to preserve the society descending from our Revolution.

I have tried here to sketch a picture, not to preach a sermon. The social scientist, if he is true to his vocation, will try to see reality without reference to his own hopes or fears. Yet it must be clear that I do not view this particular scene as a visitor from outer space. On the contrary, I find myself deeply and painfully involved in it. As a sociologist I can, indeed must, look at the religious situation in terms of what a colleague has aptly called "methodological atheism." At the same time, I am a Christian, which means that I have a stake in the churches' overcoming their "failure of nerve" and regaining their authority in representing a message that I consider to be of ultimate importance for mankind. I suppose that a phrase like "methodological subversion" would fit the manner in which, again of necessity, the social scientist looks at political reality. With some mental discipline, then, I can try to describe contemporary America as if it were ancient Rome. But I cannot escape the fact that I am an American citizen and that the future of this society contains not only my own future but that of my children. Even more important, I happen to believe in the continuing viability of that eighteenth-century vision and in the promise implied by that oath — in my own case, first taken freely and of my own volition as an adult. Both for the religious believer and for the citizen, the assessment that I tried to make here translates itself into practical and political tasks.

Notes

1. H. Richard Niebuhr, *The Social Sources of Denominationalism* (New York: Henry Holt & Co., 1929, 1954).

2. Robert N. Bellah, "Civil Religion in America," *Daedalus* (Winter, 1967) pp. 1-21; frequently reprinted; e.g., Donald Cutler (ed.), *The Religious Situation* (Boston: Beacon Press, 1968).

3. Will Herberg, *Protestant, Catholic, Jew — An Essay in American Religious Sociology* (Garden City, N.Y.: Doubleday & Co., 1955).

4. Gunnar Myrdal, *An American Dilemma — The Negro Problem and Modern Democracy* (New York: Harper, 1947).

5. See Perry Miller, *The New England Mind* (New York: Macmillan, 1939).

6. Thomas Paine's *Common Sense* was published in 1776; *The Age of Reason* in 1794. See Harry H. Clark (ed.), *Thomas Paine: Selections* (New York: Hill & Wang, 1961).

7. French *laïque*, pertaining to the laity rather than the clergy, hence secular.

8. Four distinct denominations were involved in the 1957 merger: The Reformed Church in the U.S., the Evangelical Synod of North America, the Congregational Church, and the Christian Church.

9. The original article, plus several others, are reprinted in William Lee Miller, *Piety along the Potomac* (Boston: Houghton Mifflin, Co., 1964).

10. Peter L. Berger, *The Noise of Solemn Assemblies* (Garden City, N.Y.: Doubleday & Co., 1961).

11. See Dean M. Kelley, *Why Conservative Churches Are Growing* (New York: Harper & Row, 1972).

12. See Gilbert Murray, *Liberality and Civilization* (New York: Macmillan, 1938).

13. Will Herberg, *op. cit.*

Bibliography

Bainton, Roland, H. *The Reformation of the Sixteenth Century.* Boston: Beacon Press, 1952.

Brown, Robert McAfee. *The Spirit of Protestantism.* New York: Oxford University Press, 1961.

Cavert, Samuel McCrae. *Church Cooperation and Unity in America: A Historical Review, 1900-1970.* New York: Association Press, 1970.

Collins, Sheila D. "Toward a Feminist Theology," *The Christian Century* (August 1972): 796-799.

Cone, James H. *God of the Oppressed.* New York: Seabury Press, 1975.

Ferm, Deane William. "American Protestant Theology, 1900-1970," *Religion in Life* 44 (Spring 1975): 59-72.

Ferré, Nels F. S. *The Sun and the Umbrella.* New York: Harper and Row, 1953.

Fosdick, Harry Emerson. Sermon preached at First Presbyterian Church, New York, May 21, 1922.

Graham, Billy. "Conversion — A Personal Revolution," *The Ecumenical Review* 19 (July 1967): 271-284.

Handy, Robert T. *The Protestant Quest for a Christian America, 1830-1930.* Philadelphia: Fortress Press, 1967.

Hudson, Winthrop S. *Religion in America.* New York: Charles Scribner's Sons, 1965.

Jurji, Edward J., ed. *The Great Religions of the Modern World.* Princeton, NJ: Princeton University Press, 1946.

Kelley, Dean M. *Why Conservative Churches are Growing.* New York: Harper and Row, 1972.

King, Martin Luther, Jr. "From the Mountaintop," *Renewal* 9 (April 1969): 3-5.

Marty, Martin E. *Protestantism.* New York: Holt, Rinehart, and Winston, 1972.

McCord, James I. "Whither American Protestantism?" *Theology Today* 24 (October 1967): 167-275.

Menzies, William W. "Our Heritage," *Paraclete* 9 (Winter 1975): 3-7.

Miller, Perry. *The New England Mind: The Seventeenth Century.* New York: The Macmillan Company, 1939.

Nelson, Hart M.; Yokley, Raytha L.; and Nelson, Anne K., eds. *The Black Church in America.* New York: Basic Books, Inc., 1971.

Niebuhr, H. Richard. *The Social Sources of Denominationalism.* New York: H. Holt & Co., Inc., 1929; rev. ed., 1954.

Niebuhr, Reinhold. "Nuclear War and The Christian Dilemma," *Theology Today* 15 (January 1959): 542-48.

Russell, Letty M. *Human Liberation in a Feminist Perspective – A Theology.* Philadelphia: Westminster Press, 1974.

Smylie, James H. "Sheldon's *In His Steps:* Conscience and Discipleship," *Theology Today* 32 (April 1971): 32-45.

Sweet, William Warren. *The American Churches: An Interpretation.* Nashville, Tenn.: Abingdon Press, 1947.

Tillich, Paul. "Religious Symbols and Our Knowledge of God," *The Christian Scholar* 38 (September 1955): 189-97.

Annotated Bibliography

The books and sources from which the selections for this volume have been taken, as well as the literature mentioned in the prefaces to the selections, are recommended for further reading and study. Many of the major encyclopedias provide articles and reading lists under such headings as "Protestantism," "Reformation," "Martin Luther," "Methodism," and so forth. In addition, the following works dealing with Protestantism will be found useful.

I. Basic Texts and Bibliographies

Ahlstrom, Sydney E. *A Religious History of the American People.* New Haven: Yale University Press, 1972. A massive and standard text, over 1000 pages with more than 30 pages of bibliography.

Bainton, Roland H. and Gritsch, Eric W. *Bibliography of the Continental Reformation: Materials Available in English.* Hamden, Conn.: The Shoe String Press, 1972. An indispensable guide to books and articles in English.

Burr, Nelson R. *Critical Bibliography of American Religion.* Princeton, NJ: Princeton University Press, 2 vols., 1961. A descriptive analysis of sources dealing with history, society, ideas, and the arts.

Dillenberger, John and Welch, Claude. *Protestant Christianity.* New York: Charles Scribner's Sons, 1954. A reliable text with suggestions for reading.

Marty, Martin E. *Protestantism.* New York: Holt, Rinehart and Winston, 1972. A lively and provocative narrative with a 100-page bibliography.

Smith, H. Shelton; Handy, Robert T.; and Loetscher, Lefferts A. *American Christianity.* New York: Charles Scribner's Sons, 2 vols., 1960, 1963. Inclusive anthologies of representative documents with descriptive comments by the editors.

Williams, J. Paul. *What Americans Believe and How They Worship.* New York: Harper and Row, 1969. A dictionary approach to most of the religious groups and more comprehensive than Frank S. Mead's *Handbook of Denominations in the U.S.* Nashville: Abingdon Press, 1970; although Mead's book is also useful.

Zaretsky, Irving I. and Leone, Mark P., eds. *Religious Movements in Contemporary America.* Princeton: Princeton University Press, 1974. A wide-ranging examination of the cults and sects from a sociological perspective, with 40 pages of bibliography.

II. Reformation and Later History

Bainton, Roland H. *Here I Stand: A Life of Martin Luther.* Nashville: Abingdon Press, 1950. The standarrd biography and a delight to read; extensive notes, bibliography, and woodcuts.

Brauer, Jerold C. *Protestantism in America.* Philadelphia: Westminster Press, 1965. The title describes the contents.

Brown, Robert McAfee. *The Spirit of Protestantism.* New York: Oxford University Press, 1961. Written by a Protestant who is also familiar with Catholicism.

Dolan, John P. *History of the Reformation.* New York: The New American Library, 1967. A Catholic view written by the author of the volume on *Catholicism* in Barron's World Religions Series.

Forrell, George W. *The Protestant Faith.* Englewood Cliffs, NJ: Prentice Hall, 1960. A Lutheran view of doctrine and theology.

Hillerbrand, Hans J., ed. *The Protestant Reformation.* New York: Walker and Co., 1968. A selection of documents from the Continental and British reformers.

McLelland, Joseph C. *The Reformation and Its Significance Today.* Philadelphia: Westminster Press, 1962. The first part deals with the Reformation; the second with today.

McNeill, John T. *The History and Character of Calvinism.* New York: Oxford University Press, 1954. A standard and thorough exploration of the whole history of the Reformed movement.

Outler, Albert C., ed. *John Wesley.* New York: Oxford University Press, 1964. A rich selection of excerpts by the Methodist reformer with complete bibliography.

Pauck, Wilhelm. *The Heritage of the Reformation.* Glencoe, Ill.: Free Press of Glencoe, 1961. Engaging and penetrating essays by a recognized authority.

III. Contemporary Interpretations

Altizer, Thomas J. J. and Hamilton, William. *Radical Theology and the Death of God.* Indianapolis: Bobbs Merrill, 1966. Essays by two of the spokesmen for the "Death of God" movement in the 1960s.

Bloesch, Donald G. *The Evangelical Renaissance.* Grand Rapids, Mich.: Eerdmans, 1969. An account of conservative trends.

Cobb, John C. *A Christian Natural Theology.* Philadelphia: Westminster Press, 1965. An example of "process theology," using the principles of A. N. Whitehead.

Cox, Harvey G. *The Secular City.* New York: Macmillan, 1965. A widely popular book in the 1960s which sought to interpret Christian faith by means of current secular notions and values.

Fletcher, Joseph F. *Situation Ethics.* Philadelphia: Westminster Press, 1966. The controversial view of Christian conduct in contextual and situational terms.

Hageman, Alice L., ed. *Sexist Religion and Women in the Church.* New York: Association Press, 1974. A daring and provocative series of essays, mostly by and about women.

Harkness, Georgia E. *Women in Church and Society: A Historical and Theological Inquiry.* Nashville: Abingdon Press, 1972. Just what it says, and written by a distinguished theologian who wrote a dozen books before the women's movement began.

Henry, Carl F. H., ed. *Fundamentals of the Faith.* Grand Rapids, Mich.: Zondervan, 1969. Essays by conservative theologians and churchmen, edited by the former head of *Christianity Today,* "A Fortnightly Magazine of Evangelical Conviction."

҉ Herberg, Will. *Protestant, Catholic, Jew.* Garden City, New York: Doubleday, 1960. A brilliant comparison of the three faiths, from a religious sociology point of view.

Lehmann, Paul L. *Ethics in a Christian Context.* New York: Harper and Row, 1963. An intellectually demanding discussion of the relation of theology to ethics within the "context" of the Christian community.

Tillich, Paul. *The Protestant Era.* Chicago: University of Chicago Press, 1948. Early essays on many different topics, but with five specifically dealing with "the Protestant principle." Basic for Tillich's later theology.

Washington, Joseph R. *Black Religion: The Negro and Christianity in the United States.* Boston: Beacon Press, 1964. An early examination of black theology. See also the author's *Black Sects and Cults.* New York: Doubleday, 1972.

Index

NOTES

NOTES

NOTES

Existentialism

by Wesley Barnes
256 pp., paper $2.50

Essentially and uniquely literary in nature, this book synthe-
sizes the historical, psychological, and philosophical aspects of the movement of existentialism, a movement that
cannot be justified or sustained on philosophical grounds.
The literary communications and expressions of agonized
modern man, the man of "choosing, willing, and protesting," are concisely, but thoroughly, treated as to authors
and their individual works.

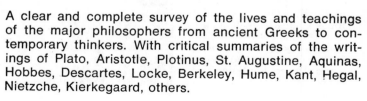

Essentials of Philosophy

by Nicholas A. Norvath
363 pp., paper $3.25   HS-C

A clear and complete survey of the lives and teachings
of the major philosophers from ancient Greeks to contemporary thinkers. With critical summaries of the writings of Plato, Aristotle, Plotinus, St. Augustine, Aquinas,
Hobbes, Descartes, Locke, Berkeley, Hume, Kant, Hegal,
Nietzche, Kierkegaard, others.

Barron's Educational Series, Inc.
113 Crossways Park Drive   Woodbury, New York 11797

On sale at your local bookseller or order direct adding 10% postage plus applicable sales tax.

CATHOLICISM
AN HISTORICAL SURVEY

by John P. Dolan
Professor of History
University of South Carolina

Catholicism traces the historical development of the religion from its Judaic backgrounds to the world-wide church of the present day. It explains Catholicism's origin and transformation in time and space as well as its complex relationships with different civilizations in the living context of history. What especially enhances the work is its selection of important documents, conciliar and papal decrees, theological tracts and sermons which reflect the mind of Catholicism in the various stages of its growth.

Pages: 256,
Size: 5⅜ x 8,
Price: **$2.95** pa.,
$8.25 cl.

Barron's
Educational
Series, Inc.

CONFUCIANISM

by Ch'u Chai
Formerly Professor of Chinese Culture and Philosophy
The New School for Social Research

and Winberg Chai
Chairman of the Department of Asian Studies
City College of New York

Confucianism is a concise history of the philosophy/religion, in regard to its origin, its development, its great exponents, and its success in dominating Chinese thought for the last 25 centuries. The authors discuss the Pre-Confucian philosophical and religious thought; trace the rise of Confucianism through Confucius, Mencious, and Hsun Tzu; examine the Confucianism of the Ch'in and Han periods; and discuss the Yin-Yang school of Confucianism.

Pages: 192,
Size: 5⅜ x 8,
Price **$2.95** pa.,
$8.25 cl.

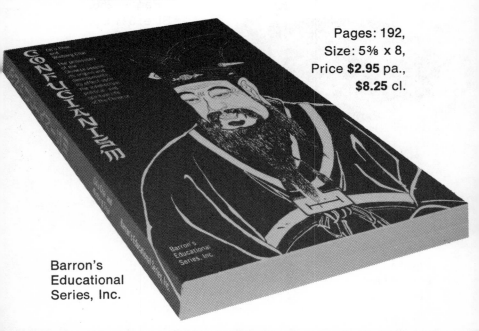

Barron's
Educational
Series, Inc.

BUDDHISM
THE LIGHT OF ASIA

by Kenneth K.S. Ch'en

Professor and Chairman of the
Department of Oriental Languages
University of California, Los Angeles

This survey of Buddhism begins with the life and teachings of the founder and then presents these teachings as systematized first by the Theravada School and later by the Mahayana School. Following a discussion of the monastic community, the book then proceeds to trace the development of the religion in Southeast Asia, Tibet, China, and Japan, ending with the treatment of the religion by the Chinese Communists in Tibet and China. Running throughout this book is the central theme —the resiliency or ability of the religion to adapt itself to all conditions and all places. The religion in one country has distinctive features not found in other Buddhist countries.

Pages: 320,
Size: 5⅜ x 8,
Price: **$3.50** pa.,
$7.95 cl.

Barron's
Educational
Series, Inc.

HINDUISM

by Troy Wilson Organ
Distinguished Professor of Philosophy
Ohio University

Dr. Organ has presented Hinduism not as an amorphous collection of beliefs and practices, but as a growing organism. The author's analysis of the motif of Hinduism is a unique contribution to the study of Hinduism as a religion. Dr. Organ is convinced that Hinduism is not an escape from the world but a program of development — a development of the full potentialities of man.

The book reflects the author's opinion that Hinduism is worthy of study not only because of its contributions to the world of religion and literature but also because it contains insights which may assist in leading Western man out of the current malaise.

Pages: 428,
Size: 5⅜ x 8,
Price: **$3.50** pa.

Barron's
Educational
Series, Inc.

ISLAM
BELIEFS AND OBSERVANCES
by Caesar E. Farah
Professor of Middle Eastern Languages and Literature
University of Minnesota

Islam relates the fundamentals of Islamic tenets, beliefs, and observances; highlights the impact of intellectualism and the rise of splinter sects; and discusses the period of renaissance brought about by modern thinking.

Students, professors, and theologians as well as general readers have found *Islam* to be an intriguing, penetrating survey of the nature of the religion. Students in comparative religious courses have praised its comprehensive, yet detailed content. Professors have acknowledged its authoritative approach. General readers have liked its simple, straightforward style — a style that conveys the complexities in simple, easily-understood terms.

Pages: 228,
Size: 5⅜ x 8,
Price: **$2.95** pa.,
$7.25 cl.

Barron's
Educational
Series, Inc.

Understanding the Old Testament

by Jay G. Williams
Chairman, Department of Religion Hamilton College

A readable, well-informed introduction to the Hebrew Scriptures, based upon the geography of Israel and the pre-Christian history of its people, recommended for students of the Bible, literature and history.　　**$3.95** pa.

Understanding the New Testament

by Francis Bayard Rhein
Assoc. Prof. of Philosophy and Biblical Literature
Madison College, Virginia

A scholarly, analytical commentary on the New Testament in the light of current advances in Biblical research.　　**$3.75** pa.

Understanding The Old Testament

Its literature, history, impact on Western culture and relevance to our contemporary society by Jay G. Williams
Barron's Educational Series, Inc.

Understanding The New Testament
Francis Bayard Rhein

REVISED

A scholarly, yet easily understood analytical commentary on the New Testament in light of current advances in Biblical research. With discussions of the background, purpose, structure, and content of each book. Brings the meaning of the New Testament into sharper focus for contemporary readers.
Barron's Educational Series, Inc.